BECOMING A LEADER In Enrollment Services

A Development Guide
For the Higher Education Professional

Roger M. Swanson and Faith A. Weese

Becoming a Leader in Enrollment Services
A Development Guide for the Higher Education Professional
© 1997 by American Association of Collegiate Registrars and Admissions Officers
All rights reserved.

Published in cooperation with Magna Publications, Inc., 2718 Dryden Dr., Madison, WI 53704
Cover design by Sonja Penner

American Association of Collegiate Registrars and Admissions Officers
One Dupont Circle, NW, Suite 330
Washington, DC 20036-1171
(202) 293-9161

Founded in 1910, AACRAO is a nonprofit, voluntary, professional education association of degree-granting postsecondary institutions, government agencies, higher education coordinating boards, private educational organizations, and education-oriented businesses. Its goal is to promote higher education and further the professional development of members working in admissions, enrollment management, financial aid, institutional research, records, registration, scheduling, academic standards, and student progress.

AACRAO adheres to the principles of nondiscrimination and equality without regard to race, color, creed, gender, sexual orientation, age, religion, disability, or national origin.

Library of Congress Cataloging-in-Publication Data

Becoming a leader in enrollment services: a development guide for the higher education professional/ [edited] by Roger M. Swanson and Faith A. Weese.
   p. cm
   Includes bibliographical references and index.
   ISBN 1-57858-002-1 (alk. Paper)
    1. Universities and colleges—Admission—Vocational guidance—United States. 2. College admission officers—United States. 3. College registrars—United States. 4. College attendance—United States—Planning. I. Swanson, Roger M. II. Weese, Faith A. III. American Association of Collegiate Registrars and Admissions Officers.
LB2351.2.B42   1997
378.1'11-dc21   97-6540
                                                                      CIP

Table of Contents

Foreward v
   Diana Guerrero

Introduction vii
   Roger M. Swanson and Faith A. Weese

Chapter 1 The Profession 1
   Wayne E. Becraft

Chapter 2 The Professional 21
   Roger M. Swanson and Faith A. Weese

Chapter 3 Communication 33
   Faith A. Weese

Chapter 4 Technology 71
   Melanie Moore Bell

Chapter 5 Leadership and Management 87
   W. Wes Williams and Sheahon J. Zenger

Chapter 6 Strategic Enrollment Management 107
   Michael G. Dolence

Chapter 7 Professional Development 135
   Roger M. Swanson

Chapter 8 Politics 151
   David H. Kalsbeek

Chapter 9 Ethics and Ethos 171
   C. James Quann and David Birnbaum

Chapter 10 Career Mobility 193
   William R. Haid

Chapter 11 Future of the Profession 207
   Nancy C. Sprotte

Appendix A. AACRAO as a Resource for the Professional. . . 217

Appendix B. Professional Practices and Ethical Standards
(Code of Ethics) 223

Glossary 225

Index. 241

Foreword

As we approach the new millennium amid the rapid changes occurring at all levels of our society, effective leadership becomes critical to our institutional and personal well-being. As enrollment professionals, we no longer operate within the narrow confines of our job descriptions. Our expertise and influence extend well beyond our institutional reporting structures. As we are confronted with changing student populations, fewer human and fiscal resources, greater demands and expectations from our publics, and accountability at every level, where can we turn for guidance as we navigate through the sea of enrollment management, information technology, student services, and faculty issues that we deal with on a daily basis? This volume will provide many of the answers and much of the direction we are all seeking.

As we assume additional responsibilities on our campuses, the need for continual professional development becomes increasingly apparent. Enrollment professionals come from varied backgrounds. Many have worked their way up through the system and may have extensive expe-

---

Diana Guerrero is Director of Admissions at The University of Texas at El Paso, is the 1995-99 AACRAO Vice President for Enrollment Management, Admissions, and Financial Aid, and has been a member of the organization for over twenty-five years. She has presented several AACRAO sessions on cultural diversity and access issues, has served as a member and chair of AACRAO's Student Access and Equity Committee, and has chaired the Latino/Latina Caucus. She is also a member of the Texas ACRAO and has chaired its EEO Committee.

Guerrero is a contributing author to AACRAO's *The Admissions Profession: A Guide to Staff Development and Program Management* (AACRAO and NACAC 1991), and to the upcoming *Handbook for the College Admissions Profession* (Greenwood Publishers 1997). Her interests include the health professions and international, transfer, high-risk, and underrepresented students. She has also visited Germany as part of a Fulbright program for international educators.

rience in some, but not all, of the enrollment services areas. Others come from the faculty or other administrative areas and may have never had direct experience in the areas which they have been assigned to lead. Still others have fallen into their positions as a fortuitous marriage of skills, interests, opportunity, and timing. Since there are still no formal training programs that prepare full-fledged registrars, directors of admission and financial aid, or enrollment managers, most of these individuals' expertise has been developed through hands-on experience, which is often fragmented and limited by the types of environments in which they have worked.

This AACRAO resource guide addresses issues involving our constantly changing profession and gives readers a firm foundation upon which to shape their futures and the tools necessary to direct the futures of the personnel they supervise. We are delighted to present authors who are respected experts in their fields and who are, above all, practitioners. They know theory, they know what works, and, collectively, they represent over 250 years of experience in enrollment services.

Share my excitement as you read and discover "We can do that!" or "I never thought about it like that before." Learn what it means to have the vision to move your institution forward while staying grounded in the present as you help your people be successful. Temper the wonders of technology with the understanding that it can never replace the subtle nuances of human communication. We can look forward to exciting, challenging times. Enjoy the journey to your professional future!

Diana Guerrero

AACRAO Vice President
for Enrollment Management, Admissions, and Financial Aid

Introduction

Our goal in producing and writing this book is to help you become a leader in enrollment services. We have tried to achieve this goal by presenting information, insights, and perspectives from recognized authorities to help you acquire important knowledge, skills, and values that are vital to your institutional success, professional growth, and career progress.

Leadership has always been exciting and challenging. Today the excitement is even more thrilling and the challenge more trying. Massive shifts in technology, dizzying changes in market pressures, demographic transformations in the workforce, fresh demands from society, and customers — whether they be our students, faculty, staff, administration, or community — as fussy and strong as ever; all come together to put us in the center of the action. Our profession claims to be caring of students and should do no less for its own professionals. Retention and growth of effective leaders and staff members are as cost-effective as retention and growth of our students.

Those who aspire to serve in senior positions in enrollment services face increasing and specialized challenges as they guide and nurture their institutions through cycles of growth and change, evolving into self-defined and continually reinvented futures. Art and science must truly converge as the modern leader crafts a mosaic of functions that co-relate to each other, to cross-campus entities, and to off-campus publics and stakeholders.

Electronic systems have broken physical barriers, from office and data communication to the teaching-learning dialectic that lies at the heart of the educational mission of our colleges and universities. Where once isolated "silos" of administrivia could operate with independence and impunity, the inter-operability of technologies and of people is now requisite for campus-wide functionality. Admissions marketing partakes of curriculum development; registration relies on electronic infrastructures; institutional research becomes an engine driving financial aid awards; academic support and orientation impact retention; student services generate happy and generous alums.

The magnitude of campus flux is everywhere. The re-engineering of institutional structure, the quantum leap-frogging progress of technology, the external demands for efficiency and productivity, the frequent changing of senior institutional guard, etc., are no longer linear or isolated. They have become our daily reality and sometimes threaten to take over our lives.

To deal successfully with these issues, we believe that leadership can be learned and must be learned — and this, of course, is what this book was written for and should be used for. We offer *Becoming a Leader in Enrollment Services* to make sure that all this chaos we face daily gives you imagination and not a headache. We want you to dream about and realize the possibilities for your leadership development now, not merely dwell on your day-to-day problems, important though they may be. Where you encounter obstacles, we want you to have the tools and the attitude to overcome them.

To help guide your professional journey in enrollment services, we have enlisted a varied, energetic, and respected cadre of AACRAO leaders and charged them to share their best guidance, insights, and perceptions. All have presented and written extensively, demonstrating their abilities as both practitioners and teachers. We sought to present them with topics critical to our profession that matched their known areas of interest and expertise. Then we pushed them hard to comply with deadlines, meet demanding form and content standards, and accept friendly but often critical reviews. We did NOT ask them to take a prescribed approach, write in a consistent style, or even agree with each other. These are people who know "what works" for them and are willing to pass along their valuable lessons and truths to those eager to learn and grow.

How can you apply their wisdom to your own job, institution, and career?

- By reading carefully and understanding the principles advanced and the applications provided

- By noting your own responses to the authors' ideas in the margins or elsewhere

- By stepping away from the "business-as-usual" attitude and opening your mind to new approaches and strategies

- By adopting the motto "think big and start small," developing a larger direction, and then taking some immediate initial steps toward its achievement

- By sharing your new plans with key and trusted individuals in and out of your office for feedback and response

- By evaluating and modifying as you progress to assess performance and adjust next steps

Advice is good only to the degree that you are able to understand it, translate it to your unique situation and environment, and learn from it for future applications.

Becoming a Leader in Enrollment Services is a book about activating leadership and planning our future. Enrollment services leaders are in increasingly greater demand as our institutions recognize the centrality of the critical missions they fulfill. The challenges, risks, rewards, and excitement are all waiting for those who are prepared and courageous. Leadership has no beginning, middle, or end. It is a journey. A true leader is continually questing, always stretching, ever seeking, constantly reaching, graciously accepting challenges and transforming them into opportunities. We hope that this book inspires, enriches, and sustains you as a leader and that it serves you as a spark plug, catalyst, and blueprint to action —and *your* success.

We offer this book in dedication to AACRAO, its members — past, present, and yet to be — and the future of our profession.

Roger M. Swanson *Faith A. Weese*
Washington, DC Phoenix, Az
April 1997

Chapter 1

The Profession

by Wayne E. Becraft

History of Enrollment Services

The professions that today include registrar, admissions officer, and enrollment services professional had their origins in the twelfth century. At that time the office of *bedel* or *beadle* began to emerge at the universities of Bologna in Italy, Paris in France, and Oxford in England. The persons in this role carried out a variety of duties, from maintaining institutional records, finances, and facilities to preceding the rectors on public occasions, collecting votes in the congregation, visiting the schools to read statutes and decrees, announcing lectures by students, and distributing lists of books available for sale (Quann and Associates 1979, 2).

By 1446, the responsibilities of the "bedel" began to change, and the registrar's office first emerged officially when an academic officer with the title of "registrar" was appointed at Oxford. This officer's duties were to give form and permanence to the university's public acts, to draft its letters, to make copies of its documents, and to register the names of its graduates and their "examinatory sermons." The position of "registrary" was created at Cambridge in 1506 with responsibilities for regulating and coordinating university ceremonies. In 1544, the duties were expanded to include the reviewing of all applicants for matriculation, and still later to act as secretary for all academic bodies (Quann and Associates 1979, 5).

Wayne E. Becraft is Executive Director of the American Association of Collegiate Registrars and Admissions Officers. He has served on numerous national higher education committees and has been a member of the Washington Higher Education Secretariat, the Alliance for International Educational and Cultural Exchange, and the Council of Higher Education Management Associations. Before assuming leadership of AACRAO, he was Director of Admission and Registration Services for the University of Maryland, University College.

In the United States, at Harvard the registrar's academic record-keeping functions remained a part-time faculty duty into the mid- nineteenth century. Yale, America's second college, followed the "bedel" tradition. At other American colleges, professors continued to serve as registrars during the latter part of the nineteenth century. At this time the registrar's role began to evolve into an increasingly professional, specialized, and full-time administrative task. Along with the college president, the treasurer, and the librarian, a review of a representative sample of thirty-two colleges and universities revealed that the registrar was among the first administrative officers to become a specialist (in 1887), preceding the creation of the office of the dean (1891), the dean of women (1896), the chief business officer (1906), and the dean of men (1920). Among colleges accredited by the Association of American Universities by 1910 — the year the American Association of Collegiate Registrars (AACR), now the American Association of Collegiate Registrars and Admissions Officers (AACRAO) was founded — 76 percent had registrars (Quann and Associates 1979, 5-7).

In the early twentieth century, the registrar's responsibilities were very broad. They included maintaining accurate records and efficient enrollment procedures, to be sure, but registrars also corresponded with prospective students, conducted high school visitations, sent and received application forms, reviewed scholarship and financial aid awards, greeted first-year and transfer students, conducted their orientation, advised them on programs and courses, counseled them on vocations and careers, scheduled classes, forecast enrollments, predicted tuition income, analyzed teaching loads, responded to questionnaires, conducted other institutional research, suggested curriculum revisions to the faculty, signed diplomas, and even shook hands with graduating seniors at commencement. At Stanford, they also handled official communication between students and academic committees, prepared all official publications, and acted as a central bureau of information about the academic work of the university (Quann and Associates 1979, 7-8).

Then, changes began to occur. Separate offices were created to provide services such as admissions, counseling, placement, and academic advising. These changes were accelerated after World War II, when, as a result of the "GI Bill of Rights," more students sought enrollment than colleges and universities could handle. As many institutions began to move to selective admission, admissions began to emerge as a specialized field. It was also at this time that junior or community colleges were developed as the new "open door" institutions. Two seminal events around this time that helped cement admissions as a separate field were the creation of the Association of College Admissions Counselors (now the National Association for College Admission Counseling) in 1937 and the addition of "and Admissions Officers" to the name of the American Association of Collegiate Registrars in 1949 (Quann and Associates 1979, 9).

While the office of admissions and the office of the registrar have clearly emerged as separate offices at most institutions, their reporting lines remain varied to this day. Some report to academic affairs through the vice president, provost, or dean. Others report to the vice president or dean for student affairs or student services. And still others report to the emerging position of enrollment services professional, which may be at the level of vice president, dean, or director. On a very few campuses, one or the other office may report to the chief external affairs or chief information management officer. The predominant pattern at this time seems to be for both offices to report through academic affairs at most four-year institutions and through student affairs or student services at some four-year and most two-year institutions.

In recent years, declining numbers of high school graduates, increased enrollment of nontraditional students, and growing competition for resources have caused many colleges and universities to realize the need to strategically coordinate the efforts of programs that attract and retain students who can succeed academically on their campuses. As a result, the practice of enrollment services — how to manage and influence the characteristics and size of student enrollments — has become critical to the survival of many institutions and crucial to the maintenance and growth of all (Hossler, Bean, and Associates, 1990). Those areas typically thought of as being part of the enrollment process include admissions, financial aid, orientation, academic advising, campus activities and residence life, career planning and placement, retention, learning assistance centers, institutional research, and faculty development (Hossler, Bean, and Associates 1990, 7-14). At many institutions the office of the registrar is also thought to be a vital element of enrollment services.

Enrollment services has taken several forms. Some institutions have reorganized the functions supporting enrollment services under a single individual, who might have the title of vice president, dean, or director of enrollment services. Others have not changed the organizational structure, but have created teams involving representatives from each of the above units to coordinate the enrollment services effort. What one sees in enrollment services, if one looks carefully, is a reassembling of the myriad functions that, in the early part of the century, were the responsibility of the registrar, and recognition that the independent units that had been created to carry out each of those functions could not, in the best interests of the institution, continue to function independently.

Why the Profession Exists and the Purposes It Serves

As indicated above, enrollment services professions exist because of a need for an array of services that do not fit neatly within the instructional components of institutions. The enrollment services professions emerged due to special needs created as colleges and universities grew in size and number. They exist to provide the administrative link between potential students, current students and parents, and the faculty of an institution. Today's enrollment services professionals are responsible for producing information and publications to assist in the recruiting, admission, and registration processes; for developing and implementing institutional policies and procedures; for enrollment planning, recruiting, admission, registration, retention, records management, advisement and counseling, and financial aid; and for data collection, entry, and reporting — all of which are required to ensure that students are enrolled in sufficient numbers to fill the classrooms of instructors and to generate budgeted levels of student fee revenue.

The enrollment services areas were professionalized with the creation of associations such as the American Association of Collegiate Registrars and Admissions Officers (AACRAO), the National Association for College Admission Counseling (NACAC), and the National Association of Student Financial Aid Administrators (NASFAA). Through these organizations, codes of ethics, standards, and guidelines have been developed that define the professions and the expectations of those involved in the various professions. The associations have developed conferences, workshops, seminars, and publications that provide training and information for those entering and advancing in the professions. They provide leadership and advocacy for those in the professions with the community, with state and federal governments, and within the institutions.

Today's associations often work together to represent the interests of their members, many times with representatives of legislative bodies and administrative departments and agencies and other relevant organizations, to craft legislation, regulations, forms, and procedures that make sense for all and lead to simplified procedures for students. Past examples of such cooperative efforts include the development of regulations for implementation of the GI Bill, the military draft, and creation of and changes in the federal financial aid programs. These are examples of how enrollment services officers, by working together, can improve their professionalism and advance their profession, as well as serve national interests related to higher education.

Today's colleges and universities, whether public, private non-profit, or proprietary, are big businesses and must be managed and operated as big businesses. Enrollment services units can no longer operate independently of other departments or units in the institution or without standards and guidelines that apply across institutions. While institutions remain extremely competitive in seeking and attracting the best students, auditors, accrediting bodies, and government agencies increasingly require that standards be followed, legal requirements be satisfied, and processes and procedures be efficient and effective. Enrollment services professionals have the responsibility to ensure that their institutions are in compliance with many of these requirements.

Reduced resources, competitive pressures, and modern management theories have led to many changes at colleges and universities in recent years which have also impacted enrollment services offices. Strategic and transformational planning, downsizing, restructuring, and process redesign are but a few examples. All of these factors provide challenges but, at the same time, increase the importance of professionalism and the opportunities to meet, share, and grow through professional associations.

Scope and Function of Those in Enrollment Services

While all of those individuals involved in providing enrollment services are working toward the same goals, their specific roles, functions, and responsibilities vary considerably. The following sketches of the primary players in each of the areas will help clarify their roles.

Admissions

The primary function of admissions is to admit students to the institution. This might involve a review of the applications, transcripts, test score reports, and other supplemental materials or it might involve simply admitting all of those who apply. The relative ease or difficulty of this process is determined by the openness of the particular college or university. Four categories of openness have been identified (Breland and Associates 1995, 9) to describe general admissions practices:

1. Any individual wishing to attend will be admitted without review of conventional academic qualifications.

2. Any high school graduate (or person with equivalent credentials) will be admitted.

3. The majority of individuals who meet some specified level of academic achievement or other qualifications above and beyond high school graduation will be admitted.

4. Among those individuals who meet some specified level of academic achievement or other qualifications above and beyond high school graduation, only a limited number will be admitted.

Obviously, the more selective the college or university, the greater and more time-consuming the admissions process. The entire higher education spectrum is represented here, from the highly selective, mostly private four-year colleges and universities to the mostly open-door community colleges. However, the degree of openness also influences the amount of effort that must be exerted to attract the number of applicants who will be admitted, with the more selective institutions requiring the greatest effort. So, the preparation of publications, marketing, recruiting, assisting and advising students, evaluating credentials, influencing financial aid offers, persuading admitted applicants to enroll, and communicating with parents and students are all part of the role of an admissions officer.

At some campuses, a committee — which may include faculty members or others outside the admissions office in addition to members of the admissions staff — actually reviews the applications and makes recommendations or final decisions on the applicants.

The admissions office is also responsible for implementing policies to increase the diversity of the student population by enhancing efforts to recruit, admit, and enroll targeted minority and underrepresented populations.

The admissions office is also often the office responsible for recruiting, admitting, and providing services for international students enrolling at the institution. This can present challenges when dealing with students who speak different languages and come from different cultures.

In addition to recruiting and admitting first-year students, admissions offices also admit transfer students. These might include students transferring from community colleges to four-year institutions, from one community college to another, from one four-year institution to another, or from four-year to two-year institutions. Transfers are one way an institution can replace first-time students who withdrew or were dismissed from the institution. In the case of transfer students, the admissions office often has the additional duty of evaluating college transcripts to determine the admissibility and acceptability of transfer credits toward degree requirements.

Finally, many four-year institutions also have graduate and professional programs. Typically, these programs have their own admissions office and admissions process, either for all graduate and professional programs or for individual graduate and professional programs. Where this is not the case, undergraduate admissions handles the processing while the departments actually make the admission decisions.

Financial Aid

Prior to the passage of the GI Bill of Rights by Congress following World War II, little financial aid was available to assist students with the costs of attending college. The primary sources of funds for paying tuition were parents and student employment. For this reason, higher education in the U.S. was viewed as elitist, since only those who could afford to pay for it could attend. With the advent of the GI Bill, the Defense Education Act, and the Higher Education Act during the middle of this century, higher education became affordable for virtually all of those who sought it. Toward the end of the century, increasing college costs and declining federal and state support have altered that reality somewhat. However, each year there are still billions of dollars in financial funds available through federal, state, institutional, and private sources. Students, in most cases, are not automatically eligible for funds. For many programs a complex process — driven by such factors as parent and student income levels, cost of tuition, number of family members in college, etc. — must be used to determine eligibility as well as level and type of eligibility.

The role of the financial aid officer is to make information available to potential students on the types of financial aid available, counsel students on the aid that might be available to them, review applications and determine eligibility and the amount of aid each individual student is eligible to receive, and work with the business office to ensure that students receive their aid in a timely and fiscally sound manner. The financial aid officer encourages students, where appropriate, to repay their loans on time so they will not go into default. He or she also prepares all required reports and requests for funds as required and submits them by the predetermined deadlines. While there are different views and some controversy on the subject, financial aid is being used increasingly as a recruiting device. In those instances, the financial aid officer must work very closely with the admissions officer to determine the most strategic use of aid resources to meet the institution's objectives in recruiting, enrolling, and graduating students.

Orientation

In addition to simply moving from high school to college, students may also experience a dramatic change in their relationship with the school. Most high schools are relatively small, enabling students to know many other students, particularly those in the same grade. The schools are usually close to home and the students generally return home after school every day. The teachers are supportive and encouraging, and virtually every student enrolls in the same or similar programs. On the other hand, many colleges and universities can appear large and impersonal. Students know few if any other students, at least at first. College campuses are often located quite a distance from home, so students are largely on their own and may return home only for holidays and summer vacations. Faculty have to be sought out if students need advice and assistance, and a multitude of programs may be available from which students may choose.

To respond to many of these conditions, colleges and universities provide orientation programs. Such programs may include tours of the campus and its facilities, opportunities to meet and talk with current students, testing to determine placement level in certain courses, short courses to help improve study skills, and opportunities to meet with key support personnel, such as academic advisors to plan academic programs and registrars to complete registration. Conducting these programs is the role of the orientation officer. Research demonstrates a positive correlation between orientation program participation and student retention.

Academic Advising

Colleges and universities typically offer a broad array of academic programs from which the student must choose. These programs might be organized into a single college or, in the case of a university, several colleges. Academic advisors may be faculty members who also advise students pursuing programs in their departments and/or colleges. Or they may be professional advisors who assist students in all programs and colleges at a particular institution. Institutions may require students to see an advisor before registration for each term, only periodically, or only at the student's initiative.

The role of the academic advisor is to assist the student in choosing a particular program and then to assist in selecting courses so the student meets the requirements of the program while also fulfilling personal interests and needs. In those institutions where transfer credits are not evaluated by the admissions office, the academic advisor usually provides this service. In many institutions, the academic advisor is also involved in clearing students who have completed their programs for graduation.

Learning Assistance Centers

Many students arrive at colleges and universities today unprepared for college in general or inadequately prepared in specific subject areas. Many colleges and universities provide programs and courses to help correct these deficiencies and increase the chances for success and retention of students until they complete their chosen programs. These might include study skills seminars, test-taking skills development, and tutoring in various subjects such as math and English.

The role of the learning services officer is to advise and counsel students on how to maximize their opportunities for success in completing their academic programs and to provide programs and courses that correct deficiencies.

Campus Activities and Residence Life

Virtually all colleges and universities provide at least some support services and activities, including student government, fraternities and sororities, entertainment programs, clubs, recreational sports programs, etc. Some also provide on-campus housing which offers student employment and programming options. All of these programs provide opportunities for students to come in contact with and get to know other members of the campus community, including other students, faculty, and staff. They also increase students' level of comfort at the institution, a factor so important to attracting and retaining students.

The role of the campus activities and residence life professional is to develop and oversee quality programs, often referred to as co-curricular programs, which, when combined with the academic programs, aim to develop the whole student.

Career Planning and Placement

In our rapidly changing society, many students are unclear and/or uncertain as to what their career path should be or what opportunities are available to them. Career planning and placement services may be needed early on to assist students in selecting a program or major field of study. The services may be sought out by students at any time if they wish to change their academic and/or career directions. Career planning and placement services may also be sought out as students near the completion of their academic programs to provide assistance in developing specific career paths and in providing information on job opportunities upon graduation, skill development to prepare for the job search (e.g., résumé writing, interviewing), and the arrangements for potential employers to meet with graduating job-seekers.

The role of the career planning and placement officer is to provide information resources on career choices and job opportunities, to counsel students in choosing career paths and related academic programs, to assist students in identifying employment opportunities, and to bring together potential employers and interested students.

Institutional Research

All colleges and universities have limited resources. In order to maximize the benefit from the existing resources, a great deal of research is necessary. Such research may take the form of outcomes surveys of recent graduates to determine what they liked and did not like about the institutions they attended, surveys several years out to determine how well their academic programs prepared them for careers, surveys of applicants who did and did not enroll to determine the factors affecting their decisions, and the compilation of data on how well students are progressing, as well as retention and graduation rates. The data derived from this research are then used to direct recruiting efforts, assist in program design, and determine services that need to be made available.

The role of the institutional research officer is to conduct surveys, compile data, provide analyses of data to help guide the institution in developing and carrying out its programs and activities and in achieving its optimum enrollment levels, and report data to presidents, chancellors, boards of trustees, state and federal agencies, and other organizations.

Faculty Development

The role of faculty in the enrollment process is often unclear to the faculty members themselves. Yet they play a vital role in developing institutional policies and can provide valuable assistance in recruitment and retention efforts. In order to gain their support and participation in the enrollment process, it is necessary to help them understand how they fit into the picture. They must understand how sharing stories of the successes of students in their programs helps encourage other students to enroll in those programs, how a heightened level of changes out of or withdrawals from particular courses may indicate dissatisfaction with those courses or the faculty members who teach them, and how conversations with current and potential students can have positive effects on retention and recruitment. Those in enrollment services need to convey to faculty their importance in the enrollment process and seek their active involvement.

Faculty, then, are pivotal to a successful enrollment services program. Not only are their teaching methods and styles important, but how they communicate with students, other faculty, and staff, and how actively they participate in recruiting and retention programs are essential ingredients to a successful enrollment management program.

Today, more than ever, faculty need assistance in the uses of new and rapidly changing technologies to improve their teaching as well as to prepare their students for careers depending on them. Instruction via open or closed circuit television, on-line instruction and the use of on-line media, and the preparation of videotaped instruction are examples of new teaching styles that require special teaching techniques. Faculty development programs can provide the special preparation required.

Registrar

Once students have been admitted to a college or university and have selected the academic program they wish to pursue, the next major step is registering for their courses. Historically, registrations have been conducted in an arena (armory, auditorium, gymnasium, or other large facility) with a large number of faculty and staff, many forms, many stations, and, often, long lines. Today, some colleges and universities still hold arena registrations. However, computers now help to reduce the number of forms and faculty and staff members required to conduct the registration and to greatly improve efficiency, so that long lines are much rarer today.

Newer forms of registration are now employed at many colleges and universities. The first to develop was on-line registration, in which students individually meet with a staff member to select their courses and the staff member immediately enters the data into the computer. This process usually takes only a few minutes, and at the conclusion the students have a completed schedule. Many campuses permit students to register on-line from computers in residence halls and libraries on the campus, from their homes, or from anywhere a computer and modem or network are available. The newest forms of registration are via the World Wide Web and via touchtone telephone. Using the latter method, students can call the campus from a touchtone telephone anywhere in the world, and often at any time of the day or night, and, by entering a personal identification number to identify themselves and code numbers for their courses, complete registration in minutes. Registration via the World Wide Web can also be accomplished in minutes from anywhere that students can access the Web. The efficiency and ease of the registration may be critical for some students in whether or not they remain at a particular institution; thus, the registrar has a critical impact on the enrollment process.

The registrar, then, is responsible for the conduct of registration. But the registrar also produces class rosters, grade lists, and grade reports, maintains student academic records, clears students for graduation, determines honors eligibility, often is responsible for organizing the commencement ceremony, and produces transcripts of students' academic records for further education, employment, or personal use. In addition, the registrar often publishes the schedule of classes for each term and frequently publishes the college catalog as well.

The registrar is usually the campus officer charged with implementation of the institution's academic policies as they relate to curriculum, educational records, reporting, and graduation requirements. The registrar also is the official charged with campus-wide compliance with certain federal regulations, the most visible of which is the Family Education Rights and Privacy Act (FERPA). Through involvement in the registration process, the preparation of the schedule of classes, and other areas of responsibility, the registrar is in a position to influence course offerings and program design, which in turn influence recruitment and retention.

Who Is the Enrollment Services Professional?

While literally everyone at a college or university can have an impact on enrollment and should be made aware of their role, it is the major responsibility for those in the positions identified above. But titles alone do not make someone an enrollment services professional. While there are few degree programs designed especially to prepare someone for a career as an enrollment services professional, and many of those currently holding the positions listed above have arrived in them through a variety of routes, today's enrollment services professional must come to the position with certain critical knowledge and skills. These typically include:

1. Excellent oral communication skills that enable one to make presentations to everyone from boards of trustees and college presidents to faculty, high school counselors, parents, and students.

2. Excellent written communication skills that enable one to develop and communicate information that will attract potential students to the campus as well as general information, course and schedule information, policies, and procedures for potential students, current students, and the campus community.

3. A thorough knowledge of computers and information systems. Virtually all colleges and universities today use computers for recruitment, admission, registration, the collection and maintenance of student data, research and analysis, and the production of reports and publications. Without a thorough knowledge of how to design and develop efficient and effective information systems, the enrollment services professional would be lost.

4. A thorough knowledge of other technologies that can be used to improve the efficiency and effectiveness of enrollment services offices. These include optical imaging, which is used to digitize and electronically store paper documents; touchtone telephone/voice response technology, which makes it possible to use the telephone for data entry and data access as well as for registration and receipt of grades; and desktop publishing, which can be used to prepare publications for printing, among other things.

5. The ability to analyze and synthesize data. Much of the work of the enrollment services professional relies on data. How data are collected, how data from different sources are brought together, and how data are analyzed will often determine the success or failure of recruitment, enrollment, and retention efforts and, in many cases, the success or failure of an institution.

6. Excellent knowledge of human resources management. The enrollment services professional is truly one who must rely on others to get the job done. It is essential that these professionals be able to select talented individuals to work in their units, motivate them to perform at their best both individually and as a team, and provide leadership and direction to the campus-wide enrollment effort.

7. Strategic and tactical planning capability. As higher education experiences more and more change — with increased dependence on technology, increased competition for students, the increased need to market beyond traditional venues, decreased resources from state and federal governments, and more and more dependence on tuition revenue to support the institution — the enrollment services professional must be astute at

planning, not only for each year's activities but also for the future. Only in this way can there be a comprehensive plan for moving the entire operation forward while still meeting each year's goals and objectives.

8. Excellent human relations skills. Virtually all members of the staff of enrollment services offices are required to interact with people — other college and university staff, high school counselors, potential students, current students, parents, and other members of the community. In essence, every staff member must be working at all times to build positive and effective relationships with all of those persons with whom they come in contact. Knowing how to interact with others, how to communicate with them positively and effectively, and, especially, how to maintain positive relationships when challenged are key ingredients for anyone engaged in enrollment services.

9. A thorough knowledge of higher education issues. During the early part of this century, there was relatively little change in higher education, so one could easily develop a basic knowledge of the issues. However, with the passage of the GI Bill of Rights following World War II, this began to change. The number of colleges and universities grew rapidly, community colleges were created, federal financial aid programs emerged, graduate and professional programs expanded, and enrollments soared. More recently, affirmative action programs have been challenged, resources have been slashed, and distance learning programs and "virtual" universities have challenged traditional pedagogical methods. In order to develop and maintain effective programs, the enrollment services professional must remain current on all of these issues.

10. A knowledge of legal issues in higher education. Laws related to affirmative action, disabilities, discrimination, privacy, etc., affect the content of publications, what questions you are allowed to ask on an application for admission, whom you admit and how those decisions are reached, and who has access to a student's records. Those in the enrollment services professions are often those responsible for the enforcement of these laws on the campus; therefore, they must be knowledgeable about

them and take the lead in sharing that knowledge with the rest of the campus community.

11. A thorough knowledge of and experience in marketing are absolute essentials for many enrollment services professionals. This is particularly true of those involved in recruiting and admission. There was a time when marketing was not even spoken about in higher education except in contemptuous terms; but today marketing is considered essential to achieving enrollment objectives. Knowing how to identify potential markets and how to reach individuals in those markets is of vital importance to developing and/or maintaining a successful enrollment program.

12. Counseling skills are valuable and/or necessary for many enrollment services professionals. While communications skills are important, knowing how to listen to someone's concerns and respond to them effectively — whether it be in dealing with the selection of a college, the choice of a degree program or which courses to take, or personal or emotional problems — requires the special skills of a trained counselor. Since enrollment services professionals at one time or another find themselves dealing with all of these situations, it is important that they have the skills to deal with them.

13. The ability to work with volunteers is often something that is overlooked. More and more institutions, particularly those that are extending their recruiting efforts outside the local geographical area and even to other countries, are asking volunteers to assist in the efforts. The volunteers may be students home for the summer, recent graduates, and parents of enrolled students. Since these individuals are not paid, other ways of motivating them must be found, and they must be trained in what to say and, perhaps more important, what not to say. This requires special skills and abilities not normally taught but ones that must be sought out by the interested enrollment services professional through special programs and publications

on the subject, which are often available from volunteer organizations.

What Type of Person Makes the Best Enrollment Services Officer?

The simple answer to this question would appear to be individuals who have the knowledge, skills, and abilities described above. However, while those are important, other factors have a bearing on the likelihood of one's entry into and success in the enrollment services professions.

Individuals should be outgoing, warm, and friendly, with a tendency toward extroversion and gregariousness. However, as with all things, moderation is essential. Being viewed as too friendly, or as pushy or obnoxious, or as trying to invade one's privacy, is not desirable.

Maintaining a positive attitude at all times is essential. It is difficult to present a positive image of your institution and its programs if you have a negative attitude. This often involves a great deal of self-control, particularly if you face challenges in your personal life.

Dedication and commitment are necessary traits. Hard work, long hours, and travel are often required of enrollment services officers. You must be willing to make a commitment to this level of involvement to be successful. If you are looking for a strictly 9 to 5 job, you probably should look elsewhere.

Political skills are also useful — not those required to run for elected office, but those necessary to deal effectively and politely with those "difficult" people who will be encountered frequently. These might be politicians seeking favors for their constituents or family members, parents demanding exceptions for their children, or other administrators seeking special favors. It is important to deal with these situations tactfully, so the persons involved feel they were heard and treated fairly. Political skills aid enrollment services officers in achieving this objective.

Entering the Profession

Enrollment services officers frequently enter the profession through work study assignments, internships, and part-time employment while in school. Such individuals are often the ones who staff information desks, prepare mailings of materials to potential students, make follow-up telephone calls to share their experiences at the institution and try to encourage applicants to enroll, lead campus tours, conduct orientation programs for new students, and assist with registration and records maintenance. Those who do well, exhibit the qualities of a good enrollment services officer, and have an interest in the profession are often selected to fill full-time positions when they graduate and positions become available.

Others coming into enrollment services may have degrees in areas such as higher education administration, student personnel counseling, marketing and/or public relations, communications, and information systems design and development, and many are beginning their career or making a career change.

Still others may come to enrollment services by virtue of employment in other departments or administrative units at the same or different institutions.

The Future of the Enrollment Services Profession

Higher education is undergoing change. For most of the '90s, colleges and universities have been downsizing and restructuring, often as a result of reductions in funding. This trend is likely to continue, as a result of continued reductions in state and federal funding and continuing pressure to reduce the rate of increase in tuition and fees. These changes affect the staff and structure of enrollment services offices. While many of the reductions are achieved by not filling vacant positions, the losses are still very real and the workload must be managed in some other way. Most often this is accomplished by doing more and more with fewer and fewer staff members, resulting in increased pressure for all. Increases in efficiency through advances in technology and the use of technology in the enrollment services area have, in some instances, helped to mitigate the impact of the staff reductions.

Changes of this nature have created a change in the makeup of the workforce in enrollment services offices, particularly in the support staff. Higher skill levels and more education and training are required to prepare individuals for even entry-level positions. In addition, rapid changes in technology and the continuing adaptation of new technologies to the enrollment services areas make it necessary to provide ongoing opportunities for staff training and development.

For much of the late '80s and early '90s, the number of students graduating from high schools across the nation was declining. Since this is the population that traditionally had made up the entering class at colleges and universities, the projected declines struck fear into the higher education community. Predictions of huge drops in college enrollment and vast numbers of institutional closings were common. Fortunately, for most this did not come to pass. The number of high school graduates did drop. But colleges and universities worked hard to offset the decreases by putting extra effort into what in the past had been unthinkable — marketing. Through increased recruiting and marketing efforts, institutions were able to raise the percentage of high school graduates going on to college. Another, unanticipated phenomenon occurred. The number of adults continuing their education or attending college for the first time increased dramatically. Many of these students enrolled in traditional daytime courses, unlike their predecessors, who enrolled primarily in evening and weekend courses often offered by a separate unit of the institution.

As a result of these changes, total college enrollment continued to climb each year, even while the number of high school graduates was declining. However, the growing numbers of adult and part-time students made it necessary for colleges and universities, enrollment services offices included, to change. In addition to further expanding all services into evening and weekend hours so that students would not have to take time off from work, new services were introduced that enabled students to conduct business from home or work and not even come to the campus. Examples include registration by mail, on-line registration, and touchtone telephone registration, which were mentioned earlier.

Rapid growth of distance learning programs, video courses, and on-line instruction, in part to meet the growing need to serve adult students wherever they might be, provides challenges for enrollment services offices that must also serve these students. While campuses earlier adjusted to the need to provide services at off-campus locations where courses were offered and during evening and weekend hours, now they are called on to provide services anywhere at anytime. This trend is likely to continue well into the future as "virtual" universities and course offerings on the World Wide Web become commonplace. Enrollment services offices will need to develop new ways to provide services to students acquiring their education through these new delivery vehicles.

The anticipated growth of proficiency-based education programs, both at the elementary and secondary levels and at the postsecondary level, will provide many new challenges to enrollment services professionals. Moving away from the Carnegie units and credit hours that have been the standards for many years will force enrollment services officers to find new ways to place value on educational experiences for purposes of admission, transfer, and graduation or program completion.

As indicated earlier, advances in computer technology have enabled enrollment services offices to become more efficient and effective and have helped to offset staff reductions in these areas. Continued improvements in hardware speed and capacity and new software packages will provide new opportunities in the future. The major development on the horizon that is foreseeable at this time, and that could significantly impact enrollment services offices in the future, is voice-recognition software. Eliminating the keyboard for data entry will eliminate a barrier to those who do not type well. It will also make it possible to transfer much of the data entry activity to the students and others, greatly improving the efficiency of the data entry process.

With all of the above changes that are occurring now or anticipated in the near future, the enrollment services profession has a bright and challenging future. However, those seeking employment in enrollment services offices now and in the future will require higher levels of education and training to be able to deal with the increased complexities of the work and the ever-increasing use of technology. Staff reductions are likely to continue; however, opportunities for employment and advancement in the profession appear strong.

References

Breland, Hunter M., and Associates. 1995. *Challenges in college admissions: A report of a survey of undergraduate admissions policies, practices, and procedures.* Washington DC: American Association of Collegiate Registrars and Admissions Officers, American College Testing, The College Board, Educational Testing Service, and National Association of College Admission Counselors.

Hossler, Don, John P. Bean, and Associates. 1990. *The strategic management of college enrollments.* San Francisco: Jossey-Bass.

Quann, C. James, and Associates. 1979. *Admissions, academic records, and registrar services: A handbook of policies and procedures.* San Francisco: Jossey-Bass.

Chapter 2

The Professional

by Roger M. Swanson and Faith A. Weese

The concept of the professional might be thought only to apply to those in the traditional professional fields related to medicine or law. However, the authors would argue strongly that it is a much broader descriptor that may, in fact, be applied to almost any individual who measures his or her life's work and actions against high moral, ethical, and functional standards. Thus, teachers, police officers, plumbers, race car drivers, and perhaps even wrestlers may consider themselves professionals in the sense that they require prescribed education and/or training, meet industry-wide qualifications, have their skills or productivity measured or certified by external standards, and have their conduct and integrity monitored or reviewed by an internal, institutional, or associational appointed body. In some professions, such oversight and control is very tight, whereas in others it may be more generalized.

In this chapter, following upon the first chapter, which defines our profession, the concept of the enrollment services professional will be explored. In actuality, all chapters that follow serve to further identify and enhance the educational, experiential, and skill qualifications that de-

---

Roger M. Swanson serves as Associate Executive Director of the American Association of Collegiate Registrars and Admissions Officers and has responsibility for professional development programs, the annual meeting, membership services, the SPEEDE/ExPRESS Project, and the Office of International Education Services. As an educational administrator, he has over thirty years of professional experience in higher education and has held university appointments through the dean and vice president level in both academic and student affairs.

Faith A. Weese is Registrar and Director of Academic Records at Grand Canyon University, where she teaches courses in journalism, publications, and communication. She has over twenty years of professional experience in the academic and enrollment services area and presents workshops, seminars, and conferences nationally in the area of leadership, teamwork, and communication. Currently, she serves as the AACRAO Vice President for Registration and Records Management.

scribe a member of our profession. Chapter 9, in particular, addresses admissions, records, enrollment management, and financial aid using ethics, good judgment, and honesty in determining what is best in a given set of circumstances as well as what is right and wrong.

The steps to becoming a leader in enrollment services lead from an initial entry point through learning and maturation to the leadership level. In actuality, that learning and growing never really stop, as one discovers that new challenges, technologies, and expectations require that our quest for professionalism will continue throughout our careers — and retirements!

The entry point may occur through any of the functional areas discussed in Chapter 1 and at any level. Many people join enrollment services right out of college, often extending the work they did as students into full-time jobs. The admissions ambassador or webmaster, part-time records assistant, or financial aid work-study student who gained experience and appreciation for the nature of our work did so well that they continued after graduation when a vacancy occurred — or was created for them.

As professionals in training, they expanded their specialty work, but then extended their skills and knowledge to new areas, such as publications, research, computer products, communications, document processing, program oversight, and supervision. They began at the extremities of the domain circles and gradually moved toward the center, soon beginning to interact with, if not overlap, the work of other domains in the process.

So, the fledgling assistant records manager discovers how the registration process, timing, and user-friendliness have significant recruitment and retention implications, how they fulfill instructional policies from academic affairs, and how they merge with, contribute to, and take from the campus MIS network. They not only gain greater understanding of these related areas, they begin to see the interconnectedness — concepts, policies, procedures, systems, services, inputs/outputs, and overall success measurements — of enrollment services units. They are on their way to becoming professionals when this greater perspective becomes their perspective.

Some newcomers to enrollment services may not work their ways from peripheral entry points, but may move into the professional realm from other positions on or off campus. It is not uncommon for a member of the campus computer center or advisement office to relocate to an enrollment services office based on demonstrated experience and transferable knowledge and skills. Often, with some good orientation and honeymoon adjustments, they may be fully integrated into their new responsibilities within a relatively short time.

Some top leadership positions, as well, may be filled from the ranks of those who head other campus units, who have enrollment services offices after transferring from another division (academic to student affairs or vice versa), or who are members of the faculty or another institution. For these, the learning curve may be steep for a time as they strive to learn the basics, understand the new culture, and develop a vision for the future.

As people are introduced by new duties, career growth, or personal interest to the concept of being a professional in enrollment services, what items should they consider as they strive to meet this new higher standard? What code or work ethic, written or unwritten, are they expected to follow? Are there levels of qualification, certification, or recognition necessary? How can they help others understand and grow to become fully realized professionals?

For starters, there are some written guidelines on this. Various policy statements from AACRAO help to provide professional standards for enrollment services officers, in particular the "Joint Statement of Professional Practices and Ethical Standards" (see appendix B). In addition, AACRAO has several publications that focus on the assessment of admissions and records offices. *The Admissions Profession: A Guide for Staff Development and Program Management* focuses on how to organize and administer the admissions office and its programs and develop effective student contact programs. *Professional Development Guidelines for Registrars: A Self-Audit* focuses on the knowledge and skills required by registrars and reviews the necessary functions of the registrar's office. The National Association for College Admission Counseling offers an extensive statement on professional ethics for the admissions/recruitment officer. Other associations (e.g., NASFAA) have developed similar documents for their respective functional areas.

Aside from the use of these field-specific guides, professionalism cannot be easily defined and is often judged according to the character demonstrated by the behavior of the individual. Some important *elements of professionalism* include:

- *Competence.* Becoming an enrollment services professional may require many hours of study and preparation. As a professional, you are expected to have a high level of expertise in a specific area or areas and are paid to apply that knowledge.

- *High standards of performance.* Most professionals expect high achievement from themselves and others. Meeting these standards is more important than the number of hours invested.

- *High standards of practice and ethics.* Professionals have a strong sense of right and wrong. They are driven by a code of ethics (e.g., AACRAO's *Joint Statement of Professional Practices and Ethical Standards*) that articulate a set of values about how they do their work.

- *Solid commitment to work and sense of ownership.* Professionals work hard and believe in the value of work. A professional meets the standards of the organization and also works to meet the higher standards of his or her own pride.

- *Collaborative spirit off campus and outside the organization and community.* Professionals value belonging to a collective body of individuals who are in an organization or association outside the immediate community, and who have similar training and work they can relate to and learn from.

- *Continuous training and education.* Professionals know the advantage and importance of staying current in their fields by a strong commitment to continuous training and study. To stay current or ahead and plan for the demands of the future, we must all be "perpetual learners."

- *Acceptance of responsibility.* Professionals impact the organization by seeking and graciously accepting and demonstrating responsibility (both credit *and* blame).

- *Seeking rewards other than* just *money.* Professionals expect compensation because of their knowledge and skills, but dollars alone are usually not their highest reward. They work at their specific profession because it gives them personal satisfaction and happiness as well as money.

"Professional" is more than just a word or a label. It means a different attitude, a different personality, and a different set of expectations from the average worker. Our average workers are important to the organization; however, they often view the world very narrowly and much less is expected of them.

Professional Characteristics

Being an enrollment services professional means that you must possess both the characteristics and skills of a professional. Skills can be learned; however, the basic characteristics of the professional are essential in becoming a successful enrollment services officer. No list could be truly exhaustive in measuring the expectations or qualities of the professional, but some are crucial. *Maturity, integrity,* and *judgment* are characteristics vital to your professional image.

Maturity

Professional maturity is difficult to describe, but the presence of it sets the leader apart from other individuals. A professional needs to look, think and act differently. In other words, he or she needs to *act the part.* A professional will need to develop some important characteristics to be truly successful.

- *Self-responsibility.* Mature people clearly demonstrate commitment and a willingness to take responsibility for not only their lives but also their work. They take charge of themselves and are accountable for their actions. They do not need to be micro-managed since they take the initiative to manage themselves. They think before they act and anticipate possible consequences of their actions, rather than acting before they think, thus producing embarrassing and avoidable mistakes. And when those occur, they will "take the heat," learn important lessons, and move forward.

- *Self-discipline.* Professionals always have self-discipline — without exception. Professional self-discipline is the understanding that moderation is important in the professional world and may need to be modified with each situation one faces. Emotions, opinions, and behaviors need to be controlled. Savvy, mature professionals know that extreme behavior is not rewarded in the workplace. Self-discipline may be easier if one focuses on the big picture. Then one can understand the broader purpose of the task or position and know where he or she fits. Professionals who demonstrate self-discipline are always growing, always striving for improvement, and they maximize the use of their time. They have identified specific long- and short-term goals for themselves, have a plan for achieving those goals, and have a desire that motivates them to continue working to achieve those goals.

- *Vision.* Professionals have vision to see the journey into the future and the destination. They are not just concerned about the job today, but build goals for five or ten years from now. Vision reaches beyond the limits of imagination. It is seeing invisible challenges and inspiring others to understand, accept, and commit to that vision.

- *Discretion.* Professionals know when to be serious and when to have fun as well as when to relax and when to work hard, depending on the circumstances. Discretion also means maintaining caring and confidentiality in all relationships.

- *Value of people.* With maturity comes a distinct realization of how important people are to an organization. Professionals understand that all people do not view the world the same way and they accept, appreciate, and celebrate the differences in people.

- *Discernment.* Professionals learn how to get along with friends, co-workers, and family. When conflict comes, it should be over important things — not small things.

- *Above and beyond.* Most professionals choose to *go beyond what is expected.* They want to expand professionally and personally by striving to grow, produce, and be greater than standard workplace expectations.

- *Positive attitude.* Maturity is not the level of experience you may have in an organization, but more so an *attitude* and the presence a positive attitude fosters. A professional attitude makes a difference. Attitude sets the tone, not only for the professional with the attitude, but for everyone near.

Integrity

Integrity is one of most important characteristics for a professional to develop. It may take years to achieve (and can be lost in a moment), but it is vital to professional success. Integrity is the characteristic that leads people to trust you and, if developed, is one of your most valuable assets. It is defined more easily by actions than words and includes:

- Modeling consistency in "words" and "walk"
- Showing accuracy, timeliness, and punctuality
- Being committed to completing the job well and *on time*
- Following through with dependability and trustworthiness
- Demonstrating honesty and ethics
- Exhibiting confidentiality
- Seeking to make a positive difference in the lives of co-workers and students
- Caring for others, on and off the job
- Showing loyalty to the institution, supervisor, and supporting staff

- Demonstrating morally and legally acceptable behavior on and off the job
- Sharing credit
- Taking responsibility for mistakes you and your subordinates make and correcting them

Judgment

Good judgment is a crucial characteristic that you must possess to be an effective professional. Know your own limits. Understand that situations may arise when you feel you need help to solve a problem. Admit it, then get it. Period. Seek out an experienced colleague, whether it be on campus or in another community or association. Learn from others and borrow from their experience. No need to spend time reinventing the wheel. There is always experienced judgment around that you can benefit from. Professionals build judgment by demonstrating the following:

- *Thinking ahead.* Think beyond today and your immediate actions. Anticipate outcomes and consequences.
- *Viewing from the top.* Good judgment requires that you understand your organization, your department, and your specific job. Know how it fits within and beyond your campus, organization, and community.
- *Understanding yourself.* Know what you are good at as well as what you are not and call for wise counsel and advice when necessary. Understand that you and your job responsibilities are part of a larger, complex, interrelated system. See yourself as part of the whole.

You could say that these characteristics also describe a saint or holy person, and yet, upon the demonstration of these, day in and day out, rest the conclusions that others will make as to our overall character and professionalism. While no one pleases everyone all the time, it is surprising how similar the perceptions are when people express their views of individuals. And this perception goes a long way in determining how much we will support, follow, vote for, respect, care for, and even love one another.

Professional Skills

Knowledge and information are important as well as good personal traits and characteristics; however, professional skills are also needed to be successful:

- *Getting results.* Getting things done is a special skill and usually the bottom line. It allows no room for whining, complaining, or excuses. Professionals find ways to get things done instead of finding excuses not to.

- *Interpersonal communication.* Becoming an effective professional means that one needs to understand the importance of people. Professionals know how to meet people, develop rapport with them, understand them, and work constantly to develop working relationships. Successful professionals have a genuine concern for people, the ability to focus on and communicate with all kinds of people, while at the same time they are willing to look you in the eye with personal integrity and conviction. Effective professionals know that the fastest way to open the lines of communication is to smile. It overcomes innumerable communication barriers, crossing the boundaries of culture, race, age, gender, education, and economic status.

- *Time management and setting priorities.* One of the most precious resources you have is your time. How you choose to spend your time is one of the most important decisions that you make on a daily basis. Plan wisely and prioritize your work.

- *Appearance.* How you look is a very important factor in creating your professional image. Without ever saying a word or doing anything, you make or break your image just by your dress, grooming, and overall appearance. Clothes express three messages: they tell something about your campus or organization, your position in the organization, and the way you feel about yourself. Pay attention to what you wear; it often dictates how you act. Know what is appropriate in your office, on your campus, or in your organization.

- *Basic office skills.* Being an effective professional not only means doing the BIG things well, it means handling the everyday things that make working in the office and with professional colleagues easier. Important skills include: telephone manners, memo writing, meeting skills, presentation skills, and computer literacy.

Recognition of how well the professional meets these standards is probably less well defined in enrollment services than in many other fields, where legal or official standards are both set and measured, either once or on a continuing basis. Some professionals require initial certification or licensure based on examinations, education levels, competency-based demonstrations, or field evaluations. The enrollment services officer may be required to have some educational qualifications, but little more is usually required in order to continue practicing. The closest most of us come is our annual job-related review or evaluation, measuring our activities against job description, goals, or outcomes.

Many of the key professionalism indicators noted above are difficult to measure accurately, except, for some, in their breech. AACRAO is currently pursuing the possibility of credentialing programs that will provide definitions of knowledge, skills, and education levels resulting from experience, degrees and course work, tests, and competencies. These, combined with professional development and training opportunities, will offer recognition of professional status for some levels of enrollment services officers. Such programs would help direct the growth of younger professionals, provide some measurement of accomplishment and status, and allow those interested to offer additional résumé criteria toward new positions, promotions, increases of duty and salary, and general self-advancement.

While evaluations of professionals are made according to the key external standards discussed above, they may also derive from measurement against the internal ethic by which a person lives and judges his or her thoughts and actions. It is this internal ethic that parents, religious leaders, and school teachers seek to instill in children so that they do the right things without immediate supervision. The same applies in adulthood and keeps us obeying the driving rules of the road, even when police officers are not around. The true professional measures every action — proposed, in process, and in retrospect — by a high internal standard. Developing that standard and then acting within its scope marks the ethical maturity of the enrollment services professional.

If this is so, where is the value of living and working toward high external and internal professional standards? Is virtue its own reward? Or are other reasons sufficiently compelling?

For bottom-line people, consummateprofessionalism would seem to render the individual more successful, employable, and happy. Many of the qualities a professional values and demonstrates are shown by business and psychological research to lead to greater productivity, increased effectiveness, and certainly stronger respect, cooperation, and reciprocity of high-road behavior. Activation of nearly every quality noted above tends to receive positive and like response. Hence, trust builds trust, caring brings caring in return, and loyalty engenders loyalty.

Does it always work? No. Do we open ourselves up to betrayal, manipulation, and disloyalty? Yes. But our experience tends strongly to show that these are the exceptions. And often our belief in others and taking risks with them actually stimulates their best response in return, as they try to live up to the esteem we have given them. In human interactions, there are no 100 percent guarantees. So we need to act with caution, care, and prudence, but also with optimism, faith, and, perhaps, acceptance of what comes back to us; offer the benefit of the doubt, but keep good notes; and learn to compromise, and perhaps, to forgive. People often find new resources to live up to expectations and will work to justify the credibility we give them. That's another thing professionals learn to do.

Wherever you choose to serve in enrollment services, or other career- or community-related areas, you can become an effective professional. You can build on your professional qualities, characteristics, and skills and use them to motivate and influence others. What sets professionals apart from other people? It is not how much education they have, how much money they make, where they come from, or whom they know. It is certainly not their age, ethnicity, gender, or occupation. It is their awareness of the needs of others and the challenges they face. It is their enthusiasm for improvement and creating new opportunities. They have a passion for a cause and want to give something back to society. In this quest, they have tapped their personal power and professional potential.

Final Words

As noted in this chapter, some professional qualities are "how-to" skills and aptitudes, while others involve philosophies and attitudes. Professional qualities and characteristics are present in all of us to some degree. To develop and use them, one does not need to study complex psychological theories. They are basic, common-sense ideas and attitudes that can individually and collectively make you a more effective professional. Professionalism is not something that you learn once and for all; it continues to evolve throughout your journey. The enrollment services professional is not just a person, and the enrollment services profession is not a department — it is an attitude of professionalism. It is an ever-evolving pattern of skills, talents, and ideas that grow and change as you do. Professionals must have a clear definition of the qualities, characteristics, and skills that are crucial for success, a vision, and an honest desire to grow and make a difference in this challenging and continuously changing world in which we live.

References

AACRAO. 1991. *The admissions profession: A guide for staff development and program management.* Washington DC: American Association of Collegiate

Registrars and Admissions Officers and the National Association for College Admission Counseling.

———. 1987. *Professional development guidelines for registrars: A self audit.* Washington DC: American Association of Collegiate Registrars and Admissions Officers.

Bennis, Warren. 1994. *On becoming a leader.* Reading MA: Addison-Wesley Publishing company

Bennis, Warren, and Joan Goldsmith. 1994. *Learning to lead.* Reading MA: Addison-Wesley Publishing Co.

Bennis, Warren, and Burt Nanus. 1985. *Leaders: The strategies for taking charge.* New York: Harper & Row.

Cabrera, James C., and Charles F. Albrecht, Jr. 1995. *The lifetime career manager.* Holbrook MA: Adams Media Corporation.

Carnegie, Dale, and Associates, Inc. 1993. *The leader in you.* New York: Simon & Schuster.

Coleman, David D., and John E. Johnson. 1990. *The new professional.* Washington DC: National Association of Student Personnel Administrators, Inc.

Connors, Roger, Tom Smith, and Craig Hickman. 1994. *The Oz principle.* Englewood Cliffs NJ: Prentice Hall.

Covey, Stephen R. 1994. *First things first.* New York: Simon & Schuster.

———. 1989. *The 7 habits of highly effective people: Restoring the character ethic.* New York: Simon & Schuster.

Hall, Edward T. 1969. *The hidden dimension.* Garden City NY: Doubleday.

Laborde, Genie Z. 1994. *Influencing with integrity.* Palo Alto CA: Syntony Publishing.

Linver, Sandy. 1994. *The leader's edge.* New York: Simon & Schuster.

Maddux, Robert B. 1988. *Building an effective student service team.* Washington DC: American Association of Collegiate Registrars and Admissions Officers.

———. 1989. *Effective interviewing to build a quality student service staff.* Washington DC: American Association of Collegiate Registrars and Admissions Officers.

———. 1989. *Effective performance appraisals for quality student service.* Washington DC: American Association of Collegiate Registrars and Admissions Officers.

Martin, William B. 1988. *Quality student service.* Washington DC: American Association of Collegiate Registrars and Admissions Officers.

Maxwell, John. 1993. *Developing the leader within you.* Nashville TN: Thomas Nelson, Inc., Publishers.

Sabath, Ann Marie. 1993. *Business etiquette in brief: The competitive edge for today's professional.* Holbrook MA: Bob Adams, Inc.

Scott, Dru. 1989. *Effective telephone communication skills.* Washington DC: American Association of Collegiate Registrars and Admissions Officers.

Seitz, Victoria A. 1992. *Your executive image.* Holbrook MA: Bob Adams, Inc.

Senge, Peter M. 1994. The fifth discipline fieldbook: Strategies and tools for building a learning organization. New York: Currency Doubleday.

Zaccarelli, Herman E. 1993. *Training managers to train: A practical guide to improve employee performance.* Washington DC: American Association of Collegiate Registrars and Admissions Officers.

Chapter 3

Communication

by Faith A. Weese

"What you are speaks so loudly I cannot hear what you say."
— *Ralph Waldo Emerson*

Even in highly technical jobs, success or failure is determined more by human relations skills than by technical proficiency. Effective leaders must learn to communicate clearly and directly — in writing, speaking, listening, and observing and through the professional image they present. How a leader communicates an attitude and vision will set the pace and tone in the workplace, which, in turn, inspires, motivates, and obtains significant (often extraordinary) results from people and builds powerful, productive teams. Whether negotiating a contract, getting an idea across in a meeting, functioning effectively with co-workers, minimizing conflict, or building collaboration, the ability to communicate with diverse people in different situations is crucial to a leader's success.

Look behind any successful leader and what will you find? Again and again, research proves that communication skills are the most essential ingredient to success. Think about the leaders you most admire. Do they get their point across, consistently? Are they able to persuade and motivate others? Do they virtually always say the right thing, at the right

---

Faith A. Weese is Registrar and Director of Academic Records at Grand Canyon University, where she teaches courses in journalism, publications, and communication. She has over twenty years of professional experience in the academic and enrollment services area.

As a professional speaker, Faith presents workshops, seminars, and conferences nationally in the areas of leadership, communication, and teamwork. Currently she serves AACRAO as Vice President for Registration and Records Management and immediate Past-President of the Arizona AACRAO. She has served on numerous state, regional, and national committees, which include, most recently, Chair of AACRAO's Publications Advisory Board and member of AACRAO's Professional Competencies and Credentialing Task Force.

time? Do they keep their heads in the face of anger and conflict? Do they project the powerful images that you are striving for? Great news! These skills are not inborn; they are learned.

Leaders who have the ability to communicate information and ideas effectively have a powerful edge, an unparalleled opportunity to persuade, motivate, and make things happen. No other skill can increase effectiveness and leadership more than being able to present yourself, your organization, and your ideas as a leader with confidence, clarity, and persuasiveness.

This chapter gives insight into the communication process and ways of improving your communication competence. It may be more important to you than you initially imagined, because communication effectiveness is vital to success in nearly every walk of life. For instance, of the seventeen factors most important in helping graduating college students obtain employment, oral communication, listening ability, and enthusiasm (all of which are basic to this chapter) were found to be first, second, and third in importance, respectively (Curtis, Winsor, and Stephens 1989). Whether you aspire to a career in enrollment services, higher education, business, industry, government, or almost any other field you can name, communication skills are likely to be a prerequisite to your hiring and your success.

A good communicator has skill — an aptitude — and a philosophy — an attitude. Your skill can be learned and polished, but what you communicate grows out of your mission, your sensitivity, courage, ethics, commitment, and vision — all the qualities that make you the leader you wish to be.

In this chapter we will consider the power of attitude as it relates to communication: how it affects relationships and how you can use it to enhance your leadership and serve your followers and constituents so they can help you make a difference. We will also look at the less obvious, more subtle elements of communication that play such a vital role in mastering productive relationships as well as the communication process.

A Fact of Life

"They that govern the most make the least noise."
— *John Selden*

It is a fact of life: we are all intensely involved in the ever-changing and expanding Information Age. As enrollment services professionals, we are deeply immersed in a communication revolution. Daily we are inundated with an explosion of information. Our campuses are getting larger, offices are increasing in size and partnering with other corporations and/or campuses, activities within our communities and on our campuses are more specialized, and more communication is needed to keep the wheels turning.

Computer technology has dramatically changed our work habits. We hold international videoconference team meetings and conduct video marketing recruitment without leaving the office. In our exploding age of technology, we quite often let our machines do the talking for us. A brief look at communications today — in particular, the Internet — reveals the most important example of a communications pattern that is being extended. The familiar communication links — letters, books, newspapers, magazines, films, and television — always told a few stories to many people. For the first time in history, many people tell stories and communicate to countless others. Over twenty million people worldwide are on "the Net," creating on-line groups, friendships, and even romances and reaching around the world in seconds. Electronic communication is expanding in countless directions — computers talk to us and to themselves and have already become a communication infrastructure for synthesizing, storing, and distributing information.

Computers, faxes, and e-mail are all important methods of communication, but they cannot replace the communication that fosters human relationships. Much energy and security can be lost through an inability to communicate or negotiate easily. This is especially true in moments of conflict or dilemma. Most of us end up trying to avoid conflict because it seems easier that way. But speaking honestly and openly in this kind of situation immediately lifts tension and makes energy flow. Conflict resolution is important in a society in which rapid change has created tension. Mediation is becoming common. Even kindergarten children are being taught how to diffuse anger and become mediators.

We are all learning how to control ourselves as well as to manage those who cannot communicate easily. This is important because the way in which people talk together in organizations is central to their ability to work together. Leaders need to notice and increase the time they spend resolving people issues — it is crucial to survival and success, but not always easy. Multi-tasking, the ability to do many things at once, is already a way of life. The telephone has metamorphosed into automatic dialer, recorder, desktop speaker, message-taker, fax, copier, and bank. Microsoft's Windows 95™ software fills a computer screen with icons that signal it is ready to perform nearly every task required to run a life or a business — but it will never completely take the place of the special touch of persuasion and negotiation that human relations skills can provide.

Communicating more does not mean we are doing it better; however, the importance of effective communication is recognized today as never before. It is an ever-evolving pattern of skills, talents, and ideas that grow and change as you do. Whatever your aspirations, you will discover the importance of effective communication in helping you achieve your goals.

The Process

The complex process of communication involves senses, experiences, and feelings. It is more than just letters, reports, telephone conversations, interviews, and e-mail. It is the action of people talking, listening, seeing, feeling, and reacting to each other, their experiences, and their environment.

We communicate for a purpose, and usually, our basic objectives in communication are:

1. To be understood exactly as we intended

2. To secure the desired response to our message

3. To maintain favorable relations with those with whom we communicate

When we examine our own campuses, we see many examples of verbal and nonverbal behavior. Those who are concerned with effective communication do not focus solely on what is said or written, but on how the person involved perceives and/or thinks about the message. Thus, we see the importance of communication to leaders. In an effort to attain organizational goals, leaders use communication to persuade, inform, and motivate people who play key roles in getting things done. Leaders almost always get their jobs done through other people. They may be skilled controllers, production supervisors, or directors, but they need people to achieve their objectives. The only way to get other people to do what the leader thinks should be done is through communication. Research further indicates that monetary rewards and fear may be effective short-run motivators, but they rarely work on a long-term basis. Communication, which often fulfills basic social and egoistic needs, can and does work as a positive motivator. At the core of effective communications is a choice we make every day — an attitude.

The Choice from Within — An Attitude

"A person cannot travel within and stand still without."
— James Allen

We live in a world of words. Attached to these words are meanings that bring varied responses from us. Words such as "happiness," "acceptance," "peace," and "success" describe what each of us desires. But there is one word that will either heighten the possibility of our desires being fulfilled or prevent them from becoming a reality within us. Our *attitude* is a primary force that will determine whether we succeed or fail.

For some, attitude presents a difficulty in every opportunity. For others, it presents an opportunity in every difficulty. Some climb with a positive attitude, while others fail with a negative perspective. The very fact that the attitude "makes some" while "breaking others" is significant enough for us to explore its importance. Our attitude actually determines our approach to life.

One of my favorite stories is about a grandma and grandpa who visit their grandchildren. Every day, grandpa would lie down for a nap; however, one day, as a practical joke, the six-year-old grandson decided to put Limburger cheese in his mustache. Before long, grandpa woke up sniffing. "Why this room stinks!" grandpa exclaimed as he got up and went out to the kitchen. But not long after he arrived in the kitchen, he decided that the kitchen smelled too. So he walked outside for a breath of fresh air. Much to grandpa's surprise, the open air brought no relief, and he proclaimed, "The whole world stinks!" How true that is to life itself! When we carry "Limburger cheese" in our attitudes, the whole world smells bad.

"The greatest discovery of my generation is that human beings can alter their lives by altering their attitudes."
— William James

Our attitude tells us what we expect from life. The world does not care what our perception is or how we view life. It marches on. Adopting a good, healthy attitude toward life does not affect society nearly so much as it affects the individual. The change cannot come from others. It must come from within. We are individually responsible for our view of life — it is our choice. Our attitude and action toward life help determine what happens to us. It would be impossible to estimate the number of jobs that have been lost, the number of promotions missed, the number of sales not made, and the number of marriages ruined by poor attitudes. But almost daily we witness jobs that are held, but hated, and marriages that are tolerated, but unhappy — all because people are waiting for others to change instead of realizing that they are responsible for their own behavior. It is impossible for us to tailor-make all situations in enrollment services to fit our lives perfectly, but it is possible to tailor-make our attitudes to fit. The behavior can be learned, and the positive outlook can become natural.

Not only does attitude determine our approach to life, it determines our relationships with people. Effective communication takes a wise combination of many methods to reach the needs of people. You must know your people, establish a relationship built on trust, and model leadership.

Establishing relationships with people can be difficult. People are funny. They want to be in the front of the line but often seem to take the middle of the road. Tell someone there are 500 billion stars and he will believe you; however, tell that same person that a bench has just been painted, and he must touch it to be sure. People are frustrating at times. They show up at the wrong place, at the wrong time, for the wrong reason. They are always interesting — but not always charming. They are not always predictable, because they have minds of their own. You cannot get along with them and you cannot get along without them. That is why it is essential to build proper relationships with others in our crowded world.

> *"The most important single ingredient to the formula of success is knowing how to get along with people."*
> — Theodore Roosevelt

The Stanford Research Institute says that the money you make in any endeavor is determined only 12.5 percent by knowledge and 87.5 percent by your ability to deal with people. As higher education professionals, we are not in the book business: we are in the *people business*.

> *"I will pay more for the ability to deal with people than any other ability under the sun."*
> — John D. Rockefeller

> *"It doesn't make much difference how much other knowledge or experience an executive possesses; if he is unable to achieve results through people, he is worthless as an executive."*
> — J. Paul Getty

Usually, the person who rises within an organization has a good attitude. Promotions did not give that individual an outstanding attitude, but an outstanding attitude resulted in promotions.

Often, our attitude is the only difference between success and failure. Certainly aptitude is important to our success in life. Yet, success or failure in any undertaking is caused more by mental attitude than by mental capacities alone.

I remember the times that I would come home from teaching school frustrated because of modern education's emphasis on aptitude instead of attitude. I wanted the students to be tested on A.Q. (Attitude Quotient) instead of just the I.Q. (Intelligence Quotient). For some students, I.Q. was high yet performance was low. There were others whose I.Q. was low, but whose performance was high. We see the same illustration in our offices everyday — and more often than not, attitude makes more difference in performance than aptitude.

A university president some years ago gave this advice to an aspiring school administrator:

> Always be kind to your A and B students. Someday, one of them will return to your campus as a good professor. And also be kind to your C students. Someday, one of them will return and build a $2 million science laboratory.

Coaches understand the importance of their teams having the right attitude before facing a tough opponent. Surgeons want to see their patients mentally prepared before going into surgery. Job-seekers know that their prospective employer is looking for more than just skills when they apply for work. Public speakers want a conducive atmosphere before they communicate with their audience. Why? Because the right attitude in the beginning ensures success at the end.

Our attitude can also give us an uncommon positive perspective. I have observed the different approaches and results achieved by a positive thinker and by a person filled with fear and apprehension. The individual whose attitude causes him to approach life from an entirely positive perspective is not always understood. He is what some would call a "no-limit person." In other words, he does not accept the normal limitations of life as most people do. He is unwilling to accept "the accepted" just because it is accepted. His response to self-limited conditions will probably be "Why?" rather than "OK." He has no limitation in his life. His strengths are not so plentiful that he cannot fail; however, he is determined to walk to the very edge of his potential or the potential of a project before he accepts defeat.

This "no limit" mindset allows a person to start each day with a positive disposition. The future not only looks bright when the attitude is right, but the present is much more enjoyable. The positive person understands that the journey is as enjoyable as the destination.

What really matters is what happens in us, not to us — in other words, it is an inside job. It's up to each one of us. Attitudes are chosen. We can *choose* the one we want. The basic core of effective communication and success on the job, as well as at home and with friends is our attitude. Simply stated, it *is* a daily decision. It determines our outlook and perspective on life, how we respond to life's pressures and daily stresses, and, ultimately, how effectively we communicate and relate to others.

A Matter of Perception

> *"I know you believe you understand what you think I said, but I'm not sure you realize that what you heard is not what I meant."*
> *— Anonymous*

Perception is the process of gathering sensory information and assigning meaning to it. Our perceptions are a result of our selection, organization, and interpretation of sensory information. Inaccurate perceptions cause us to see the world not as it is, but as we would like it to be.

Perception of Self

How we communicate depends a great deal on how we define and evaluate *ourselves*. Our definitions and evaluations of self are a result of our perceptions — although not necessarily accurate. Our "self-concept" is what we think we are. It is the total of our generalizations about self — it organizes and guides the processing of information about self.

Although our self-concept is well-formed by the time we become adults, we continue to present it publicly through various roles we take. A role is a pattern of learned behavior that people adopt to meet the perceived needs of a particular context. Based on how we appraise ourselves and how others respond to us, we may choose or be forced to model various roles. For instance, during the day we may assume the role of an enrollment services professional as a director, dean, or vice president. However, in the evening we may take on the role of father, mother, or grandparent. Everyone assumes numerous roles. Some roles that we enact in private or within the family may be different from those we use in public. The term "working self-concept" has been used to denote the specific aspects of one's identity that are activated by the role one is using at a particular time. "To some extent we become different people as we move from situation to situation" (Deaux, Dane, and Wrightsman 1993, 56).

Our "self-image" is our perception of our self-concept. It is formed through self-appraisal and is influenced by our reactions to experiences. We form impressions about ourselves partly from what we see. We look at a recent photograph and make judgments about our physical shape, dress, and facial expression. If we like what we see, we may feel good about ourselves. If we do not like what we see, we may, and should, try to change, since we know that self-image is a powerful communication tool.

In addition to our self-perceptions, our self-image stems from how others react and respond to us. People form their impressions of us by looking at the outside and making assumptions about what is on the inside. They take us at face value. It is our responsibility to establish the image we value — and establish it quickly. You never get a second chance to make a first impression.

Perception of Others

Perception also plays an important role in forming impressions of others. Because research shows that the accuracy of people's perceptions and judgments varies considerably, our communication will be most successful if we do not rely entirely on our impressions to determine how another person feels or what that person is really like. We will improve, or at least better understand, our perceptions of others if we take into account how perceptions are affected by our own self-image and self-esteem, the physical characteristics and social behaviors of the other person, stereotyping, emotional states, and cultural differences. Consider this example:

> As John finishes the beginning of his presentation to a group of enrollment services professionals in his organization, he sees several of them squinting and frowning as they look at him. As he moves into the body of his presentation, his anxiety level builds because he perceives his listeners as being critical of his ideas. Their nonverbal reactions so shake him that he stumbles through his final two most important points. After he finishes, he is surprised when several of his listeners tell him that his remarks really stimulated them to think about changes that need to be made. Then when one person comments that the glare from

the window behind him made it difficult to look at him, he realized what had really happened. Clearly, he had misinterpreted the looks on their faces.

We all carry preconceived notions around with us. In Physiology 101, we learn that much of what we see is what we are prepared to see, which is related to attitude. When Flip Wilson says, "What you see is what you get," he is not talking about attitude; he is talking about accomplishments. Certainly in an ideal world, we would judge people by what they do — not by their race or clothes or even social status. However, this is not an ideal world, and we judge others by the images they project. We can learn to improve perceptions if we look for additional information about people, actively question the accuracy of our perceptions, realize that perceptions of people may need to be changed over time, and check perceptions verbally before we react.

Differing perceptions are like filters. We each use different filters as we view the world. In other words, we each may see life through a different colored lens. When we understand about differing perceptions, or filters, we know how a police officer could obtain two diametrically opposing accounts of one accident from two eyewitnesses, how two people in an organization can have fundamentally different views of the company's purpose, and how two people can have a conversation and come away with totally different views of what was communicated.

Words alone have no meaning. Meaning is assigned through one's understanding of and experiences with a word. Communication is a *people* process rather than a *language* process. Heighten your awareness of the human interaction involved if you want to become an effective communicator. In addition to *perception*, three vital aspects and typical perception blocks that impact communication are *assumptions*, *feelings*, and *defensiveness*.

Just as we assume that our messages are clearly received, so we *assume* that because something is important to us, it is important to another, or maybe even everyone. We assume that our leadership is accepted and that everyone is looking at the problem the same way or that our perception of reality is the only one. This is not reality in any of our worlds.

A perfect example of perception is illustrated by Ed Young in one of my favorite children's books, *Seven Blind Mice,* which is based on the ancient Indian fable, the "Blind Men and the Elephant."

Seven blind mice who had never seen an elephant and had no prior knowledge of them are allowed to interact with a live elephant (actually this rather large Something that was found near the edge of the mice pond). The seven blind mice go out one by one to investigate the strange Something by the pond, and each comes back with a different idea of what it is. Argue as they might, they cannot agree.

In summary, it tells the story of seven blind mice discovering different parts of an elephant and arguing about its appearance. Only when the last mouse ventures out and investigates thoroughly do they finally learn for certain what the strange Something is — and what the whole truth is as well!

As the six blind mice began to discuss their perceptions, each could hardly believe how dense the others were for not coming to the "proper" conclusion. None of them was able to convince the others that he was right and they were wrong. And none of them would concede that the others might be right — not after what each of them had just experienced firsthand! Only after they followed the wisdom of the seventh mouse could they begin to perceive correctly.

So who was right? They all were, of course! Each of the mice had an absolutely correct, firsthand perception of an elephant. The problem was that each mouse had only one perception. And with such a limited perspective (on so large a matter), it was impossible for them to reach a mutually satisfactory conclusion, until, of course, they took proper and appropriate assessment by stepping back to see the whole and by getting a different perspective.

We make the same, or at least similar, mistakes when we make assumptions based on a limited number of perceptions. Dealing daily with massive issues such as religion, business, school, marriage, self-image, depression, relationships — the "elephants" in our lives — we have a number of perceptions on file concerning each subject. But very likely we have not accumulated enough information to form a functional view of each issue. We need a number of accurate perceptions before we make any assumptions about ourselves, our friends, our co-workers, our supervisors, or the world around us. A perception is a mental image — a mental snapshot.

In relationships in which the readings of the other person are few and far apart, the assumptions we make on our perceptions can be drastically inaccurate. A close-up of an elephant's tusk, trunk, ear, leg, or tail would not help us much in identifying an elephant, but if we had all seven images and believed that they were all accurate, we could begin to get a realistic picture. Better still, we might decide to back off from the elephant far enough to get a picture of the entire animal — or at least the side facing the camera. We might even want to get pictures from several different angles. Then, with our collection of snapshots or *per-*

ceptions, we could begin to understand how all the various pieces are part of the great whole.

You might say that we need to get a "view from the pressbox." It made sense, after someone long ago explained it to me, why our high school football coach would often quietly disappear in the middle of the third quarter. I remember near the end of football season during my senior year I looked up from the sidelines and noticed that the coach was nowhere to be seen. I couldn't figure out where he was. Near the end of the game I asked a faculty member who was sitting near me (they always seemed to know everything), "Where's our coach?" "In the pressbox," he answered quickly. "Getting a drink?" "No, getting some perspective." Well, that certainly made sense then and even more so now. There's no way any coach can keep up with all the game from the sidelines, with everyone yelling advice, parents complaining, players screaming, and, of course, cheerleaders cheering.

Sometimes we need to "get some perspective." It is vital that we keep a finger on the pulse of our own lives as well as that of our work environment and organization. Self-examination and evaluation are vital and critical to the success of any leader. It is hard to evaluate ourselves while we're in the middle of the game — tight schedules, ringing phones, and constant interruptions. My suggestion is to take some "pressbox time" and get away from everything and everyone, as often as possible or whenever appropriate, in order to see the *big picture*. A day or time like this will not just happen. We must *make* it for ourselves. We never wake up and just happen to have some free time on our hands. We each need to think about readjusting our calendars to make time in our schedule — *and take it*. We must remember that getting some *pressbox perspective* could change the whole ball game and make good communications even more effective. To really communicate with an audience, it is important to escape from the everyday routine of our own life and get inside the mindset of the audience. When speaking on effective communication and trying to get people to move out of their little world of set perceptions, I use the following illustration, which I learned from a colleague and masterful communicator many years ago:

> As the audience settles back to hear a presentation on powerful communication skills, I reach into my pocket and pull out a roll of colored tape. I tell them how each one of us lives inside a box. As I continue to speak, I peel the tape off the roll and, with a sense of style and proportion, I start to form the outline of a box on the floor. I use the tape gently, but firmly pressing it onto the carpet — enclosing myself into the box. I continue to talk as I do this and tell them that "our boxes" for

each of us are the individual routines of our lives. Many of us live very ordered lives — and enjoy it. We get up at the same time every day, brush our teeth with the same toothpaste, eat the same breakfast, read the same paper, take the same route to the same job, stare out the same window — and probably say the same things to the same people every day. Such an ordered life becomes our box. As I stand up within the box, neatly formed on the floor, I look down at the bars of colored tape and tell them they need to move out of their box. As I step out and move around, I'm looser now, the words seem to flow more easily, and the dynamics inside the room change. The room even seems bigger. I proceed to tell them that NOW I can look at the world through another person's perspective. If I'm trying to understand someone I'm working with, I try to experience what I'm asking them to do — to see how it feels, that which maybe I had only pictured in my mind before. I try to see it from their point of view, which is not always easy. Most of us operate, day after day, within the self-imposed confines of our own boxes. Communications — whether it be presentations, negotiations or just information dissemination — suffer when we never bother to find out what our audience is thinking. Before we tell somebody else what to do, we should spend a little time looking out at that person's world. My advice: "get inside and look out." In other words, learn how to step outside the boundaries and get an "outside view." Actually it's not hard to do — it just takes time.

Additional considerations might be:

- Whether you are to negotiate for a promotion or make a presentation to a superior in the office or speak to administrators in your campus community, be still and listen. Where are the problems? What are the needs? What are the expectations? Note the language you must use to be heard. See how it feels inside the pressure cooker of an administrator's office, if possible. Knowing their world is an advantage in effective communication.

- If you are going to talk to your peers, spend some time watching the manager, asking questions, sensing trouble spots. Or, at the very least, get on the phone and talk to three or four managers or co-workers to get the pulse of the office, then make calls around the region or the nation. Tell them you are preparing an important presentation to your peers, association, organization, or whatever the case. They will talk to you. Try it.

- Get out of YOUR box and find out what's happening in all those other boxes, especially those boxes where your audience lives. Remember: everyone you communicate with evaluates you and listens from inside their boxes. Dare to be different — and effective. You need to know what it's like in there if you want to be an effective communicator.

Clearly, after I finish talking about getting outside the box and carefully removing the tape from the floor, the symbolism of it stays — indelibly imprinted where effective communication skills always leave their mark ... on the memory of those listening — really listening.

If you met me for the first time, you might make certain assumptions about me. I hope you would think I was a kind and considerate person, knowledgeable about my work and professional concerns. But I doubt that you would make accurate assumptions about my whole personality. You probably would not know that I used to be a commercial calligrapher. You probably have never seen me play racquetball or swim. You would not know what kind of relationships I have with co-workers, peers, supervisors, family, or community. You would not know whether I keep a neat tidy office or leave piles of paperwork strewn everywhere. You might make assumptions about these kinds of things, but those assumptions would be based more on what you know about yourself than on what you know about me.

Though your perceptions about me could be entirely accurate, several factors might prevent you from making correct assumptions. For one thing, you simply would not have enough snapshots to get a complete picture. You would need to observe me over a longer period of time, in a variety of settings, before you could tell whether your initial readings of me were accurate.

It is in the area of making wrong assumptions based on correct perceptions that most of us miss the mark. When we are too quick, we jump to conclusions, or when we make key assumptions based on limited information, our misassumptions can lead to serious confusion. Making right assumptions based on right perceptions is never a problem. But a great many of us are guilty of forming misassumptions even though we have perceived correctly.

In this day of emotional chaos and personal confusion, the better we know ourselves and our friends and co-workers, the stronger our character, confidence, and communication. The problem with *assumptions* is that we rarely test them. In time, they become — in our minds — concrete facts. A good step in effective communications is to stop assuming that the other person understands what you are saying because you understand.

As we further examine the importance of the area of perception in communication, we will discover how to identify and maximize strengths while learning ways to compensate for weaknesses. We will see how other people think and operate as we discover the differences, and we may even begin to understand those "strange" people for the first time.

The second perception block I want to discuss is *feelings*. Feelings also play a significant role in each of our perceptions. A phrase often heard is: "Just give me the facts or the bottom line and don't get emotional." You may hear this phrase every day, in one way or another. It is often thought in our professional world that there is not room for feelings. All we want is calm, pure logic. So, what we do is weigh all our communications against the evidence, as we perceive it. After all, if I put out the facts — I know they are facts — then you ought to be able to understand my logic, right?

Wrong! The reality is that every person is involved with his feelings ALL the time. Any time we believe we are dealing with another person based solely on facts, we are dealing with partial issues and avoiding emotional contact.

One way to improve communication is to test the facts by asking the other person how he or she sees the issue. That is an easy way to take care of the problem. The way to handle feelings is to acknowledge them and deal with them instead of pretending they are not there. That's a little tougher. Most of us have been pushing our feelings and emotions down for so long that we find it hard to identify or acknowledge them.

A third perception block is *defensiveness* on the listener's part. A boss says something to a subordinate about her work, a wife admonishes her husband, a parent tries to correct a child — and a stunned look comes over the recipient's face. She may get angry, become super calm, throw up her hands and walk away, get anxious, shout back, or display any of a dozen other such reactions. The result is that the words go unheard or at least unacknowledged. Then the speaker wonders, "What made him so defensive?" Sometimes the speaker's presentation has caused the other to become defensive. A few other causes of defensive communications possibly caused by incorrect perceptions:

- Speaker's expression, tone of voice, manner of speech, or content are perceived as criticism or judgment by the listener.
- Listener perceives the communication as an attempt to control him.
- Listener perceives strategies as manipulative, game-playing, or withholding information — not playing it straight.
- Speaker shows no concern for the welfare of the other person.
- Speaker maintains poker-faced neutrality. He plays a role, rather than being a person.
- Speaker maintains an attitude of superiority.

A Verbal Language

All of the evidence clearly shows that *verbal language*, written and oral skills, are critical not only in obtaining a job but also in performing effectively on the job. For example, Bensen (1983) surveyed 175 personnel managers of the largest companies in a western state. One of the key questions asked about the factors and skills most important in helping graduating business students obtain employment. The personnel managers' responses to this question showed that the most important factor or skill considered was oral communication skills, and that number two was written communication skills.

But what about the relationship between these two skills and effective performance on the job? Most chief operating officers rate employee communication skills as vital, using such phrases as "extremely important," "very important," or "tops" (Williams 1978).

Leaders spend more time communicating than doing any other single activity. Research also suggests that people spend about 45 percent of their communication time listening. Despite this, the average listener understands and retains about half of what is said immediately after a presentation, and within 48 hours, this level drops off to 22 percent. These data would suggest that listening is one of the most critical skills in the communication process (Allessandra, Wexler, and Deem 1979, 81-118). It helps leaders to determine staff needs, problems, moods, and levels of interest.

In order to become effective communicators, leaders need to tune in not only to words and the way those words are expressed, but to nonverbal cues as well. Effective communication requires responses that demonstrate interest, understanding, and concern for your staff as well as for staff needs and problems.

Effective leaders select their communication methods on the basis of careful analysis of situational factors. The method used should depend on the specific task as well as your objectives. If the task is a lengthy message, or one requiring a permanent record, you will want to use written form. On the other hand, if speed, informality, or personal impact is important, the spoken word is often preferred. Another choice revolves around whether to communicate with a single staff member or the entire team. Person-to-person conversations allow the leader to control the flow of information and protect privacy; however, opening up communication among the entire department invites staff participation, develops commitment, and helps build team spirit. It also demands that the leader become more of a facilitator, helping the team explore problems and make progress toward goals. *Person-to-person* communication can be conducted effectively by *custom tailoring* to an individual staff member. It is not only feasible, but definitely in order. This becomes increasingly important as you develop a sound working relationship with each person in your office and throughout the campus, because an individual who is addressed singly, but in the same way as everyone else, usually resents such treatment in proportion to the degree of previously assumed familiarity. People are unique, and they like to be recognized for their differences. Leaders can choose among a variety of spoken or written communication methods.

In *spoken communication*, the person addressed is immediately aware of the conditions under which the message is shared. Therefore, speed, tone, mood, gestures, and facial expressions may seriously affect the way the individual reacts. In this respect, much of our verbal and non-verbal communication cannot be visibly absent from each other. Communicating the message effectively is dependent on the following message forms: words, paralanguage, and non-verbal behavior.

Methods used for person-to-person spoken communication include the following:

- *Informal talks* are still the most fundamental form of communication. They are suitable for day-to-day liaisons, directions, exchanges of information and progress reviews, and maintaining effective personal relations. Even if the talks are brief, you need to be sure to provide the opportunity for a two-way exchange. And if either person is likely to be emotionally involved in the subject, face-to-face exchange should always be used, in preference to writing or using the phone.

- *Appointments* are always appropriate for regular planned meetings such as progress reviews and recurring joint work sessions. The people involved should be adequately prepared to make such meetings effective by providing adequate information and limiting interruptions as much as possible. For extended projects or some new employees, many leaders have regular appointments on a daily, weekly, or monthly basis.

- *Telephone calls* are useful for quick check-ups or for giving or receiving information, instructions, or data. However, your telephone personality sometimes contradicts your real face-to-face self, so you should evaluate how you sound when talking on the telephone. And, since the impersonality of routine calls is resented sometimes, you should occasionally follow up with personal notes to confirm the message.

Written communication should include messages that are intended to be formal, official, or long-term or that affect several persons in a related way. We need to remember to use a written communication to amend any previous written communication, since oral changes risk being forgotten or recalled inaccurately or are not passed along to co-workers.

> "Writing without thinking is like shooting without aiming."
> — Anonymous

Some tips for written person-to-person communication methods:

- Interoffice memos should be used for recording informal inquiries or replies, or they could be of value if several people are to receive a message that is extensive or if data are numerous or complex. They could be a simple way of keeping your boss informed, and they can be read at his or her convenience. Memos should NOT be overused or they will lose their impact and be ignored.

- Letters are usually addressed to individuals and are more formal in tone than memos. They are useful for official notices, formally recorded statements, and lengthy communications. They are often valuable in communicating involved thoughts and ideas for future discussion and development or as part of a continuing consideration of problems.

- Reports are more impersonal than letters and are often more formal. They are used to convey information, analyses, and recommendations to superiors and colleagues. They are effective when based on the results of conferences, inspections, research, and careful thought.

With various methods of communication, how do we decide which is best? Each situation has its own best method or combination of methods. Some problems are urgent and demand immediate response, such as an informal talk, telephone call, or handwritten memo. Some employees believe only what they see on paper, so time spent communicating face-to-face with them is virtually wasted. If the same message must be conveyed to a large number of people, a memo or mass meeting is best. So it seems that the most successful communication is done by supervisors who 1) quickly analyze the situation they are encountering, and 2) effectively demonstrate the many ways of getting their ideas, instructions, and feelings across to others.

Communication Flow

Communication should not be a one-way street. As enrollment services professionals, we are the link between our staff and our own boss. We must know what our superiors expect from us in quantity, quality, and time of delivery and give this information to our staff. We are responsible for their output and we are accountable if anything goes wrong. We must tell our superiors what progress we are making and discuss with them any unexpected problems. Everyone's success depends on maintaining a continuous flow in the give-and-take of information.

For a campus to function smoothly, communication must occur in three ways. First, not only must we furnish information downward to employees and upward to our supervisor, but the employees must communicate their ideas and feelings upward to you. Second, since interdepartmental cooperation among directors and supervisors is extremely important, there must be a horizontal flow of information, too. Finally, there may also be a need to exchange information with "outside" sources, such as staff groups, external vendors, students, parents, donors, or government agencies. In effect, this creates a challenging three-dimensional communication process — up/down, left/right, and in/out.

Campus Gossip, Rumor Mills, and the Grapevine

> *"Sticks and stones may break our bones,
> but words will break our hearts."*
> — Robert Fulghum

As leaders, we constantly become aware of the fact that many people get the information they need through the grapevine rather than official channels. Listen to it, for it's one way of getting clues about what is going on, but don't depend on it to provide totally accurate information. Also, do not make a deliberate practice of leaking information to your staff through the grapevine, for your staff will then rely less on formal communication methods and more on informal (sometimes incorrect) communication.

The grapevine gets its most active usage in the absence of good communication about campus rules, employee benefits, opportunities for advancement, and performance feedback. If we don't tell our staff promptly about the things that interest or affect them, the grapevine will quickly emerge. However, much of the grapevine information will be based on incomplete data, partial truths, and outright lies. And surveys show that, even though employees receive a lot of information from the rumor mill and enjoy participating in it, they would much rather get the real story from a responsible party — their supervisor. You can prevent a lot of emotional upsets among your staff, and build a lot of good will, by spiking rumors as soon as they appear. Show staff that you welcome the chance to tell the truth.

The facts are:

1. All offices have gossip, rumor mills, and grapevines.

2. They often provide early warning signals.

3. Active grapevines may possibly indicate that employees are anxious or unhappy, or that they are not receiving proper information fast enough.

Here are a few simple tools you might consider adding to your communication toolbox to avoid rumors and improve the communication process:

- Choose the attitude that it is better to give too much information than not enough, and improve the formal information flow.

- Hold regular staff meetings. Make them as short as possible — stand-up meetings are beneficial. Share all new information. However, if there is none, encourage questions, which may uncover rumors of which you may not be aware.

- Keep a flip chart handy in your office or circulate a newsletter regularly. Encourage employees to record questions and topics that need attention at your meetings.

- Anticipate issues that might provoke negative gossip or grapevine chat. Deal with them right away — don't wait until later.

- Do not deny the truth — your credibility and trust will suffer if you do. Often, information reaches your staff before you hear it. Acknowledge the supposed information, then track down the source for the truth. When you get the facts, share them with your staff. Tell your staff whatever you can that is not confidential. To get information you must give information.
- Go directly to the source of the rumor you hear (if appropriate) and find out if you or your team will be affected. If a change is imminent, find a way to position yourself to take advantage of the situation by developing a plan to help you and your staff make the change a successful one. Be open to change.
- Maintain a positive attitude — always.

Words are the phrases we select to express the thought that we intend to communicate orally or in writing, including:

- Vocabulary
- Language
- Phrases
- Sentence structure
- Sentence clarity

> *"The difference between the right word and the almost-right word is the difference between lightning and the lightning bug."*
> — *Mark Twain*

Words have power. They can insult, injure, or exalt. They can also lead to costly errors, false hope, or disillusionment. They can evoke pride, loyalty, action, or silence, and they are critical to the influence process. However, they alone are not the sole basis for how people represent and interpret reality.

A Nonverbal Language

> *"The most important thing in communication is to hear what isn't being said."*
> — *Peter Drucker*

Talking and writing are the communication methods most frequently used, of course. But regardless of what is said, your staff will be most affected by what is communicated to them by actions. What we do — how we treat them — is the proof of real intentions. Going to bat for a staff member who needs help provides concrete evidence of how highly you value that person's contributions on your team.

Even in simple matters, such as training an employee to do a new job, the act of showing how to do it is eloquent even when no words are spoken. Similarly, going to an employee's work space to chat rather than always requesting that the employee come to your office helps project a supportive image. The best communication is to combine spoken and written words with compatible actions.

Nonverbal Communication

Nonverbal communication, or how people communicate by nonverbal means, is more ambiguous, continuous, and multi-channeled, and it gives more insight into emotional states. In addition, meanings of nonverbal communication are culturally determined and may be expressed via:

- Body language/motion (gestures, facial expressions, eye contact, posture, poise)
- Paralanguage (characteristics of the voice)
- Self-presentation (image)
- Environment (space, positioning)

Communication effectiveness, especially listening and speaking, are markedly enhanced or diminished by body language or motions. How we enter an office, how we support our message through gestures and facial expressions, and how we imply interest and vitality through eye contact and many other non-verbal cues serve as windows to our emotions, desires, and attitudes for our staff as well as our supervisors. These signals may be no more than a frown, a shrug of the shoulders, or a gesture with the hands. Sometimes, unfortunately, gestures can be misinterpreted:

- Nodding the head up and down (can imply agreement with the speaker); shaking the head from side to side (can be perceived as disagreement)
- Drumming the fingers or tapping the foot (may mean, "Hurry up. I'm impatient.")
- Raising the eyebrows (may signal doubt, surprise, or skepticism)
- Rolling the eyes (disbelief, non-acceptance)

- Wiggling a foot (bored)
- Arms crossed tightly across upper chest (unwillingness, defensiveness)

Many body movements such as these may be unconscious and might be difficult for you to change. But you should be aware that they are being perceived. You should try to assess whether people are reacting primarily to your words or to your body language. If we observe the nonverbal signals from others, these can often provide us with solid clues to what is on another person's mind. This is an important aspect of communication if we want to be perceived as an effective communicator.

Decker (1992) concluded that the words a person uses in speaking account for only 7 percent of that person's influence on others! Voice tone explains 38 percent of the impact and visual impression 55 percent. Riggenbach (1986) discusses the role of body language in various types of negotiations and claims that 95 percent of the nonverbal gestures being received during negotiations are not used by the receiver. According to Riggenbach, the nature and interpretation of body language vary among countries and cultures. Finally, Riggenbach says, "Body language shows the inner feelings and attitudes of a person — actions do speak louder than words!"

Changes in a follower's body postures and gestures often signal a change in readiness. Movement toward the front of a chair may indicate interest. Relaxation of the body may reflect acceptance. Mirroring of our nods, smiles, and gestures could also indicate acceptance.

Paralanguage

Paralanguage, or the characteristics of the voice, are important in the delivery of a message. In contrast to body language or motion, paralanguage refers to nonverbal sounds. It concerns *how* something is said rather than *what* is said. We have all developed some sensitivity to the cues people give through their voices. Two major categories of paralanguage are 1) vocal characteristics (e.g., pitch, volume, rate, quality), and 2) vocal interferences.

As a leader, you need to be aware that the use of *vocal characteristics* can be a highly versatile instrument of power. Through them, you can convey enthusiasm, confidence, anxiety, urgency, or serenity as well as other states of mind and intent. Timing when you speak, increasing or decreasing voice intensity, pausing, and varying pitch and other aspects of speech patterns can increase one's ability to influence, no matter what the audience.

Vocal Interferences

Vocal interferences are sounds that may interrupt or reduce your communication power. Some interferences may cause distraction and, occasionally, total communication breakdown. Excessive vocal interferences are bad speech habits that we develop over time. The most common interferences that creep into our speech include "uh," "er," "well," and "OK," and, of course, those nearly universal interrupters of Americans' conversation, "you know" and "like." Vocal interferences that may be minor distractions in interpersonal or group settings can be totally disruptive in public speaking. Vocal interferences are difficult to eliminate, but they can be reduced through a program of awareness and practice. By closely watching for and listening to the paralanguage of our audience, we can pick up clues about our progress in influencing any audience.

Self-Presentation and "The Image"

Self-presentation and "the image" — manifested in such factors as clothing, touching behavior, and use of time — further affect communication. People learn a great deal about you from the way you choose to present yourself nonverbally, especially through first impressions. These are remembered forever. Posture and walk are very much a part of your total appearance. Do you walk confidently or tentatively? Do you stand up straight or slouch? Clothes that don't fit, messy hair, slips that show, untrimmed nails, smeared lipstick, spotted ties, and shirts that hang out send unprofessional messages. Sloppiness is an expression of personality, and some people may draw conclusions about sloppy ways of thinking, sloppy management, and general unreliability from that kind of appearance. Some may say, "If they can't manage to pull themselves together, how can they manage anyone else?" Informality has its place in our professional world; however, knowing the appropriate time, possibly in a more casual setting, is important.

We judge by appearance more than we realize. We all carry categories in our heads of what is acceptable and what is not, and we match people to our categories. It would be useful for all of us to find out how we think others should look so that we would be less prejudiced by appearances. Here again, there are different cultural norms. Norms of hygiene are not shared by everyone in the same way. Appearance is also related to fads. Remember the outcries at the young men who wore long hair during the days of the Beatles? Young people often follow extreme fashions, and you as a leader may need to set some standards as to what can and cannot be worn to work.

Although you cannot control other people's feelings or their reactions to you, they base their perceptions on what they see — and you *can* control what you show them. There are no rules for governing the specific behaviors you should use to make an initial impact, but you need to be aware of the image you are creating.

Environmental

Environmental management communicates. In addition to the way we use body motions, paralanguage, and self-presentation, we communicate nonverbally through management of the physical environment. We need to be aware of the environment over which we can exercise control, such as space, temperature, lighting, and color. As a leader, it is important to understand how our staff views space and its relationship to you. It is important to monitor how you position yourself in relation to your staff. People have levels of comfort when it comes to how close they want you to be. The general rule is, if you are making them uncomfortable, then change. This may involve moving closer or farther away. How much control we have over space depends, of course, on whether we are dealing with permanent structures, movable objects within space, or informal space. Managing informal space requires some understanding of attitudes toward both space around us and our territory.

We are all aware that communication is influenced by the distances between people. Edward T. Hall (1969, 116-125), a leading researcher in nonverbal communication, has studied the four distinct, generally accepted distances for different types of conversations in our dominant culture:

- *Intimate distance,* up to eighteen inches, is appropriate for private conversations between close friends.

- *Personal distance*, from eighteen inches to four feet, is the space in which casual conversation occurs.

- *Social distance*, from four to twelve feet is where impersonal business such as job interviews is conducted.

- *Public distance* is anything more than twelve feet.

Note that these four distances were not determined arbitrarily; they represent descriptions of what many people consider appropriate in various situations. Individuals, do, of course, vary.

Of greatest concern to us is the intimate distance, that which we regard as appropriate for intimate conversation with close friends, parents, and younger children. People usually become uncomfortable when "outsiders" violate this intimate distance. Intrusions into our intimate space are acceptable only when all involved follow the unwritten rules. For instance, when people are packed into a crowded elevator and possibly touching others, they often try to stand rigidly, look at the door or the indicator above the door, and pretend they are not touching. Sometimes they exchange sheepish smiles and possibly acknowledge the mutual invasion of intimate distance.

Interpersonal problems occur when one person violates the behavioral expectations of another. For instance, Carol may come from a family that conducts informal conversations with others at a range closer than the eighteen-inch limit that most Americans place on intimate space. When she talks to a colleague at work and moves in closer than eighteen inches, the co-worker may back away from her during the conversation. Another example of violation of expectations occurs when people engage in nonverbal behaviors that may be considered sexual harassment. Jim, when in an apparently "playful" mood, may use posture, movements, or gestures that Carol may interpret or perceive as somewhat threatening to her. In keeping with current sentiments toward harassment, we need to be especially sensitive to others' definition of intimate space.

We must understand, however, that other people may not look at space or territory in quite the same way as we do. That the majority of our professional colleagues have learned the same basic rules governing the management of space does not mean that everyone shares the same respect for the rules or treats the consequences of breaking the rules in the same way. Thus, it is important for us as leaders to be observant so that we can be sensitive to how others react to our behaviors.

Active Listening

Communication is not just a process of sending messages. A leader must be skilled in receiving and listening. We may spend as much as 75 percent of work time in face-to-face communication (Harris 1989). As much as half of the time may be spent listening (Caudill and Donaldson 1986). Our physiology also influences our ability to listen accurately and actively. We speak at an average pace of 125 words per minute, but our brain is able to listen at a speed of 400 to 600 words per minute. Since the brain can listen faster than we can speak, a "listening gap" occurs for the average person. The "gap" allows the mind to wander to thoughts unrelated to those being expressed by the speaker and influences the ability of the receiver to accurately hear the message being sent.

> *"The best way to persuade is with your ears."*
> *— Dean Rusk*

The active listener hears and understands the message. The full intention should focus on content and intent of the speaker. Active listening is a skill that can be learned through practice and used on a daily basis. Carl Rogers, who popularized the term active listening, stated that leaders needed to listen for the content and feelings, respond to the feelings, be aware of speaker cues, and reflect back to the speaker what is heard.

Becoming an effective, active listener takes much skill and practice; however, that behavior must be developed to be a successful communicator. Through effective, active listening, the leader can develop better relationships between management and staff, increase the establishment of clear and concise goals that are understood by all, and decrease the chance of communication misunderstandings progressing to complex and costly problems.

The Teamwork Factor

The process of fully utilizing employee potential remains one of the primary responsibilities in the workplace. Our ability to get along with the people we work with is one test of our effective leadership. Recognizing, acknowledging, and accepting differences and similarities among all employees is part of our professional development process. We are each imprinted with particular ways of thinking, understanding, valuing, and conceptualizing. Our behavior reveals specific, identifiable attitudes, preferences, wants, and motives that make us feel good about ourselves.

Interpersonal communication is your informal interaction with yourself and others. The key to understanding others lies in understanding yourself. Most of us are excited about discovering people with whom we have much in common, yet sometimes our interpersonal communication fails in key places. The goal is developing and maintaining relationships.

No matter how ambitious, capable, competent, dependable, educated, energetic, responsible, serious, wise, or witty you are, if you do not relate well to other people, you will not make it. No matter how professionally competent, financially adept, and physically solid you are, without an understanding of human nature, a genuine interest in the people around you, and the ability to establish personal bonds with them, you are severely limited in what you can achieve. You will need people skills to be a leader and you definitely need them to be effective. The higher up the ladder you go, the more important personal bonding and people skills become. Leadership jobs are people skills jobs. You cannot lead people without having people skills.

I have learned that if you can give people a tool so simple that they can quickly grasp it, they will jump at an opportunity to use it. So many of us are walking through life with empty toolboxes, hoping someone will give us some equipment that will work.

Understanding individual personalities is one such tool. When people begin to understand personalities and inborn temperament traits, then it is simple to see that different is not wrong. By understanding the differences, we can also learn how to amplify our strengths and work to overcome our weaknesses. Understanding this principle is vital to effective communication. Helping people understand themselves and each other is the key to teamwork. If we do not have a way to understand personalities, we tend to judge others from our own perspective and to condemn them when they don't conform to our image. In order to see people as they really are and yet have no critical, stinging, bitter things to say, we need to understand the basic personality patterns and realize that these other people are not "out to get us." They just see life from a different point of view or through a different-colored lens. There are many books written that may help you put the pieces together in your workplace or in any type of group activity in which you need to relate to people who do not seem to see things your way.

Everyone is looking for simple tools to solve complex problems. With all the various personalities we encounter every day, we need effective skills to help give them what they want. Because all people have different needs and desires according to their own personalities, we have to learn how to meet those needs. In meeting those needs, we will understand ourselves better as well as each other. In understanding, we must be able to not only accept these differences but also to *celebrate* them. Once we realize that we can see people's personality types, how they fit, and the importance of each, it is a logical step for us to learn the basic desires and emotional needs of the people in our workplaces. These valuable pieces of information enable us to not only understand the people we work with and for, but also to help us get along with them and make all our lives easier.

Business shelves are bursting with books offering tips on managing and presentation skills. Among them seems to be an abundance of new ways to test people's personalities. Some are complex and require trained professionals and complex computer analysis systems to administer, while others arc simple question-and-answer quizzes. However, while various tests may use different labels, results on any of them should pinpoint the same basic characteristics, because these traits are who you are.

The value of understanding others can open eyes to the people around you. So many of us never look to see what is happening on the other side of us, yet all effective leaders have the pulse beat of the people surrounding them. This is just being *alert to life*. I encourage you to make a habit of observing people and tuning in to what is going on in your professional arena. You may not realize how much you are learning until you become *alert to life*.

Knowing who's who among your employees and/or co-workers is the first step in effective interpersonal communications. Knowing their differences and how they are likely to react in different situations is the second. Knowing their value to an organization, and their strengths and weaknesses and needs, is the third. Putting it all together is a process that begins with you — the leader — no matter what place in any of the organizations you find yourself in.

Important interpersonal communication skills do not come easy. Some take preparation and others take practice. Although this checklist is written primarily for those in some kind of management or leadership position, it will equally apply to many who may not at the moment be in charge. We all deal with people in relationships that are not perfect, so we may apply this advice as it fits our particular needs. To effectively communicate and lead:

1. *Examine, understand, and accept your own personality and work style.* Before trying to learn about the personalities of those you work with, take the time to evaluate your own personality. It is difficult to inspire others to introspection unless you can show what you have learned and how you have applied your knowledge. When your staff sees a kinder, maybe more understanding and gentler boss and observes that you can occasionally laugh at your own mistakes, they will want to know why.

2. *Check your own weaknesses.* It is important for each of us to recognize and understand our own weaknesses before we can understand, accept, and celebrate the same in others.

3. *Lighten up!* Don't take yourself so seriously that people do not dare to be themselves when they are near you. Humor relieves tense moments and reduces stress. I have found that most successful people have a good sense of humor. For some employees, lightening up is no problem, but for some who want the work done now or for those who insist on life being perfect, there may be a need to allow for a few minutes a day for fun. Fun,

you say? Fun at work? Yes, it is a proven fact that a "fun break" in the middle of a pressured day will increase productivity and give the workers fresh enthusiasm for the task at hand. You may get more out of your employees if you encourage them to take a guilt-free "fun break," such as a walk or other exercise, an occasional long lunch, or just time to rest. What's more, an optimistic attitude and the ability to laugh at yourself from time to time make you easier to relate to personally — and professionally. You seem more human and approachable to your superiors, subordinates, and peers. To last ... laugh!

4. *Treat supervisors, co-workers, and employees as real people with feelings.* An article in *Newsweek*, Feb. 17, 1992, reported the results of a survey aimed at finding out what motivates people to work hard and to succeed. The prime motivator, with an 89 percent positive response rate, was "self-esteem/the way people feel about themselves." Far below was fear of failure, at 44 percent, and status in the eyes of others, at 35 percent.

Stop and think about how you treat others. Does what you say to them lift their self-esteem? If it does, you are making others feel good about themselves, and they will want to work hard for you. However, if your comments, gestures, and facial expressions and commands are so authoritative and demeaning that you put down the other person, you wipe out their natural motivation and force them into working out of fear.

5. *Be a reliable leader.* Just because you are the leader and in charge does not mean that you can do whatever you want. To produce a team effort, the leader must be reliable. People must know that they can count on you to do what you say you will do. If you call a meeting, be there. If you say you will review salaries in June, do it. Do not promise things or materials that you cannot provide. If you promise a new copy machine, go out and get it. Do not use your personality weaknesses as an excuse for your lax behavior or your procrastination.

No matter what your personality or title, you need to build trust with your staff. They need to know that, if you say something, they can count on you to follow through.

6. *Analyze the personalities of your team.* Now that you have yourself in order, it is time to look at others on your team. Make a list of all the jobs under your jurisdiction, write a brief description of each job, and add a note on which personality type would function best in this responsibility. Now, observe who actually holds the positions. In how many cases do you have the right person in the right place? If you are at 100 percent, you either have fantastic analytical ability or you are very lucky. If you see that you have people struggling in their areas of weakness, begin to sort this out and shift responsibilities until the whole puzzle fits together.

7. *Staff-recruit your weaknesses.* As you look over the people you have and analyze your own abilities, you may find some gaping holes in your workplace. Determine what personalities you are missing, and then look to staff your weaknesses or the weaknesses of the organization as a whole. Recruit for the specific personality that would fit in your position, environment, and community. Experience and ability are always important, but also try to find the individual whose personality will fill in your weaknesses.

8 *Teach your team about personalities.* You will increase your understanding of the personalities you work with by becoming knowledgeable, even if you never share this concept with your staff. But if you do teach the others, you will increase productivity and office morale. Suddenly, lights will go on in their minds as they find explanations for their own desires and the behavior of others. Take time to present or give a personality workshop. It will be worth the time and effort. You will find that not only have you put people in the right places, but you will have shown them why. Morale will be high and productivity will rise. Whatever your business or profession, teach your people to understand themselves and others.

9. *Bond in your own backyard.* Practice your people skills on the people closest to you. Often, it is easy to forget that the people with whom you already have relation-

ships also need your attention, encouragement, and respect. Build a strong base of support, and hone your people skills by treating the people you know with the same consideration you would extend to someone with whom you are trying to create a new bond.

10. *Smile more!* Smiles draw positive attention to you and make you (and others) feel at ease. Top people smile more frequently — and not just because they make more money. Why do they smile? Because it reflects mood and improves attitudes — yours and others'. So smile — unless your expression would unintentionally contradict your words.

11. *Get a grip — shake hands.* Never underestimate the significance of a handshake. People draw conclusions about you in seconds with your handshake. Be firm, but not so forceful that you cause discomfort. It helps convey certainty, confidence, and competence. If you wish to convey additional warmth, use two hands.

12. *Treat everyone fairly.* At times, you will hear that the leader obviously loves or hates a certain type of personality. When this becomes public knowledge, people try to change to fit whatever they think the leader wants, and many end up wearing masks and being phonies. It is a shame that so many leaders with all kinds of education do not seem to know how to evaluate their people and encourage them to function in their strengths. If you can accept your staff as they are and not make them play an unfamiliar role, you will increase the energy and productivity of your team.

Playing an unnatural role is exhausting. Treat everyone fairly, and remember that being different does not make a person wrong.

13. *Be open and approachable.* Your attitude and physical presence should invite people to approach you and talk with you.

14. *Listen.* Others will sense your sincere interest in them if you, at appropriate times, keep your mouth shut and listen. When you do respond, zero in on something they just told you and get them to tell you more. Effective

communicators listen more than they talk, and when they listen, they *really* listen. They know that the only way to have an effective dialogue with someone is to listen effectively. Effective listening involves more than making eye contact and keeping your mouth shut. You can do that and look attentive. Instead of concentrating on the message being conveyed, your mind wanders — back to a meeting that just ended, ahead to an upcoming social engagement, or to what you will say as soon as the speaker stops to catch his breath. By allowing your attention to wander, you not only run the risk of missing important information, but you also leave a less than favorable impression on the person with whom you are conversing.

15. *Lead by example.* Your success or failure depends on the performance of those you supervise. Constantly use your people skills to motivate and encourage them. When you use people skills, you set the tone for others and lead by example. More than any other skill, people skills are observed and copied by the people around you. When you provide a model of fair treatment, sincere interest, and personal effectiveness for others to emulate, you and the entire organization benefit. One of the most important tasks you assume in positions of leadership is being an effective role model for others. Just as you got ahead by mirroring those above you, the people below you will mirror your behavior once you are the leader. If you do not like what your subordinates are doing or communicating, look at their role model — you. If you want them to do something, *you* do it first.

16. *Provide materials, workshops, books, tapes, and resources for your staff or network.* Always be on the alert for materials and programs that will help your team members feel good about themselves, provide further education, and lift team morale. We must remember that visible differences help us estimate probable personalities. There are various strengths and weaknesses in each individual, and we should examine ourselves to find out how we are doing. We must also remember that all of us are valuable parts of the big picture in our office, campus, or organization, and just because some of us are different does not mean we are wrong. We do not need to remake or reinvent ourselves, but to follow the message of that old song that

urges us to "accentuate the positive," eliminate the negative, and not mess with Mr. In-Between.

Final Words

Interpersonal communication is a process of dealing with people as individuals in order to build trust, openness and honesty in a leader/employee relationship in the workplace. To treat our employees as unique individuals, we, as enrollment services professionals, must understand what makes them different from one another. With this knowledge, we as unique leaders can go about leading our employees as unique individuals — with understanding, acceptance, and celebration of our differences.

- If you are the bright, powerful, controlling flower of the office, you already know you are a born leader and that you stand out in the crowd. Be grateful that you have a sense of humor and can tell stories that entertain the entire office, but develop a sensitivity as to when is the appropriate time for fun. You may need to speak less of what comes to mind and listen more.

- If you are a perfecting, controlling person, cheer up and realize that every group needs an organized person who is orderly and absolutely accurate. But do not expect others to become perfectionists and then get depressed when they do not improve. Even though you may be able to take control of any situation, be sure you are not so bossy that no one wants to respond to your instructions.

- If you are a peaceful, sensitive person, realize that we all love your quiet, inoffensive, and gentle nurturing spirit. But do not become so passive that you cannot make necessary decisions or offer opinions. We can't afford to sit around and wait for all those other people to improve. We have to take the first step.

- If you are a creative, inventive person who values knowledge and new ideas, do not become so involved in discovering solutions and using your brain that feelings, rules, and non-stop excitement are completely non-existent.

As a leader in enrollment services, make that effort to fit your employees together in order to create that super successful team everyone wants and dreams their workplace to be. Dare to dream.

Many of us walk through life with an empty toolbox. We want to build positive relationships in this journey through life, but we do not have the equipment we need to do so. The tools are simple, the time and training always difficult — but, if used effectively, the tools can change lives and turn an ordinary office into one of tremendous teamwork. We need to remember that when we can hammer down our own personality, we can begin to understand ourselves and build up others.

Good communication requires knowledge of ourselves and the people we work with. Leaders must understand their followers and followers must understand those who lead. Your challenge will be to communicate powerfully and with inspiration so that others embrace and support you — the key to success. As we create and communicate the visions from our heart, we powerfully connect with those we want to join us in realizing our dreams.

And you thought it was jet fuel. Diane McBarey is president and CEO of Xerox Canada Ltd. This is her quote: "If you took all the documents needed to keep a large airliner in the air and stacked them up in paper form, you'd have a pile about 45,000 feet high! — 50 percent higher than Mount Everest and, in some cases, higher than the plane is allowed to fly!" Talk about a paper monster! Apparently, "paper planes" are real after all.

Our claim to files and timetables in triplicate has complicated our desire to simply fly. Life is like that. We lose the thrill because of "administrivia." If we were in the paper business or book business, it would be a bonanza, to be sure. But enrollment services professionals are not in the paper business. We are in the *people business*. To do our job and communicate effectively, we need to keep lists; however, we must never forget that our objective is to teach people *how to fly*.

"*Think yourself empty,*
  Read yourself FULL,
    Write yourself clear,
      Speak yourself powerful,
        Choose your attitude carefully,
          Listen...and let yourself fly!"
            — "Faith"ful wisdom

References and Further Reading

Allessandra, Anthony J., Phillip S. Wexler, and Jerry D. Deem. 1979. *Non-manipulative selling*. Reston VA: Reston Publishing.

Bennis, Warren and Joan Goldsmith. 1994. *Learning to lead*. Reading MA: Addison-Wesley Publishing Company.

Bennis, Warren, and Burt Nanus. 1985. *Leaders*. New York: Harper & Row, Publishers.

Benson, Gary. 1983. On the campus: How well do business schools prepare graduates for the business world? *Personnel*, (July-August):63-65.

Booher, Dianna. 1994. *Communicate with confidence*. New York: McGraw-Hill, Inc.

Boylan, Bob. 1995. *Get everybody in your boat rowing in the same direction*. Holbrook MA: Bob Adams Publishing, Inc.

Caudill, D.W. and R. Donaldson. 1986. Effective listening tips for managers, *Administration Management* 47:22-24.

Covey, Stephen R. 1989. *The 7 habits of highly effective people: Restoring the character ethic*. New York: Fireside Books.

Curtis D.B., J.L. Winsor, and R.D. Stephens. 1989. National preferences in business and communication education, *Communication Education* 38 (January 1989):11.

Deaux, Kay, Francis C. Dane, and Lawrence S. Wrightsman. 1993. *Social psychology*, 5th ed. Belmont CA: Wadsworth.

Decker, Bert. 1992. *You've got to be believed to be heard*. New York: St Martins Press.

DePree, Max. 1988. *Leadership is an art*. Ann Arbor MI: University of Michigan Press.

Hall, Edward T. 1969. *The hidden dimension*. Garden City NY: Doubleday.

Hamilton C. and Cordell Parker. 1990. *Communicating for results*. Belmont CA: Wadsworth Publishing Company.

Harris, Tom W. 1989. Listen carefully. *Nation's Business* 77:78.

Kouzes, James M. And Barry Z. Posner. 1995. *The leadership challenge*. San Francisco CA: Jossey-Bass Publishers.

Linver, Sandy. 1994. *The leader's edge*. New York: Simon & Schuster.

Maggio, Rosalie. 1990. *How to say it*. Englewood Cliffs NJ: Prentice Hall.

Maxwell, John. 1995. *Developing the leaders around you*. Nashville TN: Thomas Nelson Publishers.

Popcorn, Faith. 1996. *Clicking*. New York: Harper-Collins Publishers, Inc.

Quick, Thomas L. 1992. *Successful team building*. New York: American Management Association.

Riggenbach, J.A. April 1986. Silent negotiations: Listen with your eyes. *Journal of Management in Engineering – ASCE*, 2(2):91-100.

Romig, Dennis A. 1996. *Breakthrough teamwork*. Chicago IL: Irwin Professional Publishing.

Seitz, Victoria A. 1992. *Your executive image*. Holbrook MA: Bob Adams, Inc.

Stech, Ernest and Sharon A. Ratliffe. 1990. *Effective group communication*. Lincolnwood IL: NTC Publishing Group.

Steward, John. 1995. *Bridges not walls*. New York: McGraw Hill, Inc.

Toogood, Granville N. 1996. *The articulate executive*. New York: McGraw Hill, Inc.

Williams, Jr., Louis C. 1978. What 50 presidents and chief executive officers think about employee communication. *Public Relations Quarterly* (Winter):7.

Young, Ed. 1992. *Seven blind mice*. New York: Philomel books, The Putnam & Grosset Group.

Chapter 4

Technology

by Melanie Moore Bell

The approach of the end of the decade, the century, and the millennium compels us to look at electronic technology and wonder where it is going and how it will affect enrollment services professionals. Lewis J. Perelman (1992, 25), the former director of Project Learning 2000 and a Senior Fellow of the Discovery Institute, wrote, "Technology is the most purely human of humanity's features, and it is the driving force of human society. The defining benchmarks of the epochs of human history are the dominant technologies: the stone age, the bronze age, the iron age, the industrial age."

As humanity enters the information age, we are again embarking on a defining moment in the history of humanity — a moment that will impact heavily upon how we interact as a society. Just how this period will shape the future of enrollment services professionals is yet unclear. However, a careful look at the key trends in information technology, as determined by Donald I. Barker (1994), provides some startling and provocative insights into the future that will affect enrollment services professionals.

Computing Power

Approximately every two years, the computing power of microcomputers doubles (Mayo 1993). This astounding rate of growth in computing

---

Melanie Moore Bell has served in higher education for twenty-four years. She was Registrar at Eastern Washington University, Registrar/Associate Director of Admissions and Records at the University of Washington, and then Registrar and assistant professor at Whitworth College before becoming University Registrar at Gonzaga University in 1992.

She wrote *Touchtone Telephone/Voice Response Registration: A Guide to Successful Implementation* (1993) and served as editor of *Research Abstracts* (American Association of Collegiate Registrars and Admissions Officers, 1989).

power has held since the early 1980s and shows no sign of abating. Conservative predictions indicate that by the year 2010, the typical microcomputer will be 1,000 times faster than today's machines.

Increases in the processing capabilities of microcomputers have already made it possible for any enrollment services professional to own a microcomputer and the software necessary to vastly reduce the work involved in writing, calculating, graphing, preparing electronic presentations, etc. As computers have become more powerful, the software for using them has become easier to learn and easier to use. For example, the graphical user interfaces, as found on the Macintosh and in Microsoft Windows, let enrollment services professionals quickly and effortlessly interact with these machines. More robust microprocessors also have provided a richer level of human-computer interaction by adding a "multimedia" dimension of sound, animation, and video.

Ever-increasing computing power is the foundation for advancing all technologies. Without this constant expansion, many, if not all, of the promising benefits of the information age would never be realized.

The Information Superhighway

Perhaps the second-most-significant technological trend is the rapid advancement and growth of switched telecommunication networks. These networks link computers together so that users can quickly and easily communicate with each other. The "mother" of all networks is the Internet, sometimes just referred to as "the Net."

The Internet is actually a collection of networks that today spans the globe. It was originally developed by the U.S. Department of Defense's Advanced Research Projects Agency (ARPA) in the 1960s and 1970s to provide military communications that could withstand a nuclear attack. The first incarnation of the Internet was called ARPANET and included only a thousand computers.

Demand for the services of the Internet by non-military researchers and scientists quickly grew. In response, the National Science Foundation implemented a new, more powerful backbone for the Net in 1986. It was called NSFNET, and the policies of "acceptable use" were widened to include researchers at universities and businesses outside the military establishment.

In the late 1980s, Congress feared we were falling behind the world in the area of super-computers and network technologies, so it passed the High Performance Computing Act. This piece of legislation, sponsored by then Senator Albert Gore, funded research to upgrade the Internet and further widen the parameter of the "acceptable use" policy to allow groups such as elementary schools, rural physicians, and libraries to participate in the benefits of the Internet. The testbed for research into this new high speed backbone for the Internet was dubbed the National Research and Educational Network (NREN), or, as the popular media have come to call it, the *Information Superhighway.*

In 1993, the National Science Foundation began the privatization of the Net by allowing companies like AT&T, IBM, and Sprint to assume the role of managers. Since then, these companies and others have announced plans for enormous investments in the National Information Infrastructure. For example, Sprint and its partners have committed to a $20 billion investment over the next decade.

In terms of speed advancements, the Internet went from 56,000 bits-per-second in the early days of ARPANET to 45 million bits-per-second by 1992 using the NSFNET backbone (Rheingold 1993, 79-80). This represents a quantum leap of unbelievable magnitude. In fact, the current speed of the network is equivalent to transmitting five thousand pages per second or a couple of encyclopedias per minute.

Nonetheless, the next step with NREN, or the Information Superhighway, is to move the Net into the gigabit range — billions and hundreds of billions of bits per second. This is equal to sending the entire contents of the Library of Congress in approximately a minute!

Historically, as the capacity (bandwidth) of the Internet has increased, the cost of transferring information has decreased. This, along with other advancements in the Net, has caused a population explosion in users and computer hosts (machines providing services on the Net). It is estimated that more than 15 million people are using the Internet at present, with a staggering growth rate of 10 percent per month (Kantor 1994).

The Internet has become the vehicle for electronic data interchange and colleges and universities around the world are moving toward transmitting admissions/financial aid/housing applications, transcripts, test scores, and many other items between institutions via the Net.

The mammoth growth in both the speed and the population of the Internet is projected to continue into the next century. Some estimate that the capacity of this Information Superhighway will increase by as much as a millionfold over the next 10 years. The rate of growth in number of users will eventually level off because, if the present rate continues, everyone in the world will be connected to the Net by the beginning of the next century.

World Wide Web

In 1993, student workers at the University of Illinois wrote the first easy-to-use browser, Mosaic; it transformed an obscure realm of the Internet called the World Wide Web (WWW) into a global phenomenon (Levy 1996, 48).

The unrelenting pace of technological revolution in telecommunications has profound implications for the future of enrollment services professionals. This trend will eventually alter almost entirely how individuals work and will open up colleges and universities to everyone around the world. For example, admissions and financial aid applications can be made from anywhere without pen and paper by providing these on the Web.

As the availability and quality of telecommunications improve, enrollment services professionals will begin to work with a more diverse and geographically dispersed student population. How will this happen? It is already happening through the emergence of "computer-mediated communications."

Computer-Mediated Communications

Computer-mediated communications (CMC) is a telecommunication technology that employs the computer as an "intermediary" to facilitate communications. At present, CMC technology primarily involves the exchange of electronic mail (e-mail) and the participation in computer conferencing. E-mail provides a convenient, fast, and easy way to dialogue with individuals around the world, while computer conferencing offers the same advantages for group exchanges of information.

Many colleges and universities are offering courses and entire degrees through computer-mediated communications. These "on-line" programs let students "check in" for new assignments, lectures, and interactive discussions at both a time and a place of their choosing. Although no one is sure just how many on-line degree programs presently exist, the growth of these "virtual classrooms" is exploding.

A *virtual classroom* is a teaching area that exists only in "cyberspace." *Cyberspace* is the term coined by William Gibson, in his science fiction novel, *The Necromancer*, to describe the conceptual space where words, images, human relationships, data, wealth, and power are manifested in digital form and manipulated by CMC technology.

The lifelong need for learning, fostered by global competition (Hammer and Champy 1993, 11-72) and the declining quality of teaching in

American universities (Anderson 1992, 45-78, and Sowell 1992, 225-303) makes on-line programs an increasingly more attractive alternative to traditional higher education. In fact, a New York University dean, Herbert I. London (1990, 35-40), has predicted the death of the university as we know it (i.e., four years of resident campus life). Although perhaps a bit premature, such pronouncements should act as a "wake-up" call for enrollment professionals. Without a doubt, in the twenty-first century, the virtual classroom will become as commonplace in higher education as the chalkboard.

Electronic Publishing

The rapid appearance of electronic journals and electronic books is causing many observers to wonder if these digital publications will replace their printed counterparts (Levin 1993, 29). Case in point: Paramount Publishing (owner of Simon & Schuster) recently launched an entire electronic publishing division. Royalynn O'Connor, associate publisher of Random House, expects that, within three to five years, proceeds from the company's electronic reference works (such as the *Random House Encyclopedia*) will exceed revenue from printed works.

Textbook publishers are also jumping into electronic publishing. For example, John Wiley & Sons, Addison-Wesley Publishing Company, and Benjamin-Cummings all have "learning packages" based on digital technology. Newspaper publishers are invading cyberspace too, with notables such as Dow Jones, the Washington Post Company, Knight-Ridder, and the Tribune Company offering electronic newspapers (Stix 1994, 110-111).

Electronic writing offers several advantages over paper-based publications. Cyberbooks, a term for electronic books coined by Ben Bova in his science fiction novel, *Cyberbooks,* are cheaper and easier to distribute than paper-based texts. They are also much easier to update and revise. And, perhaps most important, cyberbooks can take advantage of "hypertext" to provide convenient and easy navigation through mountains of information (Bolter 1990).

Hypertext is a technology that connects key words and phrases to other related source material. For example, if the word "lion" had a hypertext link to a description of the animal, an individual could read the additional information by simply selecting the word. Hypertext makes it possible to write to almost any audience level, since the reader can obtain additional explanations and resource material by using the hypertext links.

Electronic books or cyberbooks provide individuals with cheaper, more current, and easier to understand alternatives to traditional paper bound sources. As more and more information becomes digitized, the virtual classroom will surely be well-stocked with cyberbooks and cyberjournals.

Groupware

Groupware is a relatively new genre of software intended to enable groups of individuals to work more effectively together (Koreniowski 1993, 43-50). Groupware packages typically include electronic mail, document management, and data-sharing capabilities, although provisions for "whiteboarding" are also becoming common (Krammer 1994, 21). *Whiteboards* are electronic "chalkboards" that let multiple participants at different locations see and change data on a screen simultaneously.

The important role computers can play in improving the productivity of groups was first identified by one of the leading researchers in the field of artificial intelligence, Terry Winograd (Winograd and Flores 1986). Winograd became disillusioned with the precepts of artificial intelligence when the discipline failed to achieve many of the major goals set for it early on. The reason for this failure, he believes, lies in the assumption that deductive reasoning and decision-making are at the heart of successful group efforts. Instead, he persuasively argues that collaboration and communications are the real keys to successful group enterprises.

Winograd's assessment of workgroup effectiveness seems to be entirely correct, given the substantial gains in productivity reported by organizations that adopt groupware technology as a means to "re-engineer" or "downsize" themselves (Davidow and Malone 1992). In fact, groupware is the key driving force behind this modernization effort.

The chief maker of groupware is the Lotus Corporation. Its groupware product, *Notes*, is widely used. Because of the present high cost of the software, *Notes* has not made its way into higher education. As groupware technology moves into higher education, it will open up a host of possibilities for group interaction and collective projects. It will be important for enrollment services professionals to embrace this new genre of software because this technological force will reshape the structure and work environments of colleges and universities. Individuals "on the road" will be able to interact with persons in their offices or in their homes to reschedule appointments, change recruiting goals, report recruiting efforts on a daily basis, and view admissions and enrollment census, to name a few.

Multimedia

Multimedia refers to a loose collection of technologies that extend and expand the way individuals interact with a computer. Up until recently, users were limited to communicating with computers through a dull and monolithic interface based solely on text and limited graphics. Multimedia introduced a full range of new ways to exchange information between humans and computers, including high-fidelity sound, photo quality graphics, animation, and even full-motion video (Barker 1992, 8-9).

Sound, high-resolution graphics, animation, and video can vastly enrich and enhance human-computer interaction. For example, the Voyager Company used a combination of stereo sound and photo-quality graphics to create *Multimedia Beethoven: The Ninth Symphony*. This multimedia application lets individuals explore the work of Beethoven by listening to his compositions, viewing their detailed structure, and reading about how he brought them to life. Other educational multimedia applications include electronic encyclopedias complete with sound clips and photos, animated science adventures, and interactive tutoring systems that make use of audio/video clips.

Multimedia products provide a superior way to communicate with a computer because they improve the quality and increase the quantity of the information that can be exchanged. As multimedia hardware becomes "standard equipment" on personal computers, enrollment services professionals can expect a torrent of educational multimedia packages designed to make use of the wider "bandwidth" afforded by these user interface enhancements. For example, these packages will change how admissions recruiting presentations are designed and presented because they will be user-friendly and portable. Individuals preparing presentations will need to keep up with this technology because multimedia products are changing how colleges and universities "go on the road."

Intelligent Agents

As the amount of information available grows exponentially, the time and effort necessary to sort through this avalanche of data and find what is relevant and important also expand proportionally. In response to this "information overload," computer scientists and programmers have been working on a new genre of software called intelligent agents.

According to Brenda Laurel (1990, 356), a leading researcher in the area of human-computer interfaces, an *intelligent agent* is:

> A character, enacted by the computer, who acts on behalf of the user in a virtual (computer-based) environment. Interface agents draw their strength from the naturalness of the living-organism metaphor in terms of both cognitive accessibility and communication style. Their usefulness can range from managing mundane tasks like scheduling to handling customized information searches that combine both filtering and the production (or retrieval) of alternative representations, to providing companionship, advice, and help throughout the spectrum of known and yet-to-be invented contexts.

Numerous companies are planning to market intelligent agents with one of the capabilities mentioned above. For example, General Magic in Mountain View, California, offers a software package, Magic Cap, with intelligent agents (Ratcliffe 1994, 56-58). Essentially, these agents will be programs generated by one computer to tell another computer how to do a task, like making a dinner reservation, finding the best price on a car, or organizing a meeting.

The Magic Cap software is designed to run on set-tops, the devices that represent the convergence of computers with television sets. This software is intended to provide an on-ramp for individuals to the Information Superhighway while sheltering travelers on this digital highway from the complexities of the system.

Intelligent agents will offer users of the Information Superhighway a convenient means to filter and retrieve important information out of the glut of available data. Agents will sift through piles of e-mail, news feeds, and other data to quickly retrieve relevant documents. Enrollment services professionals will find agent technology particularly useful for doing research and communicating with colleagues and peers.

Videoconferencing

Videoconferencing is the ability to transmit and receive live video from one personal computer to another. This technology is, quite simply, exploding. Until recently, the cost of equipping a personal computer for videoconferencing and installing the dedicated cabling necessary for the high-volume video traffic it generates was cost-prohibitive. However, the cost of adding an audio/video board to a PC and connecting a microphone and video camera has fallen dramatically.

Announcements from companies such as Intel indicate that the hardware costs will drop even further, as much of what is needed for videoconferencing will be built right into future PCs (Ross 1994, 66-68).

Other breakthroughs in the area of compression technology, such as the CU-See-Me software developed at Cornell University, enable video signal to be transmitted over existing cable plants, such as the Internet (Perenson 1993, 30).

These innovations are quickly making the possibility of delivery of educational programs directly into homes or other remote sites a reality. Once the sole province of satellite dishes, interactive live video will soon be available to almost anyone who wants it. Within the next few years, the infrastructure and underlying technology of videoconferencing will become economical enough to let individuals around the world share their ideas, customs, and beliefs interactively and face-to-face without leaving their classrooms or homes.

The educational potential for live video in enrollment services is almost too staggering to contemplate. However, one thing seems certain: almost any conventional presentation can and will be presented using videoconferencing technology. Imagine the impact that such exchanges will have on high school visitation sessions for prospective students, college fairs, transfer student recruiting, international recruiting, etc.

Video-on-Demand

Video-on-demand is a technology for interactively selecting, playing, or pausing a movie or video stored at a remote site from the comfort of an individual's home or office. Investments in video-on-demand are skyrocketing, as major players like AT&T, IBM, DEC, and HP prepare the infrastructure and hardware to make this technology a reality (Schroeder 1994, 18). Within five years, many Americans will be sitting in their living room and instantly locating and viewing almost any movie on video.

Students and enrollment services professionals will be able to use video-on-demand to display scenes from college and university campuses, including instructors teaching courses, students performing lab experiments, athletes playing sports, and so on. In fact, Ted Turner, founder of CNN, is opening an electronic university based entirely on video-on-demand technology. Students will be able to "take" courses at the place and time of their own choosing. Although video-on-demand lacks the obvious advantages of student-teacher interaction, it will appeal to many nontraditional students who lack the time or money to attend a college or university in person. Video-on-demand will also play an important role in supplementing classroom discussions and instruction. The sheer convenience of universal access to a vast library of videos will, no doubt, enhance the present state of education and the delivery of enrollment services.

Virtual Reality

A *virtual reality* (VR) is a computer-generated, interactive, artificial world that creates, for the participants "immersed" in it, the illusion of reality. Entering a virtual reality typically involves donning a head-mounted display (HMD) that provides an all-encompassing view of the computer-generated world. To interact with the virtual environment, participants wear data-gloves, which enable the wearers to "feel" and manipulate the objects within the virtual world.

These devices combine to produce such a powerful illusion that those immersed in the environment are able to "suspend disbelief" and become full participants in the computer-generated world. In conjunction with U.S. West Communications, researchers in the Human Interface Technology (HIT) lab at the University of Washington have developed a "virtual telephone." *Televirtuality* expands the concept of videoconferencing by inserting students and teachers at distant locations into a shared virtual classroom, where others cannot only be seen and heard, but touched and interacted with directly (Johnson 1992, 20).

Electronic Data Interchange

The use of Electronic Data Interchange (EDI) to transmit student data electronically is already saving hundreds of colleges and universities the time and money once dedicated to processing paper copies of admission applications, academic records, enrollment verifications, and a growing number of additional functions. Since most of these forms can easily be replaced by electronic formats, it seems only logical to transmit their data electronically as well. It makes no sense, and it wastes time and money, to make a paper copy of electronic data, handle it twice (sending and receiving) in the process of mail transmissions, and then re-key it (subject to errors) into another computer. Electronic transfers are faster (compare only the time for double handling and mailing) and more reliable than the current paper processes on which most institutions and students now rely. The hazards of paper forms being delayed or lost (in preparation, in the mail, in receipt) can be costly to institutions and frustrating to students, for whom lost time or documents may cost admission, a place in a desired class, or the processing of a loan for tuition payment.

The foundation of EDI technology in education is the various transaction sets that AACRAO has developed and seen through the lengthy process of approval by the American National Standards Institute (ANSI). With these in place, student data transmission via the Internet, VANs (Value Added Networks), and phone lines becomes possible when sender and receiver have appropriate hardware and translation software, which is now readily available from a host of vendors who use ANSI standards. Thus, an institution may send and receive electronic data from other systems while retaining its own unique computer systems.

In addition to the common business uses of EDI (e.g., purchase orders and invoices) a variety of EDI applications in education are now available and in use across the U.S. and Canada, including:

- Application for admission
- Academic transcript (including request for/acknowledgment of)
- Enrollment verifications
- Course descriptions and catalog information
- Financial aid transactions

Developing applications are:

- Test score reporting
- Data reporting to the federal government

For limited initial resource outlay, enrollment services can realize numerous immediate and long-range benefits from the use of EDI, including:

- One-time data entry
- Reduced errors
- Improved error detection
- On-line data storage

- Faster management reporting
- Automatic reconciliation
- Reduced clerical workload and communications
- Higher productivity
- Elimination of mail and courier charges
- Reduced inventory of stocks of envelopes and security paper
- Improved production cycles
- Marketing edge in recruitment
- Uniform communication with trading institutions

Confidentiality of student data is of utmost importance, no matter what technologies are employed. Many experts feel that data may actually be more secure using EDI than current non-electronic methods. Given that the greatest threats to security lie at both ends of the transmission (by employees in the sending and receiving offices), the chance of security breeches occurring in the mail are significantly greater than those possible on the Internet, especially when dedicated lines are used. Current and future software, as well as use of the very successful EDI server available to any institution registering to use it at the University of Texas at Austin, allow for encryption in cases where institutions feel the need for higher levels of security. Other security features of EDI, including acknowledgments, digitized signatures, and encryption, authenticate data transmission and further protect student data confidentiality.

Electronic Data Interchange is improving the efficiency of enrollment systems, and as the technology improves and increases, it will be employed at a growing number of institutions in the U.S. and Canada, and eventually worldwide. Transmission of student data electronically will become routine, providing the enrollment services leader the capacity to respond efficiently and effectively to student and institutional needs and freeing personnel from the traditional time-consuming and error-prone manual processing of student information.

Implications for Enrollment Services Professionals

We wonder how the evolving tools of today — the World Wide Web, digital information, fiber optic communication, computer hypertext and hypermedia, two-way interactive video, supersonic travel, and cordless communication — will be used by enrollment services professionals of tomorrow. The array of technology products available each year multiplies: interactive text, hypermedia, virtual reality, information services, laptop and notebook computers, CD players, and interfaces between instruments, cameras, and computers, to name a few.

What future technology will look like or how it will work is difficult to imagine. But its functions are less of a mystery. The technology will provide more accurate and rapid transportation of goods, ideas, and people. This acceleration has been continuous since African villagers used their networks of "talking drums" to transmit information over distances and call people to market. The talking drums of our time are computer networks sending terabytes of encoded information and detailing complex market arrangements. The process remains similar in form and function — to communicate with distant people to enable new forms of community. The future will bring even faster technology. However, the skills needed to work in a world of rapid communication and transportation cannot be invented — they must be learned.

Enrollment services professionals will need to develop a broad, deep, and creative understanding of community, culture, economics, and international politics, past and present, and acquire social skills to work across differences and distances. This chapter has explored visions of professional change in a technology-rich environment. It has examined collaborative patterns that are possible between the higher education community and prospective students, using technological tools which may evolve new forms of community. It is the interactive patterns among people, not the medium of their interactions, that will be of greatest concern for enrollment services professionals. The ability to work well with distant partners is a skill that will be in demand in the workplace of tomorrow. The skill to use computers to work collaboratively is much more valuable to enrollment services professionals than any degree of computer literacy with the equipment of today. The equipment changes dramatically from year to year, but patterns of human interaction change at a much slower rate. Technology enables new patterns of communication with people and resources located outside the home campus.

Enrollment services professionals must understand how technology can be used across all segments of their work to provide more information on their students, to better target recruiting materials, to give students more flexibility in the delivery of education, and to respond to students more quickly. They simply cannot be successful if they are afraid of technology. They are already living in a different world compared with five years ago, and continuing technological change is moving us into a world that will demand greater familiarity with information technology as a tactical operational tool. Enrollment services professionals who are technophobic must get over it quickly by taking classes, reading books and magazines, and spending time with the technology. They absolutely must be current on what is out there and learn how they can use technology to give them a competitive edge.

Surviving the technology skills game is much like learning to play golf — at every turn there is a new technique or tool waiting to be mastered. While an individual would like to learn them all, practically speaking, it is impossible. The key is focus. Choose a few things to become good at and concentrate on these for a while before moving on. Learn to move easily from platform to platform. The home campus is usually the best place to start. Keep up with what is available.

Learn to learn and keep on learning. Expect skills gaps, but look for the two or three that will make the most difference and work on them for a stretch of time.

Get used to working on technology skills and integrating them into work. Seek new environments, new equipment, and new challenges. Learn to use strengths to compensate for weaknesses.

In a complex world of constant change, where knowledge becomes obsolete every few years, education can no longer be something that an individual acquires during youth to serve an entire lifetime. Rather, education must focus on instilling the ability to continue learning throughout life. Fortunately, the information technology revolution is creating a new form of electronic, interactive education that should blossom into a lifelong learning system that allows almost anyone to learn almost anything from anywhere at anytime.

Ever since Gutenberg, and surely since the invention of television, the attention span and the information content available to individuals have been fundamentally altered by changes in technology. These changes are accelerating, and they are bound to alter the lives of enrollment services professionals. Only by looking ahead, by being alert to both the dangers and opportunities inherent in information technology, can enrollment services professionals improve their knowledge acquisition and provide leadership on their campuses.

References

Anderson, Martin. 1992. *Imposters in the temple: American intellectuals are destroying our universities and cheating our students of their future.* New York: Simon & Schuster Publishing.

Barker, Donald I. 1992. PC AI overview: Multimedia. *PC AI: Intelligent Solutions for Desktop Computers.* (November/December): 8-9.

Barker, Donald I. 1994. A technological revolution in higher education. *Journal of Educational Technology Systems* 23(2) (Fall).

Bolter, Jay David. 1990. *The writing space: The computer, hypertext, and the history of writing.* Hillsdale NJ: Lawrence Erlbaum Associates.

Davidow, William H. and Michael S. Malone. 1992. The virtual corporation: lessons from the world's most advanced computers. *Forbes* 150(13): 102-108.

Hammer, Michael, and James Champy. 1993. Re-engineering the corporation. *Harper Business:* 11-72.

Johnson, Colin R. 1992. Virtual reality: Preview of the twenty-first century? *PC AI: Intelligent Solution for Today's Computers* (January/February): 20.

Kantor, Andrew. 1994. Internet: The undiscovered country. *PC Magazine* (March 15).

Koreniowski, Paul. 1993. Workgroup software emerges for business applications. *Software Magazine* (July): 43-50.

Kramer, Gary and Wayne M. Childs, editors. 1996. *Transforming academic advising through the use of information technology.* National Academic Advising Association, Monograph Series #4.

Krammer, Matt. 1994. Whiteboards getting better. *PC Week* (February 7): 21.

Laurel, Brenda, ed. 1990. *The art of human-computer interface design.* Reading MA: Addison-Wesley Publishing Company.

Levin, Carol. 1993. The paperless book. *PC Magazine* (December 21): 29.

Levy, Stephen. 1996. The browser war. *Newsweek* (April 29): 48.

London, Herbert I. *Death of the university: The 1990's and beyond.* Bethesda MD: World Future Society.

Mayo, John S. 1993. *Telecommunications technology and services in the year 2010.* Remarks delivered at the AT&T Bell Laboratories Technology Symposium, October 13, at Toronto, Canada.

Perelman, Lewis J. 1992. *School's out: A radical new formula for the revitalization of America's educational system.* New York: Avon Books.

Perenson, Jelissa J. 1993. Electronic field trips for the 90s. *PC Magazine* (February 8): 30.

Ratcliffe, Mitch. 1994. Let your agent do the walking. *PC World* (February): 56-58.

Rheingold, Howard. 1993. *The virtual community: Homesteading of the electronic frontier.* Reading MA: Addison Wesley Publishing.

Ross, Randy. 1994. The alternative to business travel. *PC World* (March): 66-68.

Schroeder, Erica. 1994. Video-on-demand looms. *PC Week* (February 21): 18.

Sowell, Thomas. 1992. *Inside American education: The decline, the deception, the dogmas.* New York: Free Press.

Stix, Gary. 1994. Extra! Extra! Newspaper publishers reinvade cyberspace. *Scientific American* (February): 110-111.

Winograd, Terry, and Fernando Flores. 1986. *Understanding computers and cognition: A new foundation for design.* Norwood NJ: Ablex Publishing Corp.

——— 1993. *Beyond the traditional textbook.* Higher Education Product Companion. 3(4).

Chapter 5

Leadership and Management

by W. Wes Williams and Sheahon J. Zenger

Introduction

"Leadership" is a term that is broadly used in society and loosely interpreted by the media. This has created a situation wherein the general public often misinterprets what scholars in the various disciplines and in higher education define as leadership theory. The purpose of this chapter is to clarify and discuss how leadership theory applies to the field of enrollment services, discuss the similarities and differences between leadership and management in enrollment services, and provide a practical application of these discussions for the enrollment services professional.

W. Wes Williams is an educational administrator with twenty-seven years of experience in management, public relations, teaching, and leadership at a variety of academic institutions. He is currently at West Virginia University as the Assistant Vice President for Enrollment Management and Services. He previously served as the Associate Vice Chancellor of Student Affairs and Dean of Educational Services at the University of Kansas, Dean of Admissions at Georgia State University, and the Director of Undergraduate and Graduate Admissions at Middle Tennessee State University. He also worked in secondary schools as a teacher, counselor, and principal and has taught at both the graduate and undergraduate levels in higher education. He is an active member of AACRAO and has been called upon on numerous occasions to present on the topics of leadership and management to regional AACRAOs.

Sheahon J. Zenger is the Recruiting Coordinator and Assistant Football Coach at the University of Wyoming and previously held a similar position at the University of South Florida. He most recently served five terms on the University of Kansas School of Education National Advisory Board and has worked as a reviewer for the *Journal for the Advancement of Practice and Theory in Higher Education*.

A Need for Leaders

What is leadership in enrollment services? Who can be a leader in enrollment services? How does one lead in such an environment? Before answering these questions, it is first necessary to engage in a discussion of broader issues.

It seems that, in today's splintered society, the concept of leadership has emerged as a theoretical salve to cultural wounds. Defining leadership can be overwhelming, and it is subject to as many interpretations as there are individuals. A review of the literature pertaining to leadership not only bears this out, but seemingly carries with it an undertone of crisis and confusion (Fincher 1987, 156).

> Leadership is often identified as a concept that lacks adequate definition. ... Whatever leadership is, it is presumed to emerge within groups, organizations, and societies in times of crisis. As an emergent event, leadership is thus seen as unpredictable but somewhat inevitable. An organizational or national crisis evidently produces just exactly the kind of leadership needed to cope successfully with uncertain and hostile events or forces.

Burns (1978) reiterates the notion that leadership carries with it a great deal of misunderstanding, but Foster (1989, 39) contends that "leadership is a real phenomenon, one that does make a difference." However, he adds that "before the term can be utilized meaningfully, it is necessary to try to tease out the various ways in which it has been used and to try to come to an agreement on its essential aspects." It is from this vantage point that this discussion begins.

When the concept of leadership is narrowed to the field of higher education, the definition appears to be subject to just as much interpretation as it does within a broader context. Cohen and March (1991b, 399) suggest that leaders in colleges and universities are especially susceptible to uncertainty and identify four areas of particular ambiguity: purpose, power, experience, and success. They suggest that leaders are particularly prone to confusion in these areas "because they strike at the heart of the usual interpretations of leadership."

> When purpose is ambiguous, ordinary theories of decision making and intelligence become problematic. When

> power is ambiguous, ordinary theories of social order and control become problematic. When experience is ambiguous, ordinary theories of learning and adaptation become problematic. When success is ambiguous, ordinary theories of motivation and personal pleasure become problematic.

While the general concept of leadership and the more narrow concept of leadership in higher education, or in enrollment services more specifically, continues to be subject to interpretation, the meanings are also subject to the variable of time. Maxcy (1991, 7) suggests that while "there is still an enormous conceptual confusion regarding the meanings and bearings of the term," an "enormous leap" has been made in recent years. This "leap" refers to a perceptual change in some of the literature in educational leadership, a change that now acknowledges a need for democratic and participatory direction, as opposed to bureaucratic management and administration. Not all scholars in the field buy into this notion, but a movement in this direction is a recent trend. Green (1988, 30) suggests that this shift in perspective is not unusual, and that, in trying to define leadership, one must acknowledge and be aware of the changing definitions over time, "for effective leadership in one era may be entirely inappropriate or ineffective in another."

The need to define leadership is not specific to enrollment services. The call for leadership on a global scale appears to be one of urgency. Bennis (1989, 5) clearly and emphatically makes this point as he asks the question, "Where have all the leaders gone?" In answer to his own question, he provides the reader with a walk through modern history and a laundry list of past leaders on a grand scale: F.D.R., Churchill, Eisenhower, Schweitzer, Einstein, Gandhi, the Kennedys, and Martin Luther King, Jr. He then proceeds to move forward in history with the recapitulation of the corruption of government in the United States and the fragile condition of many nations throughout the world. He brings his picture to a close by once again addressing the question of leadership (1989, 5):

> The leaders who remain, the successors and the survivors — the struggling corporate chieftains, the university presidents, the city managers and mayors, the state governors — all are now seen as an 'endangered species' because of the whirl of events and circumstances beyond rational control.

Giroux (1991, ix) sees this problem as a "crisis of authority" and narrows the perspective to that of public education. He believes that one of the foremost problems in American society is the "refusal of the American government over the last thirteen years to address the most basic issues of meaning and purpose which link public education to the development of critical citizens capable of exercising the capacities, knowledge, and skills necessary to become human agents in a democratic society."

Maxcy (1991, 1) extends Giroux's argument and calls it a "crisis facing American public education." He lists current social conditions that have led to this crisis. Among them he includes splintering of interests without consensus. "This modern collapse in leadership, coupled with a fracturing pluralism of followers, has parents, teachers, and administrators in a quandary." Gardner (1990) addresses Maxcy's question from a broader perspective and one that brings this search for the need for a definition of leadership full circle. Gardner (1990, xi) suggests that this urgent cry for leadership may simply be the way in which a culture or society expresses its anxiety, an anxiety derived from the conditions explained by Bennis, Giroux, and Maxcy:

> It would strike most of our contemporaries as old-fashioned to cry out, 'What shall we do to be saved?' And it would be time-consuming to express fully our concerns about the social disintegration, the moral disorientation, and the spinning compass needle of our time. So we cry out for leadership.

It is perceived crisis in leadership that underlies and seemingly drives the current study of leadership theory. It is a tone that permeates the literature and must be understood by the readers as various definitions of leadership are presented.

The History of Leadership Theory

In keeping with Green's notion of changing definitions of leadership throughout different eras, it is helpful to glance at the past and observe what ideas about leadership preceded this time of so-called crisis or urgency. When reflecting on leadership of the past, current authors refer to a time of romanticism (Cooper, Kempner and Amey 1993; Tierney 1993). Simply put, romanticism in leadership theory refers to the time prior to World War II (with some carryover to the recent past), when educational leaders were regarded as idealistic role models or heroes. This was a very individualistic notion and one in which the ultimate authority and responsibility (power) were given to one person. Leaders were seen as visionaries and gatekeepers of social responsibility. This concept has been termed the "great man" theory (Tierney 1993, 11):

> We once held a heroic ideal that assumed certain individuals were capable of single-handedly creating change. Such an ideal was born of romanticism in which leadership was defined in terms of 'great men' who had divine capabilities, and life was ruled by mysterious or naturalistic forces. We conceived of power in individualistic terms and believed that the human will was free-floating and capable of producing changes it desired. Individual identity was also fixed, coherent, and determined. Institutions such as church and state established categories within which individuals fit.

Some believe that the romantic notion of a heroic leader was supplanted by the modern era and the modern obsession with empirical research. This shift is most apparent in the pursuit of the scientific. Within that pursuit lies the rejection of the religious or the naturalistic, which was so closely associated with the romantic movement. "Instead, the scientific study of human progress sought to understand by rational analysis 'man's' motivations and inner drives" (Tierney 1993, 12). This can most easily be seen in the history of leadership theory in the development of books that contained lists of traits associated with effective leaders and educational administrators. The application of scientific inquiry and theory led the research down a path of categorization and quantification in an effort to analyze what worked and what did not work. The result was the production of "how-to" books on leadership and administration. Tierney suggests that the fields of psychiatry and scientific measurement are indicative of the rejection of belief in favor of measurement, and it may also be suggested that the emergence of quantification of leadership traits and behaviors was a rejection of the "great man" theory. It may also have been a step toward the belief that a greater number of individuals were capable of leading if they possessed the appropriate traits and skills naturally or acquired them through practice.

Much of this change toward measurement, categorization, and quantification was also reflected in the actual practice of educational leaders. This was evidenced in the changing roles of educational leaders following World War II, as societal demands forced these individuals to deal with issues of policy and procedure. They became fund-raisers and spokespersons for their institutions, and their administrative abilities were focused on managing and administrative team-building (Kelly 1991, 30-32). These roles were a reflection of the modernistic quest for scientific truth and rational analysis (Cooper et al. 1993, 1).

Giroux (1992, 44) suggests that in the past this process was only natural, as modernism "becomes synonymous with civilization itself" and it stands to reason that, as we progressed through the past century, we would inherently be affected as well. Aronowitz (1988, 527) extends this to the notion of control and power that may be seen within an organization operating from the vantage point of modernistic leadership: "From its very inception, science is thus an enterprise with an interest, and that interest is the prediction and control of what is considered to be 'external' nature." Embedded within this theoretical framework was the organizational perspective of "us versus them," lines being drawn in the sand, specific attention to differences rather than acceptance of the "other," limitation of voice as opposed to multivocality, and the emergence of the bureaucracy.

These are the foundations upon which leadership theory was built. What is important to note is that leadership theory has a history, and that some scholars now divide it into the romantic and modern periods of theory development. In order to understand the phenomenon of leadership in any field, it is first necessary to realize that divergence of opinion exists with respect to the concept of leadership itself, and the history behind the evolution of that debate is critical to understanding the current definitions.

Leadership and Management

In searching for a current definition of leadership, one realizes that the heroic tradition continues to influence some of the language utilized by today's scholars, including leadership definitions. The greatest example of this may be the many references in the leadership literature to the world of business. The literature is replete with terminology and examples from the corporate structure. One asks, Is leadership synonymous with management? Phrased another way, Is a leader the same thing as a manager? Rost (1991) argues that the perspective of leader equals manager is the result of the infusion of values from the industrial paradigm, dating back to the 1930s. He contends that (Rost 1991, 129):

> Confusing leadership and management and treating the words as if they were synonymous have a long and illustrious history in leadership studies. The practice is pervasive in the mainstream literature of leadership. It is pervasive in all academic disciplines where one can find the literature on leadership ... . Many scholars and prac-

titioners went even further and equated leadership with management.

However, Rost and other scholars in organizational theory do not agree with the assumption that leadership and management are one and the same. Zaleznik (1989) and Burns (1978) were two of the first scholars to challenge the manager-as-leader philosophy (Burke 1988, 44). Kouzes and Posner (1990) challenge this line of thinking in their text entitled *The Leadership Challenge* (1990). While they write for an audience primarily in the world of business, they make a clear distinction between leaders and managers, leadership and management. Kouzes and Posner (1990, xviii) assert that both managers and non-managers can lead and that both have the potential to "lead others to get extraordinary things done." Not only do they believe that managers are not leaders by definition, but that "leadership begins where management ends, where the systems of rewards and punishments, control and scrutiny, give way to innovation, individual character, and the courage of convictions."

When attempting to apply leadership theory to educational institutions, this paradox between divergent theories in the literature can become even more confusing. Codd (1989, 158) asserts that the "pervasiveness of the ideological forces involved" has led educational administrators away from recognizing and promoting "the distinctly educational features" of their organizations, and administrative theory has "become separated from educational theory with the effect of distorting and narrowing the way educational administrators interpret their roles." Burke (1988, 44) purports that the true leaders in any organization have the ability to "empower" others. He believes that this is the true distinction between managers/administrators and leaders: "My central thesis is that one's effectiveness in empowering others depends on whether one is a manager or a leader. The two processes differ significantly." He then points to work done by Wortman (Burke 1988, 44) that suggests that leaders should "think and act strategically (that is, long range), whereas managers must be more concerned with daily operations."

While there are scholars who disagree that management is, by definition, synonymous with leadership, there are others who see the application of management theory to educational institutions as one of the reasons for crisis in education. Bogue (1985, 2) suggests that "among education administrators today there are too few philosophers and too many managerial mechanics — enamored of technique, hurried and harried, seldom asking questions of purpose and meaning." He adds that faculty should be concerned with the "transfer of management concepts from private-sector settings to education institutions" and with those in powerful positions who use only "common sense" as a guide. Giroux (1991, xi) speaks to the same issues as he criticizes the trend to transfer leadership from corporate America to America's educational institutions:

> This view of educational leadership is quite paradoxical. Not only does this approach to educational reform ignore the discourses of community, solidarity and the public good, it also draws upon a sector of society that has given the American public the savings and loan scandals, the age of corporate buyouts, and the proliferation of 'junk' bonds, and has made leadership synonymous with greed and avarice. To be sure, it is precisely the business community that prides itself on abstracting leadership from ethical responsibility, subordinating basic human needs to the rules of the marketplace, and legitimizing commodification as the highest virtue of American society.

Smyth's (1989a, 170) view is similar to Giroux's, saying that to transfer meaning from the management sciences into the schools is essentially anti-educational, because one group of individuals wielding "hegemony and domination" over another group runs perpendicular to the basic definitions of education.

Maxcy (1991, 2) may add the most clarity to this argument against "management" in education. He discusses leadership within the context of individualism, community, authority, power, and control — all issues that need to be addressed in any study of leadership. He contends that educational institutions have so much bought into management theory that "gone is the interest in improving the quality of educational life for its citizens-to-be, and in its place we find management." He further concludes (1991, 7) that, even though multiple studies have now been conducted on leadership, "there is still an enormous conceptual confusion regarding the meanings and bearings of the term." He sees this confusion primarily centered around the debate between leadership as bureaucratic management and leadership as democratic and participatory direction or, stated another way, issues or authority. It is precisely these issues of authority, community, power, and control that need to be investigated as this discussion pursues a definition of leadership.

Current Definitions of Leadership

As one reads through the literature on leadership, there appears to be as many definitions as there are authors. Before discussing the role of leadership and management in enrollment services, it is first necessary to note that several definitions recur throughout the literature. For example, some scholars in the field would define leadership as the power to persuade (Bensimon et al. 1991; Gardner 1990; Holloman 1984), while others may see it as more of an ongoing process without any real intent to persuade anyone to a specific end (Bavelas 1984; Smyth 1989; Trow 1991). Some might proclaim that styles of leadership depend upon the circumstances of a given situation (Bensimon et al. 1991; Bolman and Deal, 1991) and those who adhere to this belief might, at times, run counter to those who believe that there are some definite traits and tasks (Bennis 1986; Cronin 1989; Gardner 1989) that can be attributed to successful leaders.

Other authors choose not to define leadership, but rather to discuss types of leaders or leadership. One popular theory is to differentiate between transactional and transformational leadership (Burns 1978; Cronin 1989). Cronin (1989, 53) views transactional leadership as an "exchange, usually for self-interest and with short-term interests in mind," whereas a transformational leader "so engages with followers as to bring them to a heightened political and social consciousness and activity, and in the process converts many of those followers into leaders in their own right." Yet another group of authors choose to focus on more personal explanations of leadership, such as charismatic leadership (Bogue 1985; Rosenbach and Hayman 1989; Zaleznik 1989) or leadership through consensus-building (Zaleznik 1989).

Leadership as Contingency Theory

It is not necessary to choose one form or theory of leadership to the exclusion of all others. Some scholars advocate the use of contingency theory when studying leaders. This may also be referred to as situational leadership. These individuals believe that one cannot establish lists of tasks or traits that fit all leaders in all situations. Instead, they believe that each situation demands a certain kind of leadership. Bensimon et al. (1991, 395) maintain that, "from this perspective, effective leadership requires adapting one's style of leadership to situational factors." While Bensimon et al. present contingency theory in their writing, they also contend that "little systematic application of contingency theory has occurred to determine under what conditions alternative forms of leadership should be displayed." Bolman and Deal (1991, 413) support the view that "almost everyone believes that widely varying circumstances require different forms of leadership," but also agree with Bensimon et al. that not enough research has been done in this area to support any major assertions. Zaleznik (1989, 108) contends that the amount of research is not so much the issue as is the fact that contingency theory or situational leadership "ignores the significance of personality characteristics which determine how an individual will respond." Zaleznik believes that individual leaders naturally "resort" to "habitual modes" of dealing with conflict consistent with their individual personalities and that this is contradictory to any type of theory that tries to establish particular behaviors that would be applicable to all individuals based upon given situations.

Leadership as Relationships

When studying leadership and management, one readily recognizes the importance of human interaction, or, in Kouzes and Posner's (1990, 1) words: "leadership is a relationship between leader and follower." While multiple definitions of leadership exist, the common thread of relationships unites many of the theories and specifies the role of followers as an important variable in the leadership equation. Bolman and Deal (1991, 404) concur with this line of thinking as they discuss leadership. They emphatically state that leadership is not "a thing," but rather "exists only in relationships." Bolman and Deal (1991, 404-405) continue that, within these relationships, there exist "three or four" basic answers to the question of "What is leadership?" They submit that most managers, when asked this question, will respond with "it is the ability to get others to do what you want ... leaders motivate people to get things done ... leaders provide a vision ... leadership is really facilitation."

Cronin (1989, 45) suggests that there is a great irony in the fascination that Americans have with the issue of leadership. He contends that "we have an almost love-hate ambivalence about power wielders." Americans "yearn" for leaders and leadership and at the same time detest anyone who "tries to boss us around." If one agrees with Cronin, it would be easy to see just how complicated this concept of the leader-follower relationship could become. Gardner (1990) and Kelley (1989) both raise the point that most leaders, at one time or another, have also been followers and, at times, may very well play both roles at once. In other words, an individual may be a leader in one group or setting while, at the same time, being a follower in another group or setting. Gardner (1990, 23) suggests that this relationship between leader and follower may vary from one culture to another and may depend upon whether "an organization or group is in a time of quiescence or crisis, in prosperity or recession, on a steep growth curve or stagnating." He further suggests (1990, 23) that "leaders are almost never as much in charge as they are pictured to be, followers almost never as submissive as one might imagine."

Kelley (1989) asserts that a leader does not exist without actual followers. Holloman (1984) and Gardner (1990) show support for this assertion as they both speak of followers conferring power upon the leader. Gardner (1990, 24) specifically uses the term "confer." He says he believes that "good constituents tend to produce good leaders" and that "executives are given subordinates; they have to earn followers." As Holloman (1984, 109) stated earlier, "Mere occupancy of an office or position from which leadership behavior is expected does not automatically make the occupant a true leader. Such appointments can result in headship but not necessarily in leadership." Gardner spoke of earning leadership. Holloman (1984, 112) states that, "without followership, there can be no true leadership." So, he argues that followers are "in a sense ... also leaders — they lead their leaders, select their leaders, and sometimes reject their leaders because they do not meet expectations." In keeping with this pattern of thinking, Burke (1988, 21) submits that "leadership, after all, is a reciprocal process. By definition, no followers, no leader. The followers' power is manifested when the leader does not respond to their desires." In his article on leadership and empowerment, Burke discusses, at length, this relationship between leader and follower. He also addresses differences between leaders and managers and, more specifically, the differences between followers and subordinates. In one paragraph, Burke (1988, 21) seems to capture the essence of this concept best:

> Perhaps the greatest difference between leaders and managers regarding empowerment is the type of follower and subordinate need to which each appeals. Leaders appeal to a dependency need. Managers appeal to an independency need. Followers need to have direction. Subordinates need not be cast in the role of subordinate for every aspect of their work. Yet followers and subordinates are usually the same individuals. The point is that successful leaders appeal to one need that most people have, and successful managers appeal to quite another need that these same people have

Of significance is the fact that Burke, while noting a difference between followers and subordinates, suggests that they usually are the same people. The key to understanding this concept is to acknowledge that subordinates do not have to be subordinates in all settings and in every task.

Kelley (1989, 124) argues that organizations and organizational theorists place too much emphasis on leaders and don't focus enough on "trying to cultivate leadership in the employees we already have." He has no argument with the enthusiasm that people and organizations show for leadership and for seeking out leaders, "but in searching so zealously for better leaders we tend to lose sight of the people these leaders will lead." Burke (1988) applies this analogy back to organizations and concludes that organizations do succeed, in part, because of effective leadership, but effective followership is just as important. In keeping with leadership theory tradition and the urge that leadership theorists seem to have for making lists of leadership traits, Burke set forth a short list of qualities of followers. In that list, Burke (1988, 127) suggests that effective followers "manage themselves well ... are committed to the organization and to a purpose, principle, or person outside themselves ... build their competence and focus their competence and focus their efforts for maximum impact ... [and] are courageous, honest, and credible." Phillips and Kennedy (1986) approach this issue from the perspective of the leader and purport that leaders should place great emphasis on establishing shared values among themselves and their followers.

In the organizations that Phillips and Kennedy (1986, 199) studied, "shared values" defined "the fundamental character of their organization." These same shared values also gave the organization the "attitude" that made it distinguishable from all other organizations. This attitude that originated from the shared values provided meaning for employees that allowed them to see their work as something apart from just "earning a living." Even more important, Phillips and Kennedy (1986, 199) assert that "the values really guide behavior." They see this being enacted in several ways. For example, managers may refer to the values when trying to provide guidance for subordinates; through company folklore, new employees may be told stories "that underline the importance of these values to the company." In each of these methods, Phillips and Kennedy believe that followers and leaders can come together as well as provide meaning to their work. Shared values may inherently lead to shared work and common goals as individuals "interpret these values in the context of their own jobs."

From Theory to Reality

In the frozen tundra of the Yukon, the Eskimo people have a saying about their dog sleds that connect their villages with the outside world — the speed of the pack is dictated by the speed of the leader. As you can guess, their saying refers to the pack of dogs pulling the sled and the fact that the speed of all the other dogs is dictated by the speed of the lead dog. How true this is in all forms of leadership. Peter Drucker

(Hersey 1982, 82) has indicated that a successful organization has one significant point that sets it apart from unsuccessful organizations: dynamic and effective leadership. Good managers and leaders are basic to any organization, yet they are the most scarce resource of both education and business.

Earlier we asked, what is leadership? George R. Terry (Hersey 1982, 82) defines leadership as the activity of influencing people to strive willingly for group objectives. One might also describe leadership as the influence of people to work together to achieve a common goal. Leaders must have many attributes: a leader must be able to motivate, inspire, reward, develop trust, evaluate, be a good listener, hire and train good people, be understanding and empathetic, and understand when to push and when to pull. You can probably think of many other attributes, as these are just a few that come to mind. Certainly people must have knowledge in their field. The greatest success will come to individuals who have the ability to assume leadership roles, produce cooperation and incite enthusiasm, and communicate. Another way of saying this is that leaders must have the ability to bring out the best in others. We also think of leaders in terms of having two very important qualities:

1. They have a plan and they know where they are going.

2. They are able to encourage and convince others to go along the journey with them.

Three very important characteristics of leaders are that they possess technical skills, people skills, and planning skills. As one moves along the organizational ladder, these skills are called upon in different quantities. For instance, as an assistant director of enrollment management, one may need more technical skills and fewer long-term planning or conceptual skills. As one moves to become the dean, it is obvious that more long-term planning and possibly fewer day-to-day technical skills are needed. The one consistent factor in any leadership role is the people skills. Regardless of the level at which an administrator works, the ability to effectively work with people and build a team is critical. In reading and talking with many leaders over the years, we have asked the question, "What makes a good leader?" The response is always: Having good skills. After that, it varies. But there is a common theme of having shared goals and devising means to reach those goals, being ambitious with a relentless focus on what one believes in, knowing diplomacy, having optimism even when times are difficult, and identifying and seizing opportunities when they come one's way.

If there is a common mistake made by those of us who strive to be leaders, it's often cited as a failure to see the other person's point of view.

Being a good listener and taking the time to fully understand what your staff has to share is extremely important. We, as leaders, should welcome the opportunity that people want to talk with us and share their ideas, goals, and dreams. Another frequently cited shortcoming is a failure to show appreciation or to give credit for a job well done. We all know that "thank you's" are of no value unless we give them away. They cost nothing, but all too often we are unwilling to make the time to show appreciation.

Other common faults of leaders that show up from time to time include a failure to size up a staff member correctly, lack of frankness and sincerity, being unpredictable, arrogance, failure to delegate authority, and indecisiveness. These are all areas that we, as leaders, must constantly be aware of and monitor. From time to time, we must ask for input from our staff so that we can improve as leaders.

What are the characteristics of creative leaders? Creative leaders are those who are able to bring new insight to an organization or particular work project, or who, in general, have the ability to think outside of the box. Certainly a creative leader is one who is willing to stretch organizational policy. This doesn't mean breaking the rules, but it does mean being willing to see things other than black or white and being willing to be open to new and creative ideas. Creative leaders encourage risk-taking and are available to help members of the team pick up the pieces when things don't work out. They don't dwell upon mistakes or failures, but instead dwell upon what has been learned by the mistake and how to put knowledge to good use to solve future challenges. Creative leaders have the ability to identify and hire individuals who are also risk-takers and creative themselves. Creative leaders are willing to make quality decisions quickly, when necessary, in order not to miss windows of opportunity. They are good listeners, and people on the outside have difficulty deciding if they are working or playing. To the creative leader, there's a feeling that he or she is doing both, and he or she leaves it to others to decide which is which.

To be effective, must leadership style always be the same? Since leadership is a dynamic process that may vary from situation to situation with changes in circumstances, team members, and opportunities, a single leadership style cannot take into consideration all of these variables. Cultural diversity, customs, geographical regions, traditions, and educational level are all important in determining the appropriate leadership style to be used in any situation. As a leader, regardless of the variables, it is important to set specific levels of responsibility and standards of conduct, to be willing to discipline those individuals who do not do their fair share, and, of course, reward those outstanding employees who contribute in making the organization a better place.

Good leaders also have emotions and are able to manage with their hearts as well as their minds. They reflect the old adage of "treating others as you would like to be treated yourself," one of the guiding principles in being a successful leader. It's OK to be human and to show human emotions. From time to time we all make mistakes, and it is certainly OK to admit those mistakes. Co-workers should be viewed as human beings, all of whom have unique challenges, situations, and burdens in their professional and personal lives. Good leaders recognize and try to help co-workers with all of these challenges.

A good leader also has to be ready to answer any questions that might come his or her way. Staff like to be kept informed, and they'd much rather hear about changes being made from their leader versus the grapevine. Thus, continuous and ongoing communication to team members is very important, as is receiving feedback. Sometimes, as a leader, you will specifically have to ask for feedback, as some team members may not be accustomed to telling the leader what they think. We must focus on candid conversations with staff that build trust and improve communication.

We all know how to stifle good ideas. Such statements as "It will never work," "We've never done it that way before," "We're doing fine without it," "We can't afford it," "We're not ready for it," and "It's not our responsibility" are statements we have all heard in our professional careers, and we know how they dampen enthusiasm and creativity for new ideas. If we, as leaders, are to be successful as problem-solvers and goal-setters and have the creativity to think through possible paths by which goals can be achieved, then we have to encourage our team to support us with new ideas. When was the last time you and your team members had a team meeting for no other reason than to review how things are working in your office and how they might be improved?

We all know that authority is a poor substitute for leadership. Individuals know you are the boss and, consequently, leaders understand that they do not have to remind people that they are in charge. One's title and position are important, but one's competencies and abilities are the real characteristics of a true leader when it comes to encouraging individuals to perform. Authority may be given to a person, but to be a leader, one must earn the respect of the team members. We all know that we are more likely to encourage individuals to work with us if we enlist their feelings as well as convince their reason.

Leaders are confident and optimistic about the future. They realize that there is one thing certain in life, and that is change. With the high turnover of college presidents and with sitting presidents being influenced by corporate America's "downsizing" themes, all of us are faced with change on a daily basis. Creating an organizational structure that is flexible when change occurs is very important.

Your organization should be given the opportunity to develop skills to deal with change, and expectations should be set when employees are hired that change will occur. In order to be successful, members of the team will need to embrace and celebrate opportunities for change and growth. As a leader, you will need to initiate change, set the pace, and constantly be showing others the importance of change. It has often been said that if we are not changing and keeping up, we are probably falling behind our competition. Change should be the result of *purpose*, not desperation.

A wise manager once advised, "Surround yourself with people who are smarter than you." We all realize that there is no substitute for intelligence. Good leaders are always looking for and appreciative of people who have more knowledge than they do, who have outstanding skills, and who have the understanding of how to apply that knowledge. Leaders are very secure in hiring individuals who have better skills than they do in particular areas. We all have skills, and the diversity of skills and ideas is what makes for a strong team. Leaders understand and are comfortable with individuals who have outstanding abilities, even when these abilities exceed the leader's abilities.

Today's leaders understand the importance of:

1. Personal discipline

2. Taking care of one's health

3. Being achievement-oriented

4. Having friends and developing quality relationships

5. Being willing to seize opportunities

Personal Discipline

If you are going to manage others, you certainly will need to be able to manage yourself. All outstanding managers practice a personal code of ethics on the job and off.

Taking Care of One's Health

Being able to deal with stress and fast-paced organizations through a healthy mind and body is extremely important for leaders. Having a good diet, regular exercise, and enough sleep are excellent investments in one's career as a leader.

Being Achievement Oriented

Leaders who are making a difference are results oriented. They know that the final performance of any race is measured at the finish line. Having measurable objectives and defining tasks and resources as well as early warning systems that may help identify problems before they become insurmountable are all very important in achieving goals as a leader. Likewise, as a leader it is also important, when tasks are delegated, to check the progress and follow-up often.

Having Friends and Developing Relationships

Successful leaders make sure that they have quality relationships with their co-workers, subordinates, and superiors. Developing those personal relationships through a genuine interest in other people, their dreams and goals in life, is critical. Having quality relationships will assist a leader in many ways. Having individuals who care about you and want you to be successful is a must. No leader has ever made a significant contribution without the help of many other people along the way. Seeking input from others on a regular basis with ongoing communication and collaboration will produce great rewards as a leader.

Few leaders in history have been able to stimulate individuals to action as Napoleon did. The secret of his leadership was simple: he first determined what was needed by his troops, then did everything in his power to help them satisfy their needs. We, as leaders today, must be very sensitive to our teams, their dreams, their desires, and their goals in life and assist them as well. It is my hope that each of you often ask your staff what it is that they would like to achieve. Is it the completion of an advanced degree? Is it advancement in title? Is it higher salary? Whatever it is, work with them to achieve their goals. If they know that you have interest in helping them achieve their goals, they likewise will help you achieve your goals for the organization. Life is like that: we have a tendency to help those who have helped us.

Being Willing to Seize Opportunities

Having the attitude of "What can I do something about within my own organization to make a difference?" is an important step to be successful as a leader. All too often we think in terms of "If only my boss would step forward and provide the leadership, we would achieve a particular goal or accomplish a particular task." If we wait on others, whether it be our boss or our co-workers, we may be waiting for a long time. We, as leaders, need to take the attitude, "Let me do all that I can within my power to move the organization forward." One's self-direction and motivation can work miracles if only we are willing to take the first step.

In conclusion, will all of these thoughts and suggestions be easy? The answer is "Absolutely not!" Leadership is an ongoing process that one has to work on every day. There are always changing circumstances, situations, and players that will affect you as the leader.

To be successful as a leader, I personally like the idea of taking small steps, or, better said, the "small win" strategy. Breaking apart challenges and opportunities into smaller, more controllable parts is the first step in tackling a task as a leader. A series of wins at small but significant tasks attracts support and lowers resistance to future tasks and proposals. We all know that small steps along the way build the foundation for future successes. Small requests are more likely to produce compliance and pave the way for more difficult tasks to come. Small wins are easier for everyone to comprehend and to gain a greater understanding of the final goal. Small wins produce visible results, and gradually but surely, small wins will accumulate, resulting in completion of the larger goal.

References

Aronowitz, S. 1988. The production of scientific knowledge. In *Marxism and the Interpretation of Culture*, edited by C. Nelson and L. Grossberg. Urbana IL: University of Illinois.

Bates, R. 1989. Leadership and the rationalization of society. In *Critical Perspectives on Educational Leadership*, edited by J. Smyth. Philadelphia PA: The Falmer Press.

Bavelas, A. 1984. Leadership: Man and function. In *Contemporary Issues in Leadership*, edited by W.E. Rosenbach and R.L. Taylor. Boulder CO: Westview Press.

Bennis, W.G. 1989. Where have all the leaders gone? In *Contemporary Issues in Leadership*, edited by W.E. Rosenbach and R.L. Taylor. Boulder CO: Westview Press.

———. 1986. Four traits of leadership. In *Leader-Manager*, edited by J.N. Williamson. New York: John Wiley & Sons, Inc.

Bensimon, E.M., A. Neumann, and R. Birnbaum. 1991. Higher education and leadership theory. In *ASHE Reader in Organization and Governance in Higher Education*, edited by M. Peterson. Lexington MA: Ginn Press.

Bogue, E.G. 1985. *The enemies of leadership: Lessons for leaders in education.* Bloomington IN: Phi Delta Kappa Educational Foundation.

Bolman, L.G., and T.E. Deal. 1991. *Reframing organization: Artistry, choice, and leadership.* San Francisco: Jossey-Bass Publishers.

Burke, W.W. 1988. *Leadership and empowerment.* New York: W. Warren Burke Associates, Inc.

Burns, J.M. 1978. *Leadership.* New York: Anchor Books.

Codd, J. 1989. Educational leadership as reflective action. In *Critical Perspectives on Educational Leadership*, edited by J. Smyth. Philadelphia PA: The Falmer Press.

Cohen, M.D. and J.G. March. 1991. The processes of choice. In *ASHE Reader in Organization and Governance in Higher Education*, edited by M. Peterson. Lexington MA: Ginn Press.

———. 1991. Leadership in an organized anarchy. In *ASHE Reader in Organization and Governance in Higher Education*, edited by M. Peterson. Lexington MA: Ginn Press.

Cooper, J., K. Kempner, and M. Amey. 1993. *Higher education leadership from a postmodern perspective.* Unpublished manuscript.

Cronin, T.E. 1989. Thinking and learning about leadership. In *Contemporary Issues in Leadership*, edited by W.E. Rosenbach and R.L. Taylor. Boulder CO: Westview Press.

Fincher, C. 1987. Administrative leadership in higher education. In *Higher Education: Handbook of Theory and Research*, Volume III, edited by J.C. Smart. New York: Agathon Press.

Foster, W. 1989. Toward a critical practice of leadership. In *Critical Perspectives on Educational Leadership*, edited by J. Smyth. Philadelphia PA: The Falmer Press.

Gardner, John W. 1990. *On Leadership.* New York: The Free Press.

———. 1989. The tasks of leadership. In *Contemporary Issues in Leadership*, edited by W.E. Rosenbach and R.L. Taylor. Boulder, CO: Westview Press.

Giroux, Henri. 1992. *Border crossings: Cultural workers and the politics of education.* New York: Routledge.

———. 1991. Series introduction: Toward a discourse of leadership and radical democracy. In *Educational Leadership: A Critical Pragmatic Perspective*, edited by S.J. Maxcy. New York: Bergin & Garvey.

Green, M.F. 1992. The accidental president: Views of theory and reality. *The Chronicle of Higher Education*, (February 26):A18.

———. 1988. Toward a new leadership model. In *Leaders for a New Era*, edited by M.F. Green. New York: ACE/MacMillan Publishing.

Hersey, Paul, and Blanchard. 1982. *Management of organizational behavior*. Englewood Cliffs NJ: Prentice-Hall.

Holloman, C.R. 1984. Leadership and headship: There is a difference. In *Contemporary Issues in Leadership*, edited by W.E. Rosenbach and R.L. Taylor. Boulder CO: Westview Press.

Kelley, R.E. 1989. In praise of followers. In *Contemporary Issues in Leadership*, edited by W.E. Rosenbach and R.L. Taylor. Boulder CO: Westview Press.

Kelly, F.J. 1991. Evolution of leadership in American higher education: A changing paradigm. *Journal for Higher Education Management*, 7(1):29-34.

Kouzes, J.M., and Posner, B.Z. 1990. *The leadership challenge*. San Francisco: Jossey-Bass Publishers.

Maxcy, S.J. 1991. *Educational leadership: A critical pragmatic perspective*. New York: Bergin & Garvey.

Phillips, J.R. and A.A Kennedy. 1986. Shaping and managing shared values. In *The University as an Organization*, edited by J.A. Perkins. New York: McGraw Hill Book Company.

Rosenbach, W.E., and S. Hayman. 1989. Absentee charismatic leadership: Khomeini, Gandhi and Mandela. In *Contemporary Issues in Leadership*, edited by W.E. Rosenbach and R.L. Taylor. Boulder CO: Westview Press.

Rost, J.C. 1991. *Leadership for the twenty-first century*. New York: Praeger.

Smyth, J. 1989. Preface. In *Critical Perspectives on Educational Leadership*, edited by J. Smyth. Philadelphia PA: The Falmer Press.

———. 1989. A 'pedagogical' and 'educative' view of leadership. In *Critical Perspectives on Educational Leadership*, edited by J. Smyth. Philadelphia PA: The Falmer Press.

Tierney, W.G. 1993. *Building communities of difference: Higher education in the twenty-first century*. Westport CT: Bergin & Garvey.

Trow, M.A. 1991. Comparative reflections on leadership in higher education. In *ASHE Reader in Organization and Governance in Higher Education*, edited by M. Peterson. Lexington MA: Ginn Press.

Zaleznik, A. 1989. The leadership gap. In *Contemporary Issues in Leadership*, edited by W.E. Rosenbach and R.L. Taylor. Boulder CO: Westview Press.

Zenger, S.J. 1996. *Interim leadership: The professional life history of Dr. Delbert M. Shankel*. Unpublished dissertation.

Chapter 6

Strategic Enrollment Management

by Michael G. Dolence

The Evolving SEM Concept

Strategic Enrollment Management (SEM) is not a static, but a dynamic concept that has continued to evolve rapidly over the past decade. This rapid evolution makes it such a powerful tool for academic and administrative leaders in higher education. To begin, we must understand the traditional concept; then we will explore how it is evolving.

A classic definition of SEM is that Strategic Enrollment Management is a comprehensive process designed to achieve and maintain the optimum recruitment, retention, and graduation rates of students, where "optimum" is defined within the academic context of the institution (Dolence 1993). This definition fits well within the context of traditional teaching/research/public service missions common during the later twentieth century, a period commonly referred to as the Industrial Age.

Michael G. Dolence is President of Michael G. Dolence and Associates. He consults with higher education institutions, systems, associations, and vendors nationally. He is a specialist in strategic positioning, institutional strategic planning and management processes, strategic enrollment management, information technology planning and management, linking planning and budgeting, public advocacy, and public relations.

He served as Strategic Planning Administrator for the California State University, Los Angeles; Director of Research, Planning and Policy Analysis for the Commission on Independent Colleges and Universities; author of *Strategic Enrollment Management: A Primer for Campus Administrators;* editor of *Strategic Enrollment Management: Cases from the Field;* and co-author of *Transforming Higher Education, Strategic Change in Colleges and Universities,* and *Working Towards Strategic Change.*

Within the context of the classic definition, recruitment is defined as the active process an institution undertakes to favorably influence a prospective student's decision to attend the institution (Dolence 1995). The recruitment phase begins with identifying prospects, those students who are eligible to attend and who have the characteristics of students who have shown some affinity for the institution. Recruitment ends and retention begins once the student enrolls. The root of recruitment is the student's enrollment decision process, which rests on two primary sets of variables, one centered around the student and the other around the institution. Both are in a state of radical flux as we approach the twenty-first century.

Retention is defined within the classic context as the maintenance of a student's satisfactory progress toward her or his educational objective until it is attained (Dolence 1993). Within this context, students recruited and admitted to an institution should reasonably expect that the programs, policies, procedures, and infrastructure necessary for them to successfully complete the programs to which they have been admitted are in place.

Examining the multiple factors that affect recruitment and retention decisions is one important focal point of SEM leaders. As the information age takes root in the world economy and learning assumes primacy as a universal competitive strategy, virtually all of our assumptions and underlying educational principles are being reshaped.

The key attribute that sets SEM apart from traditional approaches is that it takes a holistic, institution-wide approach. As such, it is a formal process for helping the institution to successfully meet the challenges of the Information Age. In other words, SEM is key to transforming a college or university into a twenty-first century learning organization, not just an organization of learning. As a transformational process, SEM is a means to reinvent the institution by helping to: realign the organization with the environment; redesign the organization to achieve the new intent; redefine the roles and responsibilities within the realigned, redesigned organization; and re-engineer organizational processes to achieve dramatically higher productivity and quality (Dolence and Norris 1995).

SEM: Helping Realign Higher Education with the Information Age

One of the primary challenges facing enrollment managers and their institutions is a fundamental shift from a time-out-for-education pattern of attendance to a perpetual learning model. The shift began during the 1980s and early 1990s, with the emergence of what many fondly call the "nontraditional student." Within twenty years these same "nontraditional" students became a dominant enrollment force. These students are predominantly part-time (meaning they cannot take time out to attend full-time), often take courses over a long period of time (often for eight to ten years before completing a degree or attaining another learning objective), and are highly motivated. They have joined forces with individuals who recognize that learning is the primary competitive advantage in society and have committed to learning as a perpetual lifelong endeavor. To meet their needs, we have begun to develop products and services for perpetual learners.

Perpetual learning is an educational model founded on the premise that individuals will need to avail themselves of continuous learning opportunities throughout their lifetimes in order to maintain a competitive position in society, maximize earning potential, and secure a position in life's value chain (Dolence 1994). It is a paradigm shift that parallels the transition to the Information Age and an information-based world economy (Quinn 1992).

In the perpetual learning paradigm, the key concept is that for the information age, learning must be continuous, and so must be the relationship with the college or university.

The concept of perpetual learning broadens academe's traditional base of enrollments. Perpetual learners require a combination of knowledge and skill acquisition methodologies and a supportive infrastructure in order to achieve and maintain intellectual independence. This contrasts with the seat-time model, in which the student is dependent upon the higher education provider for mode, method, and content of instruction. Independence means that the learner has more options than just the seat-time, place-bound, course-based approach that centers "education" in the classroom (Perelman 1992). It is an approach that centers "learning" within the individual.

Perpetual learning is emerging as ubiquitous, and it follows many paths, driven by multiple learner motivations. Some learning occurs in order to secure a degree. Learning may be used to develop or refine a skill or learn a trade. Learning may be undertaken to enrich life or gain technical expertise. A great deal of learning is involved in training or gaining proficiency with a particular program, tool, or platform. A vast learning demand has built up in the personal development and acquisition of basic skills. Professional domains demand continued development and certification, while still other individuals are lost and use learning to find themselves. Organizations continue to define special learning needs and enter into contracts to meet them. In order to gain a jump-start on life, others are accelerating learning at earlier and earlier ages. This wide array of perpetual learning activity may be sought by the same individuals as they move along life's path. It is in line with these multiple motivations that new SEM strategies must be built.

Confronted with this wide array of learning motivations, SEM professionals and their institutions must constantly refine their products and services. The emergence of a national learning infrastructure, already well-developed, is challenging current niche strategies and redefining organizational positions, SEM approaches, and program success as the Information Age washes over us (EDUCOM NLII Web Page). With learning at such a premium, the Information Age will also be known as the Age of Learning. Higher education must strive to meet its demands or lose its franchise. The SEM professional is key in leading the way.

SEM: Helping Redesign Higher Education's Products and Services

Twenty-first century society is emerging with at least one pivotal and consequential difference from previous societies. It is emerging as a globally networked, learning-dependent society: electronic networks are turning out to make all the difference. These networks are in and of themselves among the most powerful influences society has ever known. They have removed the barriers of time and distance from both the business and learning equation. They have dramatically lowered the barriers to learning, communication, and profit and non-profit activity. They have placed in the hands of anyone with the knowledge and infrastructure to use, it vast amounts of information and almost unlimited connectedness to others around the world. Networks have allowed direct access to the world's knowledge base without the need for an intermediary.

Indeed, the network has changed the rules, all the rules. The network has profound implications for how learning is conceptualized, how learning organizations are constructed, and how the process of learning is conducted. The implications for SEM professionals are profound.

Open Access Redefined

For years, providing access meant removing the fiscal and physical barriers to higher education. Information Age standards have created a demand for the radical expansion of the term "access" when applied to learning. Access in the Learning Age is coming to mean individuals having the combined resources of global knowledge bases at their disposal throughout their learning careers. Access to this emerging virtual learning environment holds great potential for institutions that creatively use it to build enrollment bridges to the future (Dolence 1995). The poorest of our society, who do not have access to virtual learning networks and tools, are in great peril. We stand to lose all of the ground we have gained in the twentieth century toward leveling the socio-economic playing field.

Learner-Centered

In the virtual learning environment, as in the network and the World Wide Web, the learner is always in the center of the learning domain. This phenomenon of the learner being the structural center of a virtual university redefines the relationships among and between learner, infrastructure, teacher, mentor, and curriculum. It also challenges many of the principles and practices of recruitment and retention.

Shift in Focus from Distance to Time

Because, in the Industrial Age, the center of the learning domain was the physical campus and the faculty, library, and laboratory, resources were place-bound. Distance was a primary determinant in providing learner opportunity. Providing learning opportunities to individuals geographically isolated from the physical learning centers spawned movements such as distance education. With the advent of the Internet and the World Wide Web, learning resources are ubiquitous and openly available to anyone with a digital network connection. Distance is no longer the dominant limiting parameter, but time is. Time has long been a strategic weapon of the enrollment manager, but new rules are emerging, and they mean that new strategies must be developed (Tapscott 1996).

Shift from Seat-Time Model to Perpetual Learning Model

The seat-time model, in essence, requires a significant investment in discrete learning products, such as degrees, certificates, etc. The "investment in learning" requires the learner to "take time out" and invest it, along with significant financial resources, in a learning product or products delivered over multiple years. In contrast, perpetual learning is a learning-on-demand model (Dolence and Norris 1995).

Virtual Learning Environments

The network is the fundamental organizational framework and tool of the twenty-first century. The network must also assume a central role as SEM professionals consider the redesign of higher education products and services. The transition from autonomous, hierarchical institutions of learning to globally networked learning organizations holds profound implications and opportunities for enrollment management professionals (Dolence 1996).

The explosion in use of the Internet, the World Wide Web, and other national and international networks has created an environment of vast intellectual capacity, information and knowledge bases, shared methodologies, and other knowledge tools and assets. (A list promised by the Globewide Network Academy of 251 providers of 771 programs and 9,376 courses can be found at http://www.gnacademy.org:8001/uu-gna/index.html). Network utilization is becoming virtually universal in many domains. SEM professionals must fully understand the impact of these networks as a fundamental guiding principle for redesign.

Utilization of networks is, of course, a decision for individual learners, faculty, administrators, and institutions. SEM professionals must help their institutions understand that lagging too far behind in the development and use of network learning and technological infrastructure means a high risk of being unable to participate meaningfully in network learning as it emerges. Operating an educational institution in the twenty-first century that is not a full participant in network learning will be analogous to operating an Industrial Age institution of higher education without lecture halls, classrooms, libraries, or science laboratories.

SEM Faces New Competition

SEM professionals must prepare their institutions for a radically different competitive environment as they face the twenty-first century. The first step is to develop an understanding that the information infrastructure will emerge as a primary delivery mechanism for educational materials, even for campus resident students. This has several dramatic implications.

One resulting scenario portends that, because the network is ubiquitous and open, higher education will not own the "learning" franchise as *the* provider. Instead, it will share the provider role with commercial network operators, professional curriculum developers, and other intermediaries. Competing information and learner support systems are already emerging on commercial networks. Competition will no longer be limited to other colleges and universities and some corporate training organizations, but will also include global information and learner-support providers.

Network-based perpetual learning provides a dramatically broader enrollment base for enrollment managers to cultivate. Consider that many human resource professionals, futurists, and strategic planners believe that during the Information Age, between 20 percent and 40 percent of a worker's time will be spent learning. There are currently 140 million workers in the U.S. Based on a 40-hour work week, this translates to between eight and sixteen contact learning hours per week becoming common. In fact, my own research and desk audits conducted at eleven client sites during 1995 and 1996 reveal that this is already occurring. Workers engaged in perpetual learning could mean between 560 million and 1.1 billion contact hours of learning per year.

A second resulting scenario portends that in the long term, as individuals, business, and government turn to network alternatives, the franchise of the college degree or college credit will face significant challenges from outcomes-based product developers. The contact hours calculated above may be replaced by learning outcome achievement. The learner will take as many contact hours as needed to achieve the outcome. This could render the contact hour econometrics of higher education irrelevant. These challenges will stimulate rethinking of all current course, credit, and degree programs and structures. Under the network learning paradigm, a curriculum and its delivery must be world class, relevant, and appropriately priced.

A third resulting scenario, however, may mean that the largest, most prestigious institutions will not necessarily be the most successful in the twenty-first century, although some are moving aggressively in this direction. Smaller, more focused, more nimble institutions may be able to craft world class on-line learning materials for worldwide use. In addition, other learning intermediaries may tap the academic resources at our major colleges and universities to create "learningware" to be used in virtual learning environments around the globe (Dolence 1996).

Virtual universities have the potential to be mega-learning centers on a scale not yet imagined. Consider the advent of the Western Governors Association Virtual University (Western Governors Association 1995).

> All western governors are feeling the press of increased demand on their state systems of postsecondary education. All recognize that the strength and well-being of both their states and the nation depend heavily on a postsecondary education system that is visibly aligned with the needs of a transforming economy and society. At the same time, the states' capacity to respond to these challenges is severely constrained by limited resources and the inflexibility and high costs of traditional educational practices and by outdated institutional and public policies.
>
> The governors of the western states see the exploding availability and capabilities of advanced technology-based teaching and learning as a potentially powerful means to address these challenges, and to make cutting-edge educational and assessment services much more widely available. Therefore, the governors, meeting in late Fall 1995, charged a WGA design team with creating a design plan for a western virtual university to serve the region and an implementation plan through which such an entity could be established and financed.

As the above quote from the Western Governors Association points out, the rules context is not pedagogical alone, but also political, social, and economic as well. By preparing the way through public policy, the signatories to the WGA Virtual University initiative create fertile ground for radical change. But remember: the WGA is only one example of a virtual university; there are many others that are much further along, already enrolling many thousands of learners. (A current list can be found on the Transformational Tours section of my website [http:/home.earthlink. net/~mgdolence/].)

In order to effectively meet these challenges, SEM professionals must help stimulate their institutions to rethink their basic educational strategies. This includes, but is not limited to, reconceptualizing the learning infrastructure around networks rather than physical facilities, reconceptualizing institutions as learning organizations built around essential outcomes, redefining institutional boundaries within a network model using technology, and designing new interfaces with learners.

Redefining SEM

Where is all of this leading? It is leading to new definitions and frameworks for strategically managing enrollments. Colleges and universities must design learning environments to meet their fiduciary responsibility for human capital development for the clients and the communities they serve. Within this context, SEM takes on a new meaning. Strategic Enrollment Management can be a comprehensive process designed to achieve and maintain an optimum alignment between an institution's clients' perpetual learning needs and the institution's products and services. Alignment becomes a primary function of the enrollment manager's mission, a function that provides leadership and is broader and more comprehensive than recruitment and retention alone.

Translating the alignment function into practice, however, requires incorporating it into the SEM processes of generating and retaining enrollments. The flow of enrollments is mapped against both institutional and student decisions. Table 6.1 frames the SEM process into the four classic phases (unshaded): the identification phase, the recruitment phase, the retention phase, and the sustaining phase. Two additional phases (shaded) help maintain alignment: the assessment phase and the new product development phase. These four-plus-two phases of SEM help articulate the specific transition decisions that both students and institutions face.

The assessment phase outlined above is sometimes actually called the re-assessment phase. It is the formal re-examination of fundamental options and the rules individuals use to make decisions regarding how and where they are going to meet their learning needs. In addition to increased competition from traditional institutions, new competition from "guaranteed outcomes providers" will become a greater challenge. "Guaranteed outcomes providers" guarantee that the learner achieves the desired outcomes. When coupled with convenient network delivery, start-anytime, proceed-at-your-own-pace, pay-as-you-go virtual and perpetual learning models, the guarantee is a compelling incentive.

The new product development phase requires rethinking academic products from a market-driven, learner-centered perspective. We must get over the aversion to calling what we sell a "product" if we are to preserve the processes that we so cherish.

Repackaging is an easy first step. Caution is advised. Consumers do not have to buy into your repackaging strategy. The move to revise a general education (GE) curriculum is a classic example. Institutional GE com-

Table 6.1. The Four-Plus-Two Phases of SEM

Institutional Decision (Examples not exhaustive)	SEM Phase and Key Performance Indicators	Student Decision (Examples not exhaustive)
Decision to explore traditional, digital, and virtual learning options and opportunities.	**Assessment Phase** Traditional, Perpetual, and Virtual Learning Needs and Opportunities	Looking for learning in lots of different places on the Web, at Mind Extension University, Virtual On-line University, etc.
Decision to be learner-centered and meet learner needs. Commitment to deliver. Matching needs, opportunities, and curriculum. Perpetual learning needs.	**New Product Development Phase** Phase Repackaging, Curriculum Development, Innovative Design, New Financial Models, New Delivery Models	Patience, Set Individual Goals
Image, Program Service Mix, Geographic Sphere of Influence, Admissions Standards ...	**Identification Phase** Number of Prospects, Number of Respondents, Requests for Application	The decision to examine your institution.
Application Procedures, Admission Standards, Financial Aid Policy Curriculum ...	**Recruitment Phase** Number of Applications, Number of Accepted, Number of Deposits	The decision to attend your institution.
Financial Aid Policy, Grading Policy, Student Life Curriculum ...	**Retention Phase** Number of Freshmen, Number of Sophomores, Number of Juniors, Number of Seniors, Number of Graduate Students	The decision to achieve one's pedagogical objective at your institution.
Relationship Strategy, Continuous Product Development	**Sustaining Phase** Graduates, Alumni Perpetual Learners	The decision to continue to support and acquire perpetual learning products from your institution.

mittees rushed to repackage courses into mandated curricular sequences they "judged" to be mandatory for every student. Some institutions even designated some of those courses as "you have to take it here" in an effort to guarantee quality (or ensure that they sustained enrollment and maintained their academic posts). Increasingly, learners are rejecting the judgment, and the strategy designed to guarantee quality (enrollments) is actually chasing gifted learners away, as I have learned from focus group research at client sites in 1994, 1995, and 1996.

Repackaging can be a very positive undertaking. One institution modified "Introduction to Writing" by making it fill the need articulated in its new title, "Writing: A Key Employability Skill." Demand for the material was so high that it is now using the model for a four-course sequence and my prediction is that it will develop into a certificate, then into a degree program. Another institution developed "Retail Mathematics and Economics" from curriculum elements in three departments. The course filled the first day of registration and is now taught in three local retail malls and two banks. It has become a great recruitment tool. Both of these examples are outcomes-based.

New curriculum is essential to surviving the twenty-first century — not just modernizing the content area, but the development, design, delivery, and financing models as well. An institution should be setting new curricular products (at least three to five) before consumers every year for as far into the future as one can now see. The time to develop a new curricular product must be less than a year in most cases and be approved and in service within three months after development. This means a curriculum development process that spans no more than a year. In states where a State Master Plan prohibits such rapid development and deployment, institutions will be at a serious competitive disadvantage as more nimble, responsive providers in other states begin to penetrate their market with new, innovative learning products. New curriculum is new product and it must be developed with the learners needs' and performance criteria in mind.

Developing Market-Driven Learning Products

Alignment of product design is followed by marketing. Marketing is the process of putting the right product before the right audience at the right price. Forgive the label "product," but that is what our programs are — products — and the consumers are getting increasingly more sophisticated at shopping for them, evaluating their value, and selecting them.

Marketing has its roots in product design. In higher education, product design involves curriculum and academic program development. Regardless of what we may call our programs, an institution must have a product to put before prospects. Admissions and enrollment manage-

Table 6.2 Product Development Matrix (Mix and Match)

Track	Mode of Delivery	Method of Learning	Content
Degree Track Skill Track Trade Track Enrichment Track Technical Track Training Track Developmental Track Professional Development/ Certification Track "Find Me" Track Contract Track	Classroom Directed Study Self-Guided Learning Laboratory Library Network Interactive Computer-Based Audio Tutorial Personal Tutor Concurrent Sequential	Lecture Simulation Experimentation Personal System of Instruction Team-Based Learning Cohort Learning Groups Study Groups Teleconference	Knowledge Skills Outcomes Modules

ment professionals are eager for new products. Table 6.2 sets forth a simple product development matrix, using the "track" label to capture learner motivation, the mode of delivering the learning product, and the method of instruction or learning by which the knowledge and skills content are delivered.

Each element of the matrix can be mixed and matched with other elements of the matrix to form a product. In other words, a product can be formed around learner motivation or the mode, method, or content of the learning to be undertaken. The matrix is designed to illuminate the dimensions of academic product development within a Strategic Enrollment Management context.

The "track" is a label given to a family of curricular products designed around the needs and motivations of a group of learners with common outcomes expectations. The degree track, therefore, is designed around learners whose desired outcome is a degree. The skill track is designed around learners whose expected outcome is a new, advanced, or refined skill. The trade track is for learners engaged in or desiring to enter a trade. The enrichment track is designed for individuals who learn for pleasure or enrichment. The technical track provides entry or advancement in a technical field. The training track is designed for individuals who wish to be trained to use a particular product, process, or skill. The developmental track provides learners who need to visit or revisit the basics. The professional development/certification track is designed to provide learners with a certificate of completion for professional license or continuing education mandate purposes. The "find me" track is designed to explore options, visit alternative destinations, and explore new horizons. The contract track is designed for a client to produce a desired knowledge or skill set capability for learners.

Traditional modes of delivery involve face-to-face interaction in a classroom. Within the classroom model, learners are directed to out-of-class assignments, laboratory assignments, or library assignments. The venue for each of these revolves around the physical classroom.

Directed study provides learners with a structured course syllabus detailing course objectives, learning outcomes, assignments, resources, and performance expectations. Learners complete the assignments in a prescribed, structured way while communicating frequently with faculty by telephone, Internet, World Wide Web, e-mail, mail, or fax.

Based upon informal surveys and audits conducted over the past few years, I estimate that up to 80 percent of all learning is currently self-guided.

A librarian at a national conference commented, after a talk on transforming libraries, "It's not your mother's library, is it?" Indeed, the library of today is awash with technology, connectivity, CD-ROM resources, search utilities, etc. In fact, libraries have responded aggressively to the image of trailing in the use of technology and have helped to build powerful learning infrastructures.

The dominant model for curriculum delivery is the concurrent course structure, in which learners enroll in multiple courses at the same time. However, several models of sequential curriculum delivery, in which learners enroll in only one subject at time, have emerged and grown to be very effective and attractive to learners.

When developing SEM strategies, affect what matters most. An excellent resource for enrollment managers is Ernest Pascarella and Patrick Terenzini's 1991 meta analysis titled *How College Affects Students*.

Consider, for example, some of the conclusions that Pascarella and Terenzini (1991, 88) draw after considering the research: "The weight of evidence makes it reasonably clear that in postsecondary education neither large or small classes nor lecture or discussion formats are more effective than the other in fostering the mastery of factual subject matter material." They also observe, citing McKeachie (1980), "It is probably the case, however, that smaller classes are somewhat more effective than larger ones, when the goals of instruction are motivational, attitudinal, or higher-level cognitive processes."

If we shift the frame of analysis from the "classroom" to different approaches of learning, we also find significant evidence of alternatives that have dramatic effects on learner performance that must be considered in developing enrollment management strategies. In the 1960s there emerged a learning model that argued that virtually all students can achieve mastery of any learning task if each is given enough time and receives appropriate instruction. Carroll's (1963) model and the closely related mastery concepts of Bloom (1968) have led to the development of various approaches to individualized instruction. By "individualized" we mean tunable to a specific learner's needs, not necessarily a one-to-one personal tutorial. Early approaches are exemplified by the following:

- *Audio-Tutorial Instruction (ATI):* ATI involves three components: independent study, small group sessions, and general group sessions. During independent study sessions, students work independently on learning tasks in a laboratory equipped with tapes, materials, and visual aids. During small-group sessions, students meet periodically in groups of six to ten with an instructor for the purpose of training, discussion, and quizzing. Larger general sessions are designed as a forum for the group as a whole to engage in activities such as lectures, films, and major examinations. Students using the ATI approach experienced an achievement advantage of 8 percentile points over conventional control groups. (For example, if, upon testing, the control group achieved at the 60th percentile, the ATI group achieved at the 68th percentile.)

- *Computer-Based Instruction (CBI):* CBI involves the interactive use of a computer. Programmed instruction, simulation, drill and practice, and tutorial exercises are frequently implemented in CBI. Students using the CBI approach experienced an achievement advantage of 10 percentile points over conventional control groups. (For example, if, upon testing, the control group achieved at the 60th percentile, the CBI group achieved at the 70th percentile.) Studies also showed significant positive effect on learner attitude and a reduction in the time needed for instruction.

- *Personalized System of Instruction (PSI):* PSI is conducted through small modularized units of instruction. Students use study guides to lead them through the material. The focus is upon mastery of material, with immediate feedback given on performance and tests. Students move through the material at their own pace. Tutors, proctors, or monitors are available to help individual students with problems. Occasional lectures and discussions punctuate the PSI to provide motivation. Students using the PSI approach experienced an achievement advantage of 19 percentile points over conventional control groups. (For example, if, upon testing, the control group achieved at the 60th percentile, the PSI group achieved at the 79th percentile.)

I am not advocating any particular approach here, but simply illustrating that there is a demonstrable difference in approaches that can be exploited and differentiated. These examples are provided to help enrollment managers begin the dialogue regarding mode, method, and content of instruction with academic leaders on their campus. In addition, the tools available to assist learners is also an important domain for enrollment managers to understand and fold into their SEM strategies.

Evidence that access to individual learning tools dramatically improves performance is set forth by Lewis J. Perlman (1992) in his radical assessment of the nation's educational system. Perlman found within the K-12 community that access to home learning tools could account for significant differences between low- and high-performance schools. Learning infrastructure and learning tools, therefore, can also be differentiating and exploited by enrollment managers. Table 6.3 compares differentiating characteristics (Perelman 1992, 190).

Marketing Learning Products in the Twenty-First Century

When a product appeals to a well-defined yet not necessarily small segment of the total prospect base, that segment is called a niche. Niches in higher education's prospect base may be based on track (learner interest), price, location, ease and convenience of attendance, specific program offerings, industry affiliation, research acumen, sensitivity to discrete populations (women returning to the workforce, professionals undergoing mid-life career changes), spiritual affiliations, cultural affiliations, and the reputation of faculty, alums, or specialized facilities.

Prospects can also be categorized by their affinity for various modes, methods, and content areas of instruction and learning as set forth in Table 6.2. Finding prospect groupings with common interests and characteristics is called market segmentation. Many market segments exist within the domain of any institution. Examples of market segments in-

Table 6.3: Differentiating Characteristics of Low- Versus High-Performance Schools

Differentiating Characteristics	Low-Performance Schools	High-Performance Schools
Two parents in home	74.4	83.1
Mother working while child in high school	67.5	69.1
Number of home learning tools = above average	34.6	76.4
Father closely monitors school work	64.7	71.7
Mother closely monitors school work	84.9	84.8
Father expects student to attend college	65.3	76.4
Mother expects student to attend college	67.8	79.4

clude those based upon quality (high selectivity drawing from a wide pool of applicants), regional (wider range of academic ability exhibited by applicants over a narrower geographic distribution), or local demand (high affinity over a small geographic area). Academic administrators, faculty, curriculum designers, and academic support staff are essential to aligning products with markets, and they must understand market segmentation, niche markets, and the dynamics of the marketplace.

Identifying market segments, describing their characteristics, and extrapolating them to buying behavior is a function of market research. Market research can derive strategies by finding segments of the population with a high affinity for niches peculiar to an institution in areas now underserved. Market research can also help the institution uncover new niche opportunities within segments of the population now served. It can help decision-makers identify niches and populations and provide insight into price sensitivity, financial aid, need and performance, and long-term and short-term product and program demand. The information derived from this research has little value if it is not incorporated into product design and delivery.

Market research is not supplementary to the SEM function but an integral part of its success. It must contain a solid institutional research component but must extend far beyond the domain of the institution. Demographics, lifestyles, purchasing power, buying behavior, competing institutions, commuter behavior, and a host of other research domains can be essential to the success of institutional SEM strategies. More important as the Information Age continues to evolve will be the creative mix-and-matching of track interest with mode, method, and content of learning products.

Marketing strategies are also integral to retention. Students recruited by an institution are those it must seek to retain. Students are retained when the products, services, and culture of the institution meet the expectations of the learner.

Building a Comprehensive Understanding of Enrollment Goals

The foundation of the understanding should be based on enrollment key performance indicators. Key performance indicators (KPIs) are measures that are monitored in order to determine the enrollment health of the institution. They are not broad, general, categorical metrics, such as quality, resources, satisfaction, efficiency, or effectiveness. They are specific quantitative measures that tell all academic managers whether the college or university is achieving its goals using an acceptable level of resources. KPIs are precise numbers that have one and only one definition throughout the organization (Dolence, Rowley, and Lujan 1997).

KPIs are specific, measurable indicators. For example, annual institutional FTE enrollment reflects the aggregated enrollment at the highest level. It is composed of term, component school, college, department, and course enrollments. The business school would have an enrollment KPI that contributes to the institution's overall KPI; the departments of accounting, finance, marketing, and the MBA program have enrollment KPIs that contribute to the school's KPI. KPIs thus form a pyramid, with the organization-wide KPIs sitting at the top, division KPIs sitting one layer underneath, and major unit and department level KPIs forming the foundation. In this example, annual institutional FTE represents a primary KPI, school level enrollment represents a secondary (subset) KPI, department enrollments form tertiary KPIs, and course enrollments form the base layer, or, in this case, quaternary KPIs. Secondary, tertiary, and quaternary do not mean less important; to the contrary, you can see that without all three supportive layers, there would be no annual institutional FTE enrollment.

When strategic decisions are linked with KPIs, they can be especially effective in aligning a college or university within its environment, prioritizing resource allocations and program initiatives, focusing attention, and setting a course of action for the organization as a whole. KPIs allow concrete specification of the milestones and indicators that mark institutional progress. In short, they guide the organization, ensuring that it becomes more effective and more competitive. Table 6.4 shows some examples of KPIs. The list is by no means exhaustive.

Aligning Decisions with Enrollment Goals

In order to maintain an alignment between decisions and the key performance indicators, enrollment managers need to consider the impact current strategies, goals, and objectives will have on the KPIs identified. This can be done easily using the cross-impact analysis (CIA), a Delphi technique that gives an enrollment or management team a clear vision of how each strategy, goal, and objective affects the achievement of the organization's KPIs. The CIA is conducted using a two-dimensional matrix, in which the organization's KPIs are arrayed along one dimension and the strategies, goals, and objectives are arrayed along the other. Each member of the group assesses the impact that he or she believes each trend and event would have on each KPI. The appropriate impact is marked using the scale that follows Table 6.5.

Strategies are initiatives that align, realign, or maintain alignment between the organization and the environment. They are, or should be, long-term in nature, although they may have significant short-term impact on the organization, its collaborators, and its competitors. *Goals* are milestones achieved, usually over more than one year. *Objectives* are more immediate, time-bound, and measurable desired outcomes. *Tactics* are activities that move the organization closer to achieving its goals and objectives. *Resources* are the fiscal, human, technological, and organizational inputs to the organization's operations. Table 6.5 illustrates a CIA used to evaluate the impact of current strategies, goals, and objectives on the achievement of organizational enrollment KPIs. (A complete explanation of the use of KPIs can be found in Dolence, Rowley, and Lujan 1997.)

Table 6.4: Examples of Key Performance Indicators, with Definitions

Example Key Performance Indicator	Example Definition (Excerpted from institutional strategic plans)
1. Undergraduate FTE Enrollment	Number of units attempted divided by 15
2. Graduate FTE Enrollment	Number of units attempted divided by 12
3. Tuition Revenue	Tuition revenue collected net of institutional financial aid
4. Graduation Rate	Percentage of full-time undergraduates who graduate in four years
5. Minority Enrollment	Percentage of all enrolled students who are minorities
6. Placement Rate	Percentage of graduates employed or in advanced study one year after graduation
7. Student-Faculty Ratio	Number of FTE students divided by the number of FTE faculty
8. Recruitment Yield	Percentage of students offered admission who enroll
9. Retention Rate	Percentage of students who maintain satisfactory progress
10. Break-even Major Index	Total revenue deriving from students in each major minus the attributable cost of the major department
11. Average Debt Burden	Total value of loans divided by the number of loan recipients
12. Student Satisfaction	Composite score from annual student needs and priorities survey
13. Average SAT/ACT Score	Average SAT/ACT score of incoming first-year students
14. Value of Endowment	Book value of endowment at the end of each quarter
15. Deferred Maintenance	Dollar value of maintenance backlog

Table 6.5: Sample Individual Cross-Impact Matrix for Strategies, Goals, Objectives

Key Performance Indicators						Current Strategies, Goals, Objectives
1	2	3	4	5	6+	
						Strategy 1: (5 to 10 year)
						Goal 1.1 (2 to 5 years milestone)
						Objective 1.1.1 (1 year)
						Objective 1.1.2 (1 year)
						Goal 1.2 (2 to 5 years milestone)
						Objective 1.2.1 (1 year)
						Objective 1.2.2 (1 year)
						Objective 1.2.3 (1 year)
						Strategy 2: (5 to 10 year)
						Goal 2.1 (2 to 5 years milestone)
						Objective 2.1.1 (1 year)
						Objective 2.1.2 (1 year)

6 = strong positive influence
5 = moderate positive influence
4 = weak positive influence
3 = weak negative influence
2 = moderate negative influence
1 = strong negative influence
0 = neutral, don't know, no impact, not applicable

The scale illustrated above is easy to use, but it is not the only option for scoring the CIA. Consult your office of institutional research for other options.

Aligning Policies and Procedures with Enrollment Goals

Progress toward the desired values for the enrollment KPIs can be achieved only if organizational policies and procedures facilitate the effort. Ultimately, every organizational policy and procedure should be passed through a cross-impact analysis, to measure its impact against the organization's KPIs. In this way, the academic administrators and enrollment managers can assess the impact of each policy on each goal.

A great deal of discussion is generated by such a review. As you can see from the examples in Table 6.6, the interpretation of each cross-impact analysis is case-specific. This forces the group to carefully articulate the purpose of the policy or procedure and to deal with its impact upon the enrollment goals and organizational KPIs.

Aligning Organizational Design with Enrollment Goals

Organizational design must also be aligned with articulated enrollment goals. Four components of organizational design can be evaluated using the cross-impact analysis method — organizational structure, defined functions, supportive infrastructure, and the integration of functions. The purpose of the CIA at this stage is to gain insights into the impact of organizational design on achievement of enrollment goals and organizational KPIs. *Structure* is defined as the authority, governance, and re-

Table 6.6: Sample Individual Cross-Impact Matrix for Policies and Procedures

Key Performance Indicators	Re-evaluate financial aid package (zero sum) each year	Application fee charged is three times that of competition	Freshman Year Experience program is mandatory	Incompletes revert to F after six weeks, no exceptions
FTE enrollment	1	1	2	2
Tuition rate	4	0	4	0
Graduation rate	2	0	5	2
State appropriation	0	0	0	0
Financial aid	5	3	5	3

(The numbers used in each cell of Table 6.6 correspond to the scale used in Table 6.5.)

porting relationships that establish rules of operation within an organization. It is often diagrammed in organizational charts that can be classified into organizational typologies such as hierarchical, flat, or star. When structure is combined with division, unit, and individual functions and analyzed against organizational KPIs, some interesting insights begin to emerge. The sample cross impact-analysis is set forth in Table 6.7, which illustrates an actual CIA used to evaluate four design-driven characteristics within a university.

Just as important as organizational design is an analysis of organization infrastructure. Such an analysis should include a consideration of the physical plant, telecommunications networks, administrative and academic information systems, and classroom equipment (An example is detailed in Table 6.8).

The final dimension of organizational form is how well the different divisions, units, and even individuals integrate their activity and efforts. The analysis should include judgments on the level of cross-unit integration and communication within the organization and the impact they have on enrollment goals.

SEM: A Road to Transformation

SEM is an institution-wide process and a powerful tool for change. The need to be comprehensive and inclusive cannot be overemphasized.

Table 6.7: Sample Individual Cross-Impact Analysis for Organizational Structure

Key Performance Indicators	Academic advising is under three vice president jurisdictions	Information technology is under three vice president jurisdictions	Academic program development does not include admissions recruiters	Recruitment and retention responsibility is shared by 22 offices
FTE enrollment	2	1	1	1
Tuition rate	0	2	3	3
Graduation rate	4	0	0	0
State appropriation	3	0	0	0
Financial aid	0	4	5	6

Table 6.8: Sample Individual Cross-Impact Analysis for Infrastructure

Key Performance Indicators	Administrative Information System	Academic Information System	Quality and Condition of Physical Plant	Parking Convenience and Enforcement
FTE enrollment	2	1	1	1
Tuition rate	0	2	3	3
Graduation rate	4	0	0	0
State appropriation	3	0	0	0
Financial aid	0	4	5	6

SEM crosses all functional domains and all levels within an institution. No one office, functional element, or system can be neglected without diminishing the quality of the effort. The potential benefits are numerous.

SEM can be used to stabilize enrollments. This may involve stopping declining enrollment, controlling enrollment growth, and/or smoothing out fluctuations in enrollment in order to stabilize finances. It may also mean working with individual departments to increase the number of majors, bring the department to break-even enrollment numbers, or handle over-enrollment pressures.

SEM can be used to link academic programs with recruitment and retention efforts. Too many departments and schools leave their enrollments to fate. Using the principles and practices of SEM in academic unit management and operations affords the opportunity to establish stable departments and improve both quality and retention. An important step is to align all of the academic planning, review, and evaluation processes — including program review, accreditation self-study, annual budget preparation, academic master planning, and curriculum planning — with each other.

SEM can be used to stabilize finances, including eliminating deficits, paying off debts, and reinvesting strategically. Higher education cannot fix its financial problems by working the expenditure side of the equation alone. With the costs of higher education rising consistently faster than the Consumer Price Index, and with the deep concern of the public over the continued escalation, serious long-term revenue planning must be undertaken. The link between enrollments and revenues is inexorable. In fact, enrollment planning and revenue planning go hand in hand.

SEM can be used to optimize resources. This goes beyond budget. It includes containing growth in the number of employees, redirecting and refocusing employees' efforts, optimizing campus information systems, etc. Virtually every campus in America under-exploits its existing resources.

SEM can be used to improve services. Many services are misguided, redundant, or unvalued by their recipients. SEM provides methods for dramatically improving services, including shortening response time, increasing satisfaction, and reducing overhead and paperwork.

SEM can be used to improve quality. Quality in most institutions is poorly defined. This hinders efforts to improve it. SEM can make quality more explicit, better defined, and more approachable from systematic methods of enhancement. Quality has three dimensions — inputs, processes, and outputs. SEM helps focus upon all three.

SEM can be used to improve access to information. SEM cannot be optimized without an integrated information system on-line. It also cannot be implemented if the people who run it are insufficiently trained. This does not mean that more people need to be hired. But those who can be trained need to be, and those who cannot be trained need to be replaced by people who can.

One of the most important uses of SEM is to reduce institutional vulnerability to environmental forces. Sound SEM programs continually monitor and evaluate environmental signals. It is not sufficient, however, to just monitor the environment. An institution must *act* on the signals it receives.

SEM is not a quick fix. Because at any given time an SEM effort involves evaluating last-cycle performance, implementing the current cycle, and planning for the following annual cycle, it requires approximately three years for full implementation. It is a deliberate process that requires an information infrastructure to sustain it. It can usually be developed with existing resources. It can be implemented in a

---

Editor's note:
For more information on SEM and conferences, look at the AACRAO Web site at www.AACRAO.COM or contact AACRAO, One Dupont Circle, NW, Suite 330, Washington, DC 20036-1171. Phone: 202/296-9161.

wide variety of ways and can be supported through various organizational structures. SEM calls for new levels of trust and cooperation from those involved in different aspects of the process. Its success rests on sound, ongoing planning and evaluation. SEM requires leadership from all levels. Leadership means new levels of professionalism.

References

Bean, John C. 1996. *Engaging ideas: The professor's guide to integrating writing, critical thinking and active learning in the classroom.* San Francisco: Jossey-Bass Publishers

Berge, Zane L. and Mauri P. Collins, eds. 1995. *Computer mediated communication and the on-line classroom.* Cresskill NJ: Hampton Press.

Bloom, Benjamin. 1968. Mastery learning. *Evaluation Comment* 1(2).

Burstein, Daniel and David Kline. 1995. *Road warriors: Dreams and nightmares along the information highway.* New York: Dutton.

Carroll, J. 1963. A model of school learning. *Teachers College Record,* 64: 723-733.

December, John, and Neil Randall. 1995. *The world wide web unleashed.* 2nd edition. Indianapolis IN: SAMS Publishing.

Dolence, Michael G. 1993. *Strategic enrollment management: A primer for campus administrators.* Washington DC: American Association of Collegiate Registrars and Admissions Officers.

———. 1994. Bringing about transformations. Presentation at the Strategic Enrollment Management Conference of the American Association of Collegiate Registrars and Admissions Officers. Cincinnati, November 14-17.

———. 1995. The ABC's of SEM. Preconference Seminar presented at the Strategic Enrollment Management Conference, American Association of Collegiate Registrars and Admissions Officers, North Carolina, November 11, 1995.

———. 1995. Developing a strategic plan for enrollment management. Preconference Seminar presented at the Strategic Enrollment Management Conference, American Association of Collegiate Registrars and Admissions Officers, North Carolina, November 11, 1995.

———. 1996. Transfoming small colleges for the information age. Presentation at the National Small College Admissions Conference. Nashville, July 22.

Dolence, Michael G., and Donald M. Norris. 1995. *Transforming higher education: A vision for learning in the twenty-first century.* Ann Arbor MI: Society for College and University Planning.

Dolence, Michael G., Daniel James Rowley, and Herman D. Lujan. 1997. *Working toward strategic change: A step-by-step guide to the planning process.* San Francisco: Jossey-Bass Publishers.

EDUCOM NLII Web Page [http://www.educom.edu/program/nlii/nliiHome.html]

Galsky, A. ed. 1991. *The role of student affairs in institution-wide enrollment management strategies.* Washington DC: National Association of Student Personnel Administrators.

Gates, Bill. 1995. *The road ahead.* New York: Viking.

Gouillart, Francis J., and James N. Kelly. 1995. *Transforming the organization.* New York: McGraw-Hill, Inc.

Harasim, Linda M., et.al. 1996. *Learning networks.* Cambridge MA: MIT Press.

Hossler Don. 1986. *Creating effective enrollment management systems.* San Francisco: Jossey-Bass Publishers

Hossler, Don. and John P. Bean and Associates. 1990. *The strategic management of college enrollments.* San Francisco: Jossey-Bass Publishers

Ihlanfeldt, William. 1980. *Achieving optimal enrollments and tuition revenues: A guide to modern methods of market research, student recruitment, and institutional pricing.* San Francisco: Jossey-Bass Publishers

Ingersoll, Ronald J. 1988. *The enrollment problem: Proven management techniques.* New York: Macmillan Publishing Co.

Kemerer, Frank, gentlemen. Victor Baldridge, and Kenneth C. Green. 1982. *Strategies for effective enrollment management,* Washington DC: American Association of State Colleges and Universities.

McKeachie, Wilbert. 1980. Class size, large classes, and multiple sections. *Academe,* 66:24-27.

Morton, Michael S. Scott, ed. 1991. *The corporation of the 1990s: Information technology and organizational transformation.* New York: Oxford University Press.

Negroponte, Nicholas. 1995. *Being digital.* New York: Knopf.

Pascarella, Ernest T., and Patrick T. Terenzini. 1991. *How college affects students: Findings and insights from twenty years of research.* San Francisco: Jossey-Bass.

Perelman, Lewis J. 1992. *School's out: A radical new formula for revitalization of America's educational system.* New York: Avon Books.

Quinn, James Brian. 1992. *Intelligent enterprise: A knowledge and service based paradigm for industry.* New York: Free Press.

Rowley, Daniel James, Herman D. Lujan, and Michael G. Dolence. 1997. *Strategic change in colleges and universities.* San Francisco: Jossey-Bass Publishers.

Stanek, Purcell, et al., 1995. *Electronic publishing unleashed.* Indianapolis IN: SAMS Publishing.

Tapscott, Don. 1996. *The digital economy: Promise and peril in the age of networked intelligence.* New York: McGraw-Hill.

Tinto, Vincent. 1987. *Leaving college: Rethinking the causes and cures of student attrition.* Chicago: University of Chicago Press.

Waitley, 1995. *Empires of the mind: Lessons to lead and succeed in a knowledge based-world.* New York: William Morrow and Co.

Western Governors Association Virtual University. Web site. http://www.west-gov.org/smart/vu/vu.html

Chapter 7

Professional Development

by Roger M. Swanson

As enrollment professionals, we have the privilege of working at institutions of higher education. We enjoy on a daily basis the excitement, resources, and opportunities that come with a career dedicated to the advancement, enrichment, and growth of individuals. Our environment is committed to learning, both that which occurs in the academic setting (via coursework, degrees, etc.) and in the non-academic setting (life in the residence halls, student activities, artistic and cultural programming, etc.).

In this milieu, rich with people and facilities (e.g., libraries, worldwide computer access, cutting-edge research laboratories, visiting performing artists, city/community networks, etc.), it is only natural that an important part of *our* jobs is continuous learning. As we provide essential services to support the activities of our primary campus populations, we

---

Roger M. Swanson serves as Associate Executive Director of the American Association of Collegiate Registrars and Admissions Officers, and has responsibility for professional development programs, the annual meeting, the SPEEDE Project, and the Office of International Education Services.

As an educational administrator, he has over thirty years of professional experience in higher education. He has held university appointments at the dean and vice president level in both academic and student affairs at California Polytechnic State University (San Luis Obispo), Arizona State University, and the University of Illinois. Also, he has been employed as a consultant at universities, colleges, and community colleges, and has held leadership positions in regional and national professional organizations.

Among his many professional publications and presentations are two books, *The Freshman Writes* (on college-level composition) and *Training New College Admissions Recruiters: A Guide for Survival and Success*. He received the Crystal Apple Award for Excellence in Teaching from the Council for the Advancement and Support of Education and the Distinguished Service Award from the Pacific Association of Collegiate Registrars and Admissions Officers.

must pursue our own acquisition of knowledge and skills to enhance our qualifications for our job and career. Furthermore, as leaders and managers of enrollment services staff, we have an obligation to assist them in their development, particularly given the rapidity of change in all elements of our professional lives. While such education may take the form of specific training (e.g., how to utilize new computer software), it may also extend to affective areas, such as change management or customer service.

This chapter will explore three areas of professional development: formal education, developmental education, and staff development.

Formal Education

Chances are you would not be in your current position without completing some level of formal higher education. The days are gone when staff positions in enrollment services at the level of assistant director or above can be "worked up to" by those without a minimum of the bachelor's degree. Often, personnel classification systems that may be mandated by the state, the institution, or union contracts or agreements require a very specific level of formal education for each position at an institution. For some positions, even "years of experience" may not substitute for a necessary degree.

For virtually every professional-level position, the baccalaureate is the minimum required degree. While new staff may be hired fresh from their undergraduate experience with little or no direct experience (particularly as admissions recruiters), it is extremely unlikely that they will be considered as applicants without the requisite B.A, B.S., or similar foundation degree. Direct experience in the particular enrollment service area (e.g., as a student "ambassador" or tour guide, student assistant in the records office) can be most advantageous to get that first position out of college. However, it will be required for nearly all positions beyond entry-level, especially without more advanced graduate credit or a degree. Many today who have extensive experience but no college degree find it difficult, if not dishonest, to extol the value of degree completion to potential applicants and families or to deal on an even footing with campus staff and faculty colleagues.

The master's degree now tends to be "preferred" for the associate director and required for the dean or director, the latter often advertised as "doctorate preferred." Those planning to advance in the profession with only the bachelor's degree are faced with the need to manage a full-time job while also working on advanced degrees. One advantage is that many institutions offer a significant tuition or registration fee discount, making continuation of formal degrees somewhat less painful financially. However, a "one-course-a-term" rate extends time to completion significantly, especially for admissions staff with heavy distance travel demands.

The doctorate tends to be the degree of advantage for those at or striving for top-level enrollment positions at the dean or vice president level. This achievement demands a life-dominating commitment and should not be undertaken lightly or without recognizing and planning for impacts on job, finances, family, and activities. While the doctorate is usually a research-oriented degree, the practicing enrollment services leader often lacks time to pursue research while facing the demands of his or her position. On the plus side, those holding this highest degree have experienced the full gamut of formal education and can stand toe-to-toe with faculty and peer colleagues. An additional advantage may be the acquisition of some level of faculty status with teaching options and other perquisites that may be negotiated.

Due to the level of commitment required to pursue and finish a doctorate degree, only those who are convinced of its necessity for their career advancement or who genuinely enjoy the curriculum, research, and writing associated with it should embark upon it. The "opportunity" costs involved include time away from job, family, or other pursuits (e.g., research); foregone income from other sources (publications, consulting, etc.); impacts on health, family, and friends; and costs of tuition, travel, books, etc. These factors make the determination to achieve the doctorate a "life decision." Unfortunately, close does not count: many who call themselves "ABD" (all but dissertation) or even 99 percent completed still do not possess the degree.

This advice is not given to dissuade anyone from attempting advanced degrees. It is, rather, to present the reality of what it may involve, so that young professionals know what they are getting into and have the wherewithal to persevere through to the end.

The subject matter of degrees is relatively flexible in the enrollment services profession. People holding all manner of bachelor's degrees are hired in enrollment offices if they have demonstrated the skills needed for the individual positions. Experience clearly counts as a supplement to the baccalaureate degree. Master's degrees similarly offer considerable variety, though they are often more closely aligned with the functions of the offices sought. For example, finance degrees may often benefit financial aid administrators, marketing or business degrees enhance the admissions professional, and computer or information system degrees support the registrar's office's more technical functions. Doctorates tend to be even more function-related, many now coming in the general area of higher education administration, with specialties, coursework, or thesis work in the enrollment office of choice area.

A final word on formal degrees should go without saying and touches on our later chapter on ethics. That is, never market or present yourself as having degrees you haven't earned. Whether you make citations on your vita or references in your conversation related to degree attainment levels, write or speak only about what you have earned (honorary degrees do not count) or have noted as being in progress. To do any more may be disastrous to your integrity and hence your career, as more and more employers require transcripts verifying educational claims prior to confirmation of employment. By means of any falsification of accomplishments, you are not only acting unethically, you are risking all that you are and have done in the likely event of exposure. Your image of integrity is your most precious asset: lacking that, degrees, experience, publications, or anything else will not mean much when it comes to getting or keeping a position in the enrollment services profession.

A new area of formal educational preparation is developing on the horizon, for which we may use the general term enrollment services professional credentialing. In many professions, individuals achieve various levels, grades, or proficiencies that are measured via completion of training and testing of knowledge, skills, or competencies. Examples in the field of secondary education would be teacher credentialing or certification (often defined by state standards), particularly in more specific areas such as special education, reading specialist, etc. A movement is clearly afoot presently to offer credentialing training and certification within the enrollment services profession. Unlike some fields, which require various levels for employment or advancement, ours would provide optional programs to enhance the individual's knowledge and experience and provide additional evidence of capability relating to advancement through promotion or hiring. Watch the information that will be available on these opportunities from AACRAO, which will be providing the leadership and direction for this movement. You may want to explore certification options for yourself or for your staff members as they become available.

Your Professional Development

While completion of a given degree may mark the end of your "formal" education, the rapidity of change in our world demands that your "informal" education or professional development never stop. We are challenged by deciding first what we need to know and then how to learn it. Because we cannot be experts in everything, we must focus our interests and energies, always maintaining the macro view but working from it to the micro areas that play to our unique interests, special talents, or immediate needs. This larger view keeps us knowledgeable on all fronts and, most important, allows us to put things in perspective, an ability most crucial in keeping our professional and personal balance or center in life.

A plan for developing your focus, from broad to more narrow, would include:

1. Developing global awareness of our world and the changes it is undergoing

2. Maintaining a comprehensive overview of higher education and the interrelated elements combining to affect it

3. Achieving a broad understanding of all aspects of our expanding field of enrollment services on a continuing basis

4. Observing where the most advanced thinkers and their campuses are going in our field and what they are doing successfully

5. Determining how we can advance our own campuses and enrollment offices within areas we can impact or control

6. How we can develop areas of more defined scope in which we might become experts and leaders — usually those we enjoy and in which we have the most capability

Let's explore these in greater depth.

No matter where we happen to be living, we can have access to incredible quantities of information about what is happening throughout the world via newspapers, magazines, radio, television, and computer electronic media. Events and trends across the globe may have local impacts now more than ever. The expansion of trade to former Eastern bloc countries or China can change our monetary exchange rate, our curriculum, the origin (or study abroad options) of our students, and our admissions, records, financial aid, and other policies and procedures. A distant company's or government's economic decision can affect plant closures or expansions in our towns, with resulting changes in our institutional enrollment patterns.

The enrollment services leader is now one who, more than ever, makes surveillance of national and international issues and events a part of daily activity. Assessing the possible effects on our work and personal lives becomes a necessary part of our planning, forecasting, and preparation. Envisioning threats and opportunities before others perceive them and translating them to our local environments becomes an unofficial, but critical part of our job descriptions.

Oversight of higher education in particular helps us put these larger perspectives into sharper focus. We cannot help but expect that trends toward greater accountability by state governments, changes in corporate and foundation giving, learning media newly available to vast new segments of our populations by software companies, swings in public confidence in colleges and universities, concerns about safety and security — and the list goes on — will all translate into items for our attention and action at our campus level.

Moving to the next level below, the enrollment services professional must keep up on the broader field of higher education, globally as well as nationally. Even though our expertise may not be in international education, the events occurring throughout the world are bound to touch our country, state or province, and campus. Watching these trends and changes helps us predict and prepare for similar ones in our own worlds. The best way to understand other higher education cultures would be, of course, to experience them firsthand. Be on the lookout for opportunities through government programs, grants and contracts, private foundations, and your own travel resources (vacations, visits to relatives, research, etc.) to visit foreign institutions or education ministries, talk to your counterparts, and exchange material and correspondence (Internet mail now facilitates this greatly). If travel possibilities are limited, consider meeting with visiting higher education officials or faculty to your campus, city, or region. Also, think about working with your own faculty who may be developing reciprocal relationships with foreign academic institutions for research, student or faculty exchanges, partnerships and consortia, etc. And finally, if none of these is possible, continue reading newspapers and new publications in international education — many from AACRAO and NAFSA (The Association of International Educators) — to be knowledgeable of this increasingly important international perspective.

Focusing on the United States, national higher education poses a challenge in itself for anyone to stay current in any comprehensive sense. The best single source remains *The Chronicle of Higher Education*, our "trade" newspaper providing weekly coverage of world and national higher education. In addition, it offers everything from announcements of meetings and conferences to position vacancies and personnel changes. Its annual fall supplement, devoted to facts and figures of American higher education, is a most valuable source of information for use in your reports or requests for support. If you are not on *The Chronicle* "routing list" and receiving a copy within a week of its issue, you may want to invest your budgeted funds or even your personal dollars to subscribe — and then pass it on to enhance the awareness of your staff. Copying articles of significance for your own files or to share with selected others will help build your resources and professional image.

The topic of higher education is one that is constantly discussed in a variety of media, from television to news magazines to daily newspapers. Many periodicals actually have an education section that deals on an issue-by-issue basis with topics related to it. Coverage, both fact- and opinion-based, can be a valuable source of current and future directions in higher education and should be monitored for the value it may offer.

Moving to the more focused area of enrollment services, beyond *The Chronicle* and popular news coverage media lie a plethora of periodicals, publications, and electronic resources for your professional awareness. Many, particularly those issued by national associations, relate to the specific unique needs defined by your interest or your campus, e.g., state/private, regional/state, community college/liberal arts, etc. Others concern specific interest or function areas at the campus level, e.g., the variety of admissions publications and information from associations (AACRAO, National Association for College Admission Counseling), other non-profits, testing agencies (College Board, ACT, ETS), and others (Noel-Levitz, software vendors). Often, membership or subscription is prerequisite to receiving periodicals or discounts on publications, but some may be had for the asking — or the borrowing.

Of great value to many are the various Internet listservs, including REG-IST-L for records personnel, ENROLL-L for admissions/enrollment management folks, STUATH-L for those involved with student athletes, and others relating to financial aid, foreign students, institutional research, etc. Subscribing to them is free, but care should be taken to select only those of major interest, since the number of messages on a daily basis can be staggering. You may want to partition your Internet file to segregate listserv messages so they do not preclude you from reading e-mail of urgency or importance, or even setup a separate email account just for listserv messages, to read at your leisure. Not all information on the listservs is valuable or even accurate, so you must take what you read as opinion, some of which can be verbose, emotional ("flaming"), and even unprofessional. Let the reader beware. Listservs can be especially useful to obtain "survey" information: throwing out a question about "how does your campus do ..." will often yield a strong response rate.

Members of AACRAO with Internet connections automatically receive the *AACRAO NetNews,* which includes news of importance, member job changes, position notices, conference and meeting announcements, notices of new publications, content of proposed or new federal regulations, etc.

The growth of World Wide Web sites provides another fascinating source of information — if you have the time, curiosity, access, and inclination. Seeing what other campuses and organizations do in setting forth admissions and registration materials and actual processes can spark your creativity and initiative. Whether scanning a viewbook, going on a "virtual" campus tour, perusing a catalog or class schedule, submitting an admissions application, or registering for classes, you will have a sense of what's possible and actually being done. And knowing what your primary competitors are doing is a vital part of directing your campus' efforts to be a contender or even the "step ahead" that can lead to greater enrollment success for you.

Printed publications, as well as the listserv and WWW resources, offer excellent strategies for keeping in touch with what many of the leaders of our profession are saying and doing. These days, it is not enough just to "keep up": the goal is be out in front, particularly in areas that directly affect your success. Hence, the importance of tuning into what the "best and brightest" are doing, not merely to mimic or replicate, but to use them as a catalyst for your own unique directions.

One of the best ways to do this is person-to-person networking. The telephone, fax, and Internet allow us to do this easily, regularly, and relatively cheaply. However, the chance to meet our colleagues face-to-face is a key reason to attend conferences, meetings, workshops, and seminars whenever possible. Sure, the program sessions will provide usually top-rate demonstrations of "what's hot" and what is really working, but interchange one-on-one with the "movers and shakers" can not only offer you expanded insights, but will often serve as a trigger for you to plan the transformation of your own office(s) and campus. Whether such meetings take place at receptions, during breaks, in the hallway or taxicab or airplane, over drinks, or in the technology center or exhibit hall, they can provide you with some of the most valuable "free" consulting you will ever get. And remember not to forget: sharing is a two-way street.

For any professional meeting you expect to attend, plan a specific agenda or set of goals you want to achieve. For example:

- Know whom you want to meet with, what you want to discuss, and what specific new items you want to bring back that will make that critical difference in your job.

- Consider making appointments ahead of time so that you do not miss meeting someone who has the answers to your questions.

- Bring along (or send in advance) materials that can help him or her understand your issues.

- Take notes so that critical points are not forgotten. Follow up as needed back on campus for clarification or more input.

- Maintain contact, and perhaps schedule a site visit to see firsthand how a particularly successful function works, perhaps even doing some videotaping for your staff, colleagues, or superiors.

- Always show appreciation for time and talent given and give credit where credit is due.

You will find that one of the virtues of being in our profession is that your colleagues are very giving people. With perhaps the limited exception of proprietary information (e.g., details of marketing plans), enrollment services people delight in helping their counterparts. From formal consulting (including on-site visits) to forwarding results, data, or materials, they tend to give freely and share generously with their professional friends.

Just as important and necessary is your ability to inform and gain support from your peer colleagues and superiors on campus. A college or university is made up of many quasi-independent units (like yours) that have their assigned functions but that must interrelate successfully for them to fulfill their missions. More than ever, particularly with shared electronic information systems (mainframes, comprehensive databases, LANs), departments and divisions are co-dependent upon each other for data, services, and support. Admissions, records, and financial aid, for example, are closely intertwined with each other, just as they are with such offices/functions as orientation, retention activities, business affairs/bursar, residence life, and so on. As a result, a large portion of your time will be spent in communication with your counterparts in these and similar offices as you cooperate to address the many issues that can be resolved only through joint effort.

Leaders today will be successful not only to the degree they are able to direct their own staff, but also through how well they can generate support from among their peers and top-level administration. This means that much of your time needs to be spent on:

- Giving and getting information from across the campus; forging alliances over common values and needs
- Sharing resources where joint projects benefit many
- Developing "outside" revenue streams as well as maintaining or increasing regular budget sources
- Determining and "using" campus politics to advantage
- "Educating" key power brokers as to your office's needs and successes
- Serving generally as advocate and spokesperson to off-campus audiences (community, region, legislators and their staffs, public interest groups, churches, coordinating councils, foundations, government entities, etc.)

These functions "out of the office" can take a great deal of time and energy. While some will occur in "official" interchanges (committee meetings, information briefings, newsletters, etc.), a number will take place in more social environments (e.g., at sports events, receptions, dinners, picnics, and a variety of informal gatherings). No matter what the event, you are always "on call" to be the expert, the representative, and the spokesperson. Even when conversation may seem to be casual or unplanned, you may find yourself enjoying an unexpected opportunity to influence colleagues or facing a confrontation out of which you may be quoted for weeks to come.

Up to this point, the areas reviewed have focused primarily on developing a broad leadership and management perspective to offer the necessary breadth of knowledge and skills to be effective. The final area to explore has to do with narrowing the focus and gaining the depth in a few more limited areas which can have a direct positive impact on your position responsibilities, but which also can provide you with a fertile field for growing your special expertise and developing your leadership across the campus and/or the profession.

You might start by asking yourself some questions:

- What is it about your job that you most enjoy and are really good at (or in which believe you have the most potential)?
- Do you seem to be best with people, information, or "things"?

- Are there parts of your job you like to pursue during your non-working hours through talking, reading, writing, computer exploration, or just plain thinking?
- If you could single out one part of your daily routine to do all the time, what would it be?
- Does that one part reflect a continuity through your past experience in the kind of work or play you have succeeded in and found to be "fun"?

Addressing these questions — and ones like them — will help you home in on areas that will offer the most rewards for pursuit and quality effort.

Having identified potential areas for further endeavor, you will want to spend more time to learn:

- Who the current experts are
- Who is presenting or writing on related topics, and where
- How outside resources (vendors, consultants, non-educational businesses) connect
- Where "benchmark" excellence may be found on other campuses or other environments
- What the future trends may be

Your research will probably confirm a lot of what you already know, but you will also discover much that is new and exciting.

How can you find answers to these questions? Most will come from the resources already covered, including publication searches, reviews of conference presentations, and personal contacts with those most knowledgeable. The further you go, however, the fewer items of "new" information you will be able to find. And this situation suggests, at least for the present, that your research phase may be concluding.

Now your thinking will be informed and may be equal to or beyond what is current in the area. Your expertise may now be moving into the "cutting edge," where you are entering new territory. Whether it is conceptual or applied, you will want to begin organizing, developing, "proving" (via hard-evidence scientific method or results-driven outcomes), and explaining your expertise in terms of:

- What it is
- How it functions

- What it means
- Why it works
- What its costs/benefits are
- What its limits are
- Where it can be applied
- What can be expected
- What other research bears upon it
- Who are the other experts
- What the next steps are

Part of our obligation as professionals is sharing our successes with our colleagues, just as (noted earlier) they are willing to share with us. Considering the best venue for that sharing may be a next step, and the variety of resources noted above will provide possible outlets. Conference planners and publications directors are always looking for new and valuable material to place before their audiences. Do not hesitate to contact them for opportunities to present, discuss, review, and promulgate what you found workable and worthwhile. If you have found particularly valuable additions to the current body of knowledge, think about possible business opportunities, ranging from selling them to commercial enterprises (e.g., software companies, product manufacturers), forming your own company or joining an existing one, or doing part- or full-time consulting. Many of your colleagues in enrollment services do some or all of these. These activities not only contribute to the overall progress of our profession, but they can be stimulating, fun, and even lucrative to those who are willing to take the initiative.

Staff Development

Having been "outward"-oriented to this point, you will want to turn your focus back to your own office and campus environments. As an accomplished or evolving expert in many areas and having control over and access to considerable information, you are in an excellent position to advance your own ideas and agendas and assist your staff toward their own professional growth.

Within your own sphere of direct influence (those staff and functions reporting directly to you), your leadership will define the mission, goals, objectives, and strategies as you move along the continuum of your

Professional Development

plans for the future. Much is written and available in many media (tapes, workshops, CD-ROM) on the key elements of effective leadership, and you are directed to Chapter 5 of this book for a discussion of this topic. Suffice it to say here that your primary job is to define and measure success for your direct reports and their functions, to motivate all your staff toward the vision you see for the future, and to provide the resources (budget, staff, space, equipment) to enable them to reach set goals. All easier said than done.

As both a leader and manager of your staff, one of your primary responsibilities is to ensure their ongoing education (new knowledge), enhancement of skills, and fulfillment of potential — or, in a phrase, professional development. You become a teacher, coach, mentor, exemplar, and role model for what you want them to know, to do, and to become. Some of the ways you can promote their professional growth include your support for their:

- Earning college credit and progressing toward degree completion, via use of tuition discounts (if your campus offers such), work time for classes, etc.

- Attending area workshops and seminars that focus on specific learning outcomes, by covering the costs, offering release time, etc. (Some of these by private agencies or by state and regional ACRAO groups can be fairly inexpensive.)

- Hearing faculty, staff, or outside speakers on campus who offer programs, lectures, debates, or panel discussions on topics related to position tasks or duties

- Having in-service presentations by other staff members or outsiders during work hours (even as simple as speakers during "brown-bag" lunches)

- Going to professional association conferences, including the annual meetings of AACRAO, NACAC, NASPA, NASFA, NAFSAA, College Board, ACT, EDUCOM, etc., or one of the 30 plus state and regional ACRAO conferences held annually

- Utilizing the huge array of learning media, from audio/videotapes to CD-ROMs to computer disk tutorials

- Accessing the many periodicals and new publications in our fields, from AACRAO publications (e.g., *Data Dispenser, College & University,* NetNews) to *The Chronicle of Higher Education* to function-focused magazines on personal computing, electronic data interchange, marketing, records systems, organizational development, financial aid, etc.)

- Providing opportunities to subscribe to listservs for those who may find the information exchanges directly relevant to their work (e.g., REGIST-L, ENROLL-L, STUATH-L)

Professional development can also happen during the ordinary course of a business day if you, as the educator, can help staff make even routine occurrences into learning opportunities. Having them review or edit drafts of reports, accompany you to key meetings or briefings, or join you as a guest at social events can expand their knowledge and perspectives.

Often, you are helping to effect a positive attitude as you are to offer specific information or skills development. Undoubtedly, the best single act you can do to create a positive climate for teamwork is to have people included and "in the loop" of information, input, and recognition. And just taking a "time-out" to assess, analyze, and evaluate a situation is so valuable to increasing staff insight, not just into surface issues but also into underlying causes, motives, and predicted outcomes. One of the best ways to learn to think like a leader is to be exposed to the full dimensions of how good leaders think. So having a short session on "How did we do?" "What really happened?" and, especially, "What did we learn?" can be the most valuable "on-the-job" training we can offer. It also has the salutary result of building trust, an absolute ingredient to all effective relationships.

Final Words

Professional development can be defined broadly or narrowly, related to yourself and your staff, and continued throughout your professional (and personal) life. If we do not learn and grow, we cannot advance, change, or be effective. Not to engage professional development options leads to stagnation, lethargy, and, ultimately, retrogression. In an age of increasing rapidity of change, we have no real choice but to engage creative, attractive, and results-producing methods of moving ourselves and our staff members toward new information, capabilities, and perspectives. As noted in the opening sentence of this chapter, we are so fortunate to be spending our working days at colleges and universities, places of learning for all of us. As an enrollment leader, your responsibility for professional development is one of the most serious you undertake as a member of the higher education community.

Resources

Bennis, Warren. 1994. *On becoming a leader.* Reading MA: Addison-Wesley Publishing Company.

Bennis, Warren, and Joan Goldsmith. 1994. *Learning to lead.* Reading MA: Addison-Wesley Publishing Company.

Bennis, Warren, and Burt Nanus. 1985. *Leaders.* New York: Harper & Row, Publishers.

Bennis, Waren, and Robert Townsend. 1995. *Reinventing leadership.* New York: William Morrow and Company, Inc.

Covey, Stephen R. 1994. *First things first. New York: Simon & Schuster.*

———. 1989. *The 7 habits of highly effective people: Restoring the character ethic.* New York: Simon & Schuster.

Depree, Max. 1988. *The art of leadership.* Ann Arbor MI: University of Michigan Press

Dolence, Michael G., and Donald M. Norris. 1995. *Transforming higher education.* Ann Arbor MI: Society for College and University Planning.

Mackenzie, Alec. 1990. *The time trap.* New York: AMACOM, a division of American Management Association.

Maddux, Robert B. 1988. *Building an effective student service team.* Washington DC: American Association of Collegiate Registrars and Admissions Officers.

———. 1989. *Effective interviewing to build a quality student service staff.* Washington DC: American Association of Collegiate Registrars and Admissions Officers.

———. 1989. *Effective performance appraisals for quality student service.* Washington DC: American Association of Collegiate Registrars and Admissions Officers.

Martin, William B. 1988. *Quality student service.* Washington DC: American Association of Collegiate Registrars and Admissions Officers.

Scott, Dru. 1989. *Effective telephone communication skills.* Washington DC: American Association of Collegiate Registrars and Admissions Officers.

Senge, Peter M. 1990. *The fifth discipline: The art and practice of the learning organization.* New York: Currency Doubleday.

———. 1994. *The fifth discipline fieldbook: Strategies and tools for building a learning organization.* New York: Currency Doubleday.

Zaccarelli, Herman E. 1993. *Training managers to train: A practical guide to improve employee performance.* Washington DC: American Association of Collegiate Registrars and Admissions Officers.

——— 1987. *Professional development guidelines for registrars: A self audit.* Washington DC: American Association of Collegiate Registrars and Admissions Officers.

——— 1991. *The admissions profession: A guide for staff development and program management.* Washington DC: American Association of Collegiate Registrars and Admissions Officers and National Association for College Admission Counseling.

Chapter 8

Politics

by David H. Kalsbeek

Organizations as Political Arenas

The challenge we face is formidable — to integrate our institutions' planning, policies, programs, and practices to achieve optimal enrollments. The challenge is great because we have to effect change throughout our organizations — and organizations do not change easily. From the two-year college to the research university, from the liberal arts college with 400 students to the land-grant university with 50,000, America's institutions of higher education are very complex organizations. They involve many interdependent people and offices with limited resources engaged in varied and continuous interactions in pursuit of diverse goals in extremely challenging and rapidly changing times. Understanding how such organizations work is not a simple task, but it is critical for successful leadership in enrollment services in an era in which the need for leadership is greater than ever before.

Making change happen in colleges and universities, as in any organization, requires skill in "getting things done," in initiating and sustaining action, in translating intentions into reality, and in taking great ideas and successfully implementing them. Some suggest that the most widespread

---

David H. Kalsbeek is Associate Academic Vice President for Enrollment Services at Xavier University in Cincinnati, Ohio. Prior to assuming that position in 1993, he spent eleven years at Saint Louis University (MO) as Director of Student Life Studies, Assistant Vice President for Student Development, Acting Dean of Undergraduate Admissions, and Associate Vice President for Enrollment Management. He has made numerous presentations at professional conferences and published numerous articles on student development and enrollment management.

problem in our organizations today is the inability to get things done, to implement desired changes. Pfeffer[1] (1992, 8) quotes Richard Nixon, who noted that "It is not enough for a leader to know the right thing. He must be able to do the right thing ... . The great leader needs ... the capacity to achieve." Leadership for enrollment management and enrollment services is all about accomplishing change in our organizations, about the ability to successfully get things done, though doing so may tug at the status quo and challenge established ways of being and doing and thinking about higher education.

How do we get things done in organizations? One way is through *formal authority,* by relying on our hierarchically structured organizations where those at higher levels direct all of the activities in lower levels under their purview. We often behave as if following the traditional chain of command is the *only* way to effect change and get action, and we thereby impose substantial limitations on ourselves and our efforts. Enrollment management, by definition, requires us to accomplish our objectives through extensive cooperation and collaboration with colleagues and partners *outside* our direct "reporting channels." Even at the very top of our enrollment management organizations, the authority we have is extremely limited when compared to the scope and breadth of what we need to do to achieve our enrollment objectives. We cannot rely solely on traditional authority structures to get things done and effectively lead an enrollment management effort.

An organizational culture with *shared vision and common goals* is an increasingly popular prescription for getting things done in organizations. Building a strong climate and culture in support of certain goals certainly can relieve an organization from depending on authoritative hierarchy for direction. But in our complex academic environments with extremely diverse "cultures" among faculty, student affairs staff, and students, and with our many widely divergent goals, it may be unrealistic to rely on a "shared vision" to mobilize the type of synchronized, synergized, and comprehensive effort required to achieve strategic enrollment goals.

A third and primary means by which we get things done in organizations is through *organizational politics* — using power and influence as a way of getting things done in an environment where other ways and means may not be sufficient. Colleges and universities, like any other organizations, are arenas for daily politics, and achieving enrollment

---

[1] This chapter, with its focus on politics as how we "get things done," is guided by the perspective of Jeffrey Pfeffer in his provocative 1992 book, *Managing with Power: Politics and Influence in Organizations.* Pfeffer's approach to describing the political skill and will required for organizational leadership is the basis for this chapter.

management goals requires us to understand that our "organizational life is dominated by political interactions" (Bacharach 1982, 1). But what does it mean for organizations to be "political"?

Most of us have grown up with a very traditional, even naive, view of organizations and of politics. This view leads us to define political behavior as how we manipulate situations, people, and information to our own advantage, calculatingly catering to what others above us in the organization value or desire, believing that getting ahead may require behaviors that are less than forthright, honest or ethical. "Politics has come to mean actions that are in the service of our own self-interest" (Block 1987, xiv). We all encounter ample instances in which such behaviors in fact occur in our organizations.

But the politics of organizational life are natural processes by which we get things done. The fact is that all organizations have limited resources, limited people, limited time and energy, limited opportunities to take action; influencing how the limited resources of the organization are acquired and channeled in specific directions is at the heart of organizational politics (Block 1987, 7). "Behaving in a manner labeled as political is nothing more than a process of influence. ... On this basis, most aspects of life in organizations can be identified as political" (Kakabadse and Parker 1984, x). And it is on this basis that we move beyond seeing the politics of the college or university as "the corrupting and unpleasant side of human nature" (Kakabadse and Parker 1984, x) and begin to see it as a natural and necessary dimension of organizational life as we try to influence the way we get things done.

Developing the political will and skill to get things done in complex organizations is critical for leadership in enrollment services — especially since many believe that colleges and universities are *intensely* political organizations. Warren Bennis, former college president and organizational theorist, noted that "university politics make other kinds seem as fierce as shuffleboard" (Kanter and Stein 1979, 316). But a text on *leadership* in enrollment services cannot make simple or simplistic prescriptions for greater political effectiveness. The key to political effectiveness for enrollment services is to understand and appreciate the inherently political nature of organizational life, to understand how such dynamics define and determine what it means to "lead" enrollment services, and what it means to "get things done" in the college and university setting. How is political influence exercised in an organization? Addressing that question is the purpose of this chapter.

Sources of Political Influence: Authority and Information

Countless texts on effective management offer "how to" tips on effecting change in organizations, on "empowered" leadership, and on building political clout. Sources of political influence include everything from personal charisma to office location. Though simple prescriptions may not always apply in every college and university setting given the extreme diversity of America's higher education institutions, two universal sources of political power in our organizations are *formal authority* and *information*.

Authority and Organizational Structure as a Source of Political Influence

Influence in enrollment services does stem directly from formal organizational and authority structures. Understanding our organizational charts (e.g., who reports to whom and who has formal responsibilities for what functions) is a necessary step in understanding sources and patterns of influence in the organization. A traditional "tree-diagram" is the way we typically think about how organizations are designed and structured; it is our mental map of the arena in which we work. The hierarchical organizational chart determines in very real ways the political playing field of our organizations since it outlines the "authority structure" which drives how decisions are made and how resources are allocated. Individuals with *authority* have potentially great political influence in an organization; their position gives them that prerogative since it dictates the resources they can control.

But while the organizational chart is a necessary tool for understanding the power and influence that come with authority, it is far from sufficient in accounting *fully* for how influence is exercised in the university setting. In fact, the way decisions and issues actually are influenced often bears little resemblance to the formal authority structure. While individuals may only have *authority* over subordinates, they may *influence* up, down, and across the organization; while they control resources directly under their purview, they can influence resource allocations campus-wide.

So as we seek to understand the organizations in which we work, the formal organizational structure offers great insight into the structure by which political influence is exercised. Clearly such power comes from being in a position to control resources ranging from human to fiscal to information resources, space allocations, and the time and attention of both organizational leadership and staff. But Bacharach and Lawler (1982) define this type of power as a "static, stable feature of organizations." Real influence, on the other hand, is a "fulcrum of change" in organizations, a more dynamic dimension of politics by which we get things done. Leadership requires understanding how political influence may transcend organizational boundaries and hierarchies and thereby energize the enrollment management effort.

We all have anecdotes of the departmental secretary, the budget director, or the personnel specialist who, while not having formal authority over enrollment services, wields great influence over how resources can be used and how activities are implemented. Even more important, in the college and university setting it is the faculty who, while not appearing on the administrative organizational chart, have great influence. Faculty determine the parameters within which policies can be developed, strategies crafted, and programs implemented. Their influence, independent of any traditional hierarchical authority, stems from their centrality in the university's mission. The story is told of how Dwight D. Eisenhower, in his first address to the faculty as the new president of Columbia University, assured them of his commitment to integrally involve faculty in the leadership of the university; the response from the faculty leadership was simply, "Mr. President, we *are* the university." Failure to appreciate the unique political reality that, in our academic organizations, "there is no rank higher than professor" can easily be a fatal flaw in developing and implementing enrollment management initiatives.

Information as a Source of Influence

Information is a source of power and influence. Information is an especially critical and influential resource when an organization faces increasing competition, greater uncertainty in the environment, greater expectations for performance, and more diversified activities (Galbraith 1973; Kalsbeek 1994). All of these factors are characteristic of higher education and, particularly, the enrollment services environment today: a far more competitive environment, extreme uncertainty about which means best achieve certain ends and about what the future holds, a tremendous (and occasionally unrealistic) expectation for the performance of enrollment services staff, and an increasing diversity — in academic programs and among students enrolling in them. In such an environment, it is extremely difficult to get things done, and information becomes a source of considerable political influence precisely because it appears to provide some certainty and remove uncertainty, to provide some ballast amidst the turbulence, and to give some reassurance that we are not flying completely blind.

A story is told of how David Berlo, past president of Illinois State University, discovered the political power of information in the movies he watched as a child. In the old Westerns, the person with authority was obvious — the colonel of the cavalry post had all the trappings of power — the crisp uniform, the nicest house on the post, the finest horse; most of all, he was in the position to tell everyone else what to do as his organization pursued its appointed objective: to keep the frontier safe from hostile tribes. But the person *really* in control of the organization's pursuit of its goals was someone who had no formal authority and none of the trappings of power — *the scout*. The scout was not part of the line organization in the cavalry; he was in a staff role, with no authority to tell anyone else what to do. But in those old Westerns, he and he alone had the information required for the cavalry to succeed in getting things done — he alone understood the Indians. As he shared that information with those formally in charge, he actually controlled the organization's outcomes. The lesson is clear: those who control information exert tremendous influence on organizational leadership. Leadership in enrollment services is largely a scouting expedition (Kalsbeek 1995).

Why Enrollment Management is a Political Process

Organizational life is intertwined with politics, with processes of influence and power. However, some conditions create an organizational dynamic in which political processes are *especially* prevalent (Pfeffer 1992), namely, when there is considerable *uncertainty,* conflict or substantial *disagreement* about means and ends, an *absence of a clear paradigm,* and an increasing task *specialization* within the organization. Political processes are clearest in interdependent systems and when change efforts focus on substantial resource bases, such as budget allocations or re-organizations. The enrollment management process exhibits *all* of these characteristics so it is not surprising that it is an extremely political process on most campuses. Leaders need to appreciate why the enrollment management process is such fertile ground for organizational politics.

First, higher education operates in an extremely uncertain environment — especially regarding enrollments — and that pervasive uncertainty makes politics a way of life for enrollment managers. We face uncertainties regarding federal and state policy, about the long-range consequences of short-term solutions, about the increasingly competitive climate, about the future viability of our tuition pricing structure, and so on. Charting a course of action, maneuvering in such "permanent whitewater" (Vaill 1991), and effecting change amidst the volatility of uncertain times requires political adeptness. As we try to influence multiple and often conflicting institutional priorities and respond quickly and flexibly to new opportunities and unanticipated challenges in a very uncertain terrain, political will and skill are tested by often entrenched and conservative organizations.

In doing enrollment management, there is also inherent conflict — fundamental disagreements and widely varying points of view about enrollment goals and the means to achieve them. Enrollment goals are often diametrically opposed (e.g., ensuring access versus increasing revenue by raising tuition) as are the various means of achieving them (committing funds to merit scholarships versus need-based grants), creating all the ingredients for conflict. Enrollment goals favored by faculty often conflict with those favored by the governing board, by the finance vice president, or by the students. "If everyone agrees on what to do and how to do it, there is no need ... to attempt to influence others" (Pfeffer 1992, 176). Such consensual agreement is hardly ever the case in enrollment management, so political skills are required to ensure that enrollment initiatives move through the potential quagmire of college and university dissent and conflict.

This built-in conflict is exacerbated by the increasing *specialization and professionalization* of the academy. Not only are universities organized around specialties among our faculty and academic disciplines, but the history of higher education administration is one of increasing professionalization and specialization — especially in the area of enrollment and student services. This contributes further to a predictable divergence of perspectives, since professionals, by definition, bring to their work an allegiance to "professional" guidelines, practices, standards, and commitments — all of which dictate multiple views on priorities and practice. Such divergence of opinion, coupled with the fact that enrollment management as a professional practice is still in its infancy, contributes to an *absence of any clear or singular "paradigm,"* an absence of any overarching or uniform perspective that guides our work. All of this creates an environment where political processes dominate daily life and are essential to overcoming barriers to effective action and change caused by organizational and professional fragmentation.

Politics is a natural way of getting things done in enrollment management because, by its nature, enrollment management relies on an interdependence of many departments, functions, and processes. If enrollment management could be organized in isolation from all other activities and domains of the university, we could rely on formal authority to get things done; the person in charge could simply direct the effort. But enrollment management, by definition, is a process whereby we attempt to integrate *all* of the university's programs and practices and policies related to achieving enrollment outcomes (Kalsbeek 1993); such integration transcends traditional organizational structures and is, therefore, highly interdependent. So getting things done cannot simply be through authoritative mandate; it requires exercising political influence.

Interdependence is also driven by the scarcity of resources in our organizations. "Slack resources reduce interdependence, while scarcity increases it" (Pfeffer 1992, 40). If the admissions office had all the resources it needed to produce its own marketing campaign, it would not have to depend on the marketing department. If enrollment services had its own technical staff, interdependence with the computing center would not be an issue. With sufficient resources, each college could manage its own scholarship processes without relying on the financial aid office. But limited resources require us to work interdependently. Moreover, in an era of scarce resources, all departments are playing a zero-sum game. Each department's resource gain is *necessarily* another's loss. In such an environment, politically influencing how resources are allocated becomes a natural and necessary objective and a key to successful leadership.

Finally, organizational politics really come into play when decisions relate to a *substantial resource base* or to *organizational re-alignment;* again, this is, by definition, what enrollment management is all about. For many colleges and universities, the enrollment management process not only affects but singularly determines the resource base for the institution. Tuition dependence means that the institution's lifeblood is its enrollment, so everyone has an interest in influencing that process, thereby politicizing the enrollment management effort. In addition, reorganizing the university for enrollment management is a frequent recommendation, combining into a common cluster of departments those functions most critical to the enrollment process (e.g., admissions, financial aid, registration and records, advising, and other student services). Campus discussions of how to best manage enrollments and provide enrollment services inevitably lead to discussions of the optimal mix of departments and functions under an enrollment management umbrella. Such discussions are an affirmation of the importance of formal authority structures in getting things done in organizations, but they also politicize the process. Any attempt to re-organize challenges the status quo, shakes up established patterns of authority and control over resources, and creates a highly political debate in which many interest groups are vested.

Getting Things Done in Enrollment Services: Some Key Political Skills

Framing

Establishing the framework within which issues are viewed, decisions made, problems defined, and solutions considered is tantamount to determining the result. Framing — the intentional process by which we set the context for any decision or policy debate — is a way of exercising influence and is, therefore, a key political skill (Pfeffer 1992). The types of decisions and actions we pursue in enrollment management can be viewed in many different ways from different perspectives. We "frame the debate" by how we define the salient issues at stake, set the agenda for considering options, and pose the questions to be answered. All of this is a way of influencing the outcome. We also "frame" issues and decisions by the way we gather the data that will "percolate into the climate of informed opinion" and the way we share information that will "constitute the intellectual capital" upon which decision-makers draw in the course of their work (Weiss 1980; Kalsbeek 1992).

Framing is a political process by which innovation and change happen. "Yet we often show little foresight or consciousness about how frames of reference are set" (Pfeffer 1992, 206). Particularly important is the appreciation of the impact of precedent, the influence that history has on the policy process. While an enrollment management perspective may be new to a given campus, all decisions about recruitment and retention strategies inevitably unfold within history, within a rich context of prior commitments and past choices that color or frame the way everyone appraises the present situation and evaluates options for future action. Historical precedent is a powerful predictor of future action because we all naturally rely on the familiarity and certainty of prior experience in deciding our preferred options. History frames possible futures. Herein lies the promise and the pitfall for new enrollment managers. Being new to a campus can free one from the blinders of historical precedent and more easily allows decisions to be reframed; but successfully getting things done also requires understanding the historical context that frames enrollment issues for those who have been around for some time.

Senge (1990) challenges us to become more skilled at identifying the "mental models" that determine what we can do by shaping how we view the situation at hand. Mental models are the deeply ingrained assumptions, generalizations, pictures, or images that influence how we understand the world and how we take action. New ideas often fail to be implemented because they conflict with deeply held images and assumptions of how the world works, images that limit us to familiar ways of thinking and acting and deciding. Senge's work on mental models offers many promising tools for leaders wanting to influence fundamental change.

So getting things done in enrollment management requires leaders to be adept at identifying those assumptions and beliefs that frame the policy arena, those mental models that determine how our organizations define problems and solutions — and then reframing them in order to effect change. Political effectiveness lies largely in our ability to influence the ways in which decisions and discussions are framed.

For example, how financial aid strategies are evolving on many campuses illustrates the power of how assumptions and mental models frame decisions and determine new courses of action. Historically, university leaders viewed institutional financial aid only as a budgeted expense, a cost, appearing on the ledgers like the loss from a casualty (Casteen 1996). Viewed in this way, good decisions sought to minimize the expense. Enrollment managers are reframing the policy discussion by defining institutional aid as a leveraged discount; viewed in this way, enrollment strategies seek not to minimize the cost but optimize the investment. An entirely new range of strategic opportunities come to mind when traditional mental models are challenged and issues reframed.

Similarly, the traditional way of describing the college enrollment process is as a "funnel"; such imagery shows the inter-relatedness of our marketing efforts to our admissions process and our yield strategies. But as a mental model, a funnel connotes some sort of natural cascading or filtration of students from one level (applicants) to another level (enrolled students), leading to a conclusion that forcing more in at the top (more applicants) will naturally lead to more at the bottom (more freshmen). We know this is not how it works. reframing the mental model can be as simple as inverting the image — turning the funnel into a pyramid that more clearly describes the actual dynamics of enrollment management (Kalsbeek 1996).

Information Management and Analysis

As noted earlier, information and the level of certainty it can provide for enrollment management is a powerful political resource. Pfeffer notes that the prevailing (though mistaken) belief that there is a "right answer" to most problems and that this answer can be discovered through sufficient analysis of information gives those who have information and who shape the analysis of that information great influence in most organizations. Therefore, information management is a key political skill for enrollment management.

Now with the rapid developments of information and communications technologies that provide unprecedented access to vast information resources from every personal computer, the political dynamics of information are changing practically overnight. It was over twenty-five years ago that Galbraith (1973, 42) noted that:

> We cannot foresee the ramifications of information instantaneously available everywhere in the organization. Information is a source of power, so the present power structure is threatened. Most of our attitudes and behaviors still reflect hierarchical and sequential processing of data.

While access to information is a base of political influence, the rise of computing networks and on-line data resources means that mere access to information may not provide the edge it once did. The way information flows through our networked organizations no longer precisely parallels the way other resources are channeled. So a key political skill is to view organizations not bureaucratically (with emphasis on how certain functions and departments are organized) but informatically, focusing on information and communications processes that formally and informally influence how things get done. Infosclerosis, the hardening and constricting of information arteries through an organization (Kalsbeek 1989), often determines the political capacity to exert influence on the decision process; intentionally constricting or widening information flow can either help or hinder the enrollment management process.

For example, developing and implementing integrated student information systems is critical to improving enrollment services. This process, however, inevitably touches off political battles over information access, spawns volatile discussions of "need to know" policies, and triggers "turf wars" over data ownership. As another example, routinely sharing students' on-line admissions records with academic department chairpersons can positively influence how advisors place freshmen in their initial math courses and, thereby, promotes student success and retention; sharing such information can also invite faculty criticism of admissions decisions and standards as they attempt to influence such decisions. All decisions about information access, information dissemination and information systems are inherently political.

Enrollment management decisions are invariably complex, multidimensional decisions. As such, analysis alone can seldom resolve the problems at hand or provide singular direction for decisions. We all know that multiple arguments on many sides of an issue can be supported from the same information with different analyses. Therefore, there is always room for the advocacy of information that supports a favored position; there is always opportunity to use information and analysis selectively to influence the decision process (Pfeffer 1992, 258). The political use of information involves the skill to develop, manage and present information persuasively in order to exert influence on the policy or decision process. The creative graphic display of quantitative data and understanding how statistics can be used to manipulate opinion (Tufte 1983; Paulos 1995) are skills of the politically effective enrollment manager.

The successful enrollment manager also understands the dynamics of information use (Kalsbeek 1994). Information is used to make decisions, such as when market research focuses recruitment strategies on those areas where the university has strong visibility or draw. But a more frequent use of information is as it enlightens issues, as it challenges assumptions, as it helps frame policy discussions, or as it defines problems rather than leads to solutions. The same market research that is used to make recruitment decisions is also used when it subtly challenges a dean's longstanding assumptions about the number of potential students interested in certain majors or a president's assumptions about the institution's market presence beyond a 300-mile radius. Though no immediate decision outcomes from that information may be apparent, it is nonetheless used. When information is deliberately gathered and presented in order to make such points and influence the perspective of various stakeholders in the decision process, then the information intentionally is being used politically. This constitutes a powerful skill for the political leadership of enrollment services.

Structuring the Organization and the Decision Process

It is not surprising that a typical approach to increasing political influence is to restructure an organization in order to obtain greater control over desired resources or expand the decision authority. Establishing a "higher" or "broader" position in an organizational hierarchy provides access to information, greater access to those with formal authority, jurisdiction over critical decisions, and responsibility for allocating valued resources. However, a distinguishing feature of enrollment management as practiced in higher education today is the multiple organizational structures found to be successful, the widely varying models and structures currently in place to achieve enrollment objectives, even among fairly similar institutions. There is no one best way of structuring organizations to provide enrollment services, no one structure that optimizes political influence in getting things done in enrollment management. But while there may be no one best structure, whatever structure is established clearly has political consequences and those consequences relate directly to natural "spheres of influence." Political skills for enrollment services include knowing how organizational structures and decision processes influence outcomes.

It is true that one's perspective on certain issues and one's ability to act on that perspective are directly determined by his or her place in an organization; in other words, where you stand usually depends on where you sit. Persons with different positions in an organization have different perspectives on what resources are expendable, what courses of action are feasible, what are tractable problems, what goals are paramount, and what information is meaningful. Kanter and Stein suggest that this is the central source of organizational tension and the key to organizational politics (Kanter and Stein 1979, 304).

Currently, enrollment services or enrollment management responsibilities generally are centered in either the student affairs or the academic affairs divisions of the university structure, and the different perspectives dominating these two domains of the academy are clear and distinct (Blake 1979). So, for example, when enrollment officers sit within student affairs, their most direct sphere of influence is within that domain. Since they naturally have more frequent contact and collaboration with their immediate colleagues in residence life, student activities, and student services, they can readily influence and be influenced by those colleagues. The enrollment management agenda naturally includes issues related to student affairs and likely is guided by a student affairs perspective; the organizational sphere of influence grants legitimacy to that agenda and fosters that perspective. It is understandably harder, then, to exercise influence among faculty, deans, and academic administrators, and harder to influence enrollment-related decisions about course scheduling, faculty development, the academic probation policy, etc.

When enrollment management responsibilities are centered in the academic arena, on the other hand, the immediate sphere of influence is radically different, focusing far more readily on academic and faculty issues. The greater challenge then becomes to influence enrollment-related decisions in the student affairs area related to campus housing, student orientation, discipline, Greek life, etc. For every political advantage of an organizational arrangement there is a disadvantage, and the greatest strength of any approach is simultaneously its greatest weakness. Understanding these differences and converting natural obstacles to opportunities is a real political skill.

Politically structuring the enrollment management effort does not always require vast re-organization of standing divisions of the college or university. Task forces and committees and work teams are also structural mechanisms for effecting change. They can be political approaches to either institutionalizing power and influence or diffusing responsibility for decisions and actions. In many organizations, a more participatory approach to making decisions has become a means to better manage interdependence, to bring together diverging interests, and to acknowledge the co-existence of numerous stakeholders (Kanter and Stein 1979). On the other hand such participatory approaches can drain an organization's most precious resource — the time and attention of its personnel — and can heighten expectations for involvement beyond what is feasible.

Politically skilled leaders know that committees are tools of political influence, vehicles for politically co-opting others. By inviting known or potential adversaries or opponents into a decision process, one can thereby achieve some affiliation or allegiance with a task or issue or outcome among those outside the immediate sphere of influence. For example, establishing an enrollment planning committee consisting of representatives of various colleges or departments builds greater ownership for the process among those who could perhaps be its most vocal critics. Involving faculty on an admissions committee, students on a calendar committee, or alums on the marketing task force are examples of how to exert political influence by structuring broader involvement in decision processes.

Language, Symbols, and Ceremony

We live and work in cultures that celebrate ritual, ceremony and symbols. It seems that higher education organizations particularly are enamored with and reliant upon these features of organizational life. As Senge (1990) and Pfeffer (1992) point out, change is fueled by desire, by emotion, by factors that may not appear objectively rational. The power of symbols, ceremonies, and ritual is the power to trigger emotional support and enthusiasm and commitment for our goals, our efforts and our institutions — and thereby make things happen.

Rituals and ceremonies abound in our efforts to manage college enrollments as we serve and educate our students. Commencement exercises in full academic garb, freshman orientation programs, dean's lists, spring break, homecoming, final exams, tenure and promotion, Greek rush, and countless campus myths that are repeated by generation after generation of students — all are part of the rich tapestry of ritual and ceremony in the academy. We use all of these to build morale and loyalty, to promote certain values, to sanction certain behaviors, to reward and celebrate accomplishments, to establish our identity and distinctiveness, to initiate newcomers to the campus culture, and so on. They become the means by which we build and sustain the emotion and commitment that is so critical to the life and vitality of the academy; leaders in enrollment services must understand and appreciate the pervasive power of such parts of campus life.

Pfeffer notes that even meetings are organizational ceremonies that send important messages and support the pursuit of political goals. Meetings ceremonially can reassure groups of their importance, keep focus on or elevate certain issues, or allow a "public" demonstration of authority or expertise and thereby send a politically charged message. The politically skilled leader recognizes the multiple roles meetings can serve in our organizations and makes the most of them to get things done.

We use symbols to influence action in organizations. Office space, location, and design are all important symbols of power and influence, speaking directly to the basic territorial instincts of the human animal and communicating clear messages of status and authority. Titles are symbols that we use to effect change; promotions and other public recognitions of achievement or merit carry great symbolic weight. Memberships on committees, parking and library privileges, the grade or classification of an office's support staff (e.g., secretary or executive secretary or administrative assistant) can all be viewed as ways in which influence is wielded through the intentional manipulation of symbols.

Language is a powerful means of exercising political influence. The words we use in our conversation, discussion, and policy discourse carry great influence in our organizations and in our profession. For example, just our choice of "enrollment management" versus "enrollment services" as a rubric for describing our efforts has political significance; the symbolism and connotations of each vary widely and will meet with varying degrees of support and success on different campuses. Our professional practice is sprinkled with language and symbols drawn from industry, from strategic planning, from the exploding computing and telecommunications field, and from psychology and education. The language of marketing long ago entered our professional lexicon and continues to redefine the scope and nature of our work, with mixed results. The language of price discounting, borrowed from fields of economics and business, does not just passively accompany the emergence of new approaches to our work; this new language actively and fundamentally redefines, redirects and reframes our perspective on our work and, in effect, transforms that work. As we choose the words we use, our rhetoric, and our jargon, we are, in effect, manipulating symbols that influence, positively or negatively, how we get things done in our organizations.

Part of attending to the language of enrollment management is the development of a "unity of voice" throughout our own enrollment services effort. Pfeffer notes that those organizations that achieve a common sense of identity, a shared perspective, consensual support for goals and objectives, and a certainty of purpose are far more influential in gaining control of resources (fiscal, human, technological, etc.) than those organizations with a less-refined, less-defined "paradigm." When an entire enrollment services division achieves such a unity of voice, it is often clearly reflected in the language that is used. With a unified voice, internal and external communications are improved with clear and consistent messages, concerted action is easier to achieve, conflict is minimized, and the entire enrollment effort presents a unified front as it attempts to exert influence throughout the organization. Developing political influence in a university can begin with a comprehensive staff development program to ingrain enrollment management principles and perspectives throughout the enrollment services organization, to develop consensus commitments to enrollment goals and strategies to achieve them, and to develop a common language that ties it all together.

Interpersonal Influence: The Organization as a Social Occasion

All organizations have in common the simple fact that they are social settings, social occasions where people live and work, interact, and form meaningful relationships with one another. The interpersonal dynamic of organizational life underlies all of our political activity; we do enrollment management in social settings. It is the pervasive yet often indescribable network of interpersonal relationships and the influence accompanying those relationships that we typically mean when we refer to an institution's "political environment."

The persistent theme of this chapter is that the political nature of our work is both natural and necessary; so too with the interpersonal network of colleagues which defines the social systems of our organizations. Interpersonal networks evolve not only because of our natural needs for human interaction, but because such interaction is how things get done. When goals are in conflict, outcomes uncertain, and stakes high, few choose to act in isolation. We naturally seek out the opinion and judgment and perceptions of others, particularly those who we find share some basic similarities with us (similar responsibilities, professional background, personality, etc.). Naturally, and perhaps necessarily, our interpersonal network comes to shape our view of our world, our definition of our problems and opportunities, and our assessment of possible solutions. As Pfeffer notes, our thoughts and actions become "socially anchored." Our decisions are influenced by the interpersonal exchanges that are spawned as we actively satisfy our craving for "the comfort and certainty of shared opinion" (Pfeffer 1992, 208). Such interpersonal influence on how we get things done is part of the political landscape; the effective leader develops organizations that foster interpersonal networks in support of the goals and objectives of the institution.

From a management perspective, the interpersonal network improves our efforts in several ways. By learning from others, we can often expedite our decision-making and problem-solving, since we may avoid learning from scratch what others already know. In other words, the interpersonal and social networking in and about our organizations helps to economize our information processing, providing shortcuts to the pressing need for continual learning in our rapidly changing field. It also provides opportunities for more divergent thinking, as multiple points of view tug at our assumptions and mental models. This is why Senge (1990) calls for the intentional and widespread development of team learning as a key element in keeping organizations vital and vibrant. Many campuses have experienced great success in enrollment management by establishing ongoing interdivisional teams with a commitment to getting things done through persistent interpersonal interchange; this is all part of political leadership in our social organizations.

In all social systems, but particularly in colleges and universities with the type of human services effort we are engaged in, cooperation and collaboration are essential. Ensuring such cooperation and collaboration is a key political skill for leadership in enrollment services. To get things done, we have to get along, and "getting along" in our organizations often involves being able to transact business in a pleasant and effective manner, even with people we may not particularly like but whom we need in achieving our goals. It is not uncommon to have the political climate described in terms of the level of collegiality that pervades the organization. Political leadership, therefore, includes nurturing a civil, courteous, and collegial climate in which diversity and differences are welcomed and in which there are rewards for working well together as professional colleagues.

Finally, the politics of interpersonal influence hinge on the notion of reciprocity. We depend on others to get things done, and they depend on us. The admissions officer depends on the financial aid counselor to expedite an award package for an irate parent. The retention officer needs the collections manager to cancel a late fee for a needy student whose parents missed a payment. The registrar needs the computing staff to revise the format of the grading rosters two terms earlier than initially planned. The underfunded minority affairs director depends on financial support from some campus auxiliaries for the Black Student Association telemarketing campaign. All of these types of interdepartmental dependencies occur every day and generally result from one person obliging another's requests.

A natural ingredient for success in our highly interdependent social systems is this pervasive sense of reciprocity and interpersonal obligation. The negative connotation of organizational politics focuses on quid pro quo exchanges, cutting deals, favors exchanged for explicitly requested favors in return. These are certainly a part of the political reality in most organizations. But the more generalized, diffuse, and pervasive reciprocity by which we try to help colleagues get things done, knowing that we thereby generally improve our likelihood of getting our things done, is a powerful organizational dynamic which politically skilled leaders recognize, encourage, and reward.

Conclusion

The political processes which dominate organizational life are more than just an academic interest, and political skills are more than just a part of the repertoire of professionals seeking career advancement. Political influence is the way by which things get done in our colleges and universities — and the things to be done in enrollment services and for enrollment management goals are of great consequence to our institutions, our communities, and our society. Despite the frequent criticism and calls for reform, American higher education is one of the greatest success stories in the modern world. The political dynamics by which we collectively and continuously move our organizations forward are an integral part of this success and, therefore, are part of solving many of our society's pressing needs; the issues and challenges faced in enrollment management are often at the heart of it all.

Successful leadership in enrollment services certainly requires developing political skill, the capacity to exert influence throughout the institution in pursuit of enrollment management objectives. But while political skill is necessary, leadership also demands political will, the desire and courage to be in the arena, to avoid being passive in the face of the overwhelming challenges we face, and to act politically to influence how intentions become reality. In organizations like colleges and universities, nothing happens unless someone pushes. The challenge we all face in enrollment management is how to push forward, how to solve the many problems facing our institutions, how to exercise the influence required to make things happen — and then having the will to do what it takes. Knowing how to get things done and then having the political will to do it is the key to successful leadership for enrollment services.

References

Bacharach, Samuel, and Edward Lawler. 1982. *Power and politics in organizations.* San Francisco: Jossey-Bass.

Blake, Elizabeth. 1979. Classroom and context: An educational dialectic. *Academe,* September:280-292.

Block, Peter. 1990. *The empowered manager: Positive political skills at work.* San Francisco: Jossey-Bass.

Casteen, John. 1996. Unpublished speech at the CASE Conference on Ensuring Higher Education's Affordability, Washington DC.

Galbraith, Jay. 1973. *Designing complex organizations.* Reading MA: Addison-Wesley Publishing.

Kakabadse, Andrew, and Christopher Parker, eds. 1984. *Power, politics, and organizations: A behavioral science view.* New York: John Wiley & Sons.

Kalsbeek, David H. 1989. Managing information resources. In *Student Services: A Handbook for the Profession,* edited by U. Delworth and G. Hanson. San Francisco: Jossey-Bass.

———. 1992. *Exploring information as a user construct: Case studies of information use in the enrollment management policy process.* Unpublished doctoral dissertation, Saint Louis University.

———. 1993. *The two faces of strategic enrollment management: A boundary spanning perspective.* Presentation at AACRAO's Strategic Enrollment Management Conference, St. Louis MO.

———. 1994. *Defining information needs for strategic enrollment management.* Presentation at AACRAO's Strategic Enrollment Management Conference, Cincinnati OH.

———. 1995. *Scouting: New roles and responsibilities in an era of accountability.* Keynote address to the Jesuit Association of Student Personnel Administrators, San Diego CA.

Kalsbeek, David H. 1996. *Developing learning organizations for strategic enrollment management.* Presentation for the National Association of Student Personnel Administrators (NASPA) Annual Conference, Atlanta GA.

Kanter, R.M. and Barry Stein, eds. 1979. *Life in organizations: Workplaces as people experience them.* New York: Basic Books, Inc.

Paulos, John Allen. 1995. *A mathematician reads the newspaper.* New York: Basic Books.

Pfeffer, Jeffrey. 1992. *Managing with power: Politics and influence in organizations.* Boston MA: Harvard Business School Press.

Senge, Peter. 1990. *The fifth discipline: The art and practice of the learning organization.* New York: Currency Doubleday.

Tufte, Edward (1983). *The visual display of quantitative information.* Cheshire CT: Graphics Press.

Vaill, Peter. 1991. *Managing as a performing art.* San Francisco: Jossey-Bass.

Weiss, Carol with M. Bucuvalas. 1980. *Social science research and decision making.* New York: Columbia University Press.

Chapter 9

Ethics and Ethos

by C. James Quann and David Birnbaum

Introduction

In the United States, academic administrators have always played unique and significant roles, different and more powerful than their counterparts in collegiate institutions in other nations (Mayhew 1979, 75). As principal academic or student services administrators, admissions and records professionals advise the academic or student services vice president or president and other chief officers of the institution and assist with policy formulation by providing, in addition to regular duties, reports, analyses, and recommendations. Admissions and records leaders also provide important links to the faculty governing unit in the development of admission and academic policies. This role in policy formation is facilitated by the fact that admissions directors, registrars, and other enrollment services officers serve on key policy-making committees and commissions, often serving as chairs, executive secretaries, or ex-officio resource persons. These multifaceted responsibilities are bene-

---

C. James Quann is Registrar Emeritus and Research Coordinator for the Office of the Provost at Washington State University. He recently retired after serving as Associate Registrar and University Registrar and Editor at that institution for twenty-nine years. He also served as Interim Vice Chancellor for Student Affairs, University Registrar, and Director of Student Information Systems at the University of California at Santa Cruz, as Dean of Men and Director of Student Activities at Central Washington University, and as Dean of Men and Director of Housing at Eastern New Mexico University. He is the lead author of *Records Management for the 1990s and Beyond* (1996) and *Admissions, Academic Records, and Registrar Services* (1987).

David Birnbaum is an attorney in the Office of General Counsel for the University of California, a position that he has held for thirteen years, with responsibility for both advisory work and litigation in such areas as right to privacy, due process, student discipline, and student records. Prior to coming to the University of California, he worked in litigation for the law firm of Gibson, Dunn, and Coutcher in Los Angeles and litigated civil rights cases for the U.S. Department of Justice in Washington, DC.

ficial to the institution, the faculty, and current and prospective students, since these officers have a broad range of responsibilities, including the interpretation and application of admission policies and academic rules and regulations.

The words "professionals," "leaders," and "officers" are intended to describe the role and function of enrollment services administrators and are meant to be interchangeable. These administrators are, or should strive to be, true "professionals," they certainly are "officers," and they should be effective "leaders." The subjects of professionals and professionalism are well covered in Chapter 2. Leadership is a significant expectation and responsibility of any professional, and most college and university presidents expect enrollment services personnel to provide effective leadership in academic and student services matters.

But what are the attributes of an effective leader? According to researchers Clement and Rickard (1992, 18), effective leaders in higher education must exhibit at least three personal qualities:

- *Integrity*, involving trust, honesty, loyalty, courage, and willingness to take risks

- *Commitment*, evidenced by a positive attitude toward working with students and faculty, enthusiasm, joy, optimism, and passion for student services work

- *Tenacity*, focusing on a strong work ethic, perseverance, patience, and follow-through

If one adds to these qualities the principles of fairness, faithfulness, and equal treatment, the stage is set for a discussion of "ethical leadership and decision-making."

Organizational Codes of Ethics

Most professional organizations publish a litany of ethical standards and expectations and commend them to their members, but these statements are usually general in nature. As an example, AACRAO regularly publishes a code of *Professional Practices and Ethical Standards* (AACRAO 1995, xi). AACRAO's code lists thirteen commandments, each applicable to our professional duties in a global sense. The thirteen points contain expressive phrases such as "adhere to the principles of," "participate in and contribute to," and "develop and implement." Such phrases speak well of professional goals and expectations, but they are of little help when it comes to solving everyday ethical problems.

This chapter will explore various guideposts that will assist the enrollment services professional when making ethical decisions. Then, borrowing terminology from our colleagues in economics, ethical issues and decision-making on a micro- and macro-basis will be discussed. Micro-issues refer to particular or singular cases, such as *individual* students; macro-issues include relationships with larger sectors, such as all students.

Ethical Guideposts for Decision-Making

In *Ethical Problems in Higher Education*, George Robinson and Janice Moulton set forth a core set of general ethical principles to be used to determine ethics and morality when making ethical decisions and judgments. They are the principles of (1) fairness, (2) maximizing benefits, (3) universalization, and (4) treating others as ends in themselves, not merely means (Robinson and Moulton 1985, 7-8).

According to Robinson and Moulton, the *principle of fairness* means that persons who are equal in aspects relevant to a particular situation should receive equal treatment. Applying the *principle of maximizing benefits* involves weighing the costs and benefits of an act or decision and deciding the scope of the problem. Who should be considered — the people in the immediate situation, those outside who may be affected, or others, such as future students? The *principle of universalization* asks, "What might happen if everyone did it?" *Universalization* has to do with setting precedents. When one person does something, others may want to do it too, and then everyone in a similar situation should be able to do it. The *principle of treating others as ends in themselves, not merely as means* entails treating others with respect and dignity and recognizing that they have desires and plans that should be considered.

Another useful set of ethical principles or guideposts for decision-making is offered by Karen Kitchener in *Applied Ethics in Student Services* (Canon and Brown 1985, 17-27). They are (1) to do no harm, (2) to benefit others, (3) to be just, (4) to be faithful, and (5) to respect autonomy.

Kitchener suggests that in *doing no harm*, we honor the obligation to avoid actions that may inflict either physical or psychological injury. The act of *benefiting others* is self-explanatory. *Being just* means giving appropriate attention to ensuring equal treatment to all those for whom we have responsibility. *To be faithful* means keeping promises (contracts), telling the truth, being loyal, and maintaining respect and civility in human discourse. *Respecting autonomy* means acknowledging the right of individuals to decide how they live their own lives as long as their actions are legal and do not interfere with the rights and welfare of others.

The guideposts set forth by Robinson and Moulton dovetail with those promulgated by Kitchener. Robinson and Moulton's *principle of fairness* coalesces with Kitchener's *being just and faithful*. Robinson and Moulton's principle of *maximizing benefits* agrees with Kitchener's principle of *benefiting others*. Robinson and Moulton's principle of *treating others as ends in themselves, not merely as means* equates with Kitchener's *respecting autonomy*. And Kitchener's *do no harm* is a universal principle that should be added to any set of ethical guidelines.

Both sets of principles are offered for administrators to follow as they approach the various ethical dilemmas and decisions that must be made in their professional lives. Many of these principles should be applied when considering a decision or judgment in any given case. Often, the considerations implied in each principle will be in agreement and will lead to a proper, if not easy, decision. In other instances, two or more of the principles may conflict, as in one of the case studies that follow, wherein the administrator must decide between the rights of the individual and the rights of the group.

When making decisions, admissions and records administrators should be aware of and should observe the guideposts mentioned above. In addition, such administrators should always use "common sense." According to one ethicist, "common" sense defines what any reasonable person in charge would do in a situation, given the knowledge available to him or her at the time of the decision (Kimbrough 1985, 19). The same ethicist observes that, to have good common sense, an administrator must have some or all of the following qualities:

- Exhibiting foresight, sagacity, and skill in performing basic administrative tasks
- Considering data and alternatives within the time frame available for action
- Observing precautions
- Exhibiting emotional control, even in crisis

The next two sections of this chapter deal with actual case studies that exemplify the types of dilemmas that admissions and records professionals face on a daily basis. Each case is followed by commentaries that highlight the issues and proposed solutions. One or more of the principles set forth by Robinson, Moulton, and Kitchener, mixed with a dash of "common sense," may be applied to each decision.

Ethical Considerations and Decisions — a Micro-Approach

The case studies presented hereafter are individual in nature and use the pronouns "she" and "he" or the adjectives "male" and "female." Each case is based on a real situation in an AACRAO institution, but the names of the institutions are omitted and the genders used are arbitrary. Readers should feel free to substitute "he" in place of "she" and so forth.

FERPA and the "Do Not Release" Dilemma

Case: Several years ago, a student completed the required paperwork to have the registrar's office withhold her public or "directory information," unless release was authorized in writing by the student. This "do not release" provision is in accordance with the Federal Family Educational Rights and Privacy Act (FERPA). The student graduated four years ago and left the "do not release" flag in place. You, the records officer, get a call from a prospective employer who wants to hire your graduate, but only if you can, within twenty-four hours, verify the degree and dates of attendance. What do you do?

Discussion: This problem occurs on our campuses nearly every day, and under FERPA these records cannot be released without permission of the former student, nor can the records officer even indicate that the student was ever enrolled at the institution. Yet, in this case, if the records are not released within twenty-four hours, the former student will be harmed. But if the records officer were to release information without the former student's approval, a commitment would have been broken and the institution and records officer would be subject to censure and possibly litigation.

So a stalling tactic is in order. Take the name, address, and telephone number of the prospective employer and indicate that the appropriate records will be checked and the telephone call will then be returned. If the records office files maintain telephone numbers of alums, the simple thing to do is call the former student (even if it must be done after the normal workday), explain the situation, and ask if the alum wants the records released. If she says yes, ask that she immediately fax to the office a short letter identifying herself and giving her approval *with signature* so that the prospective employer can be informed. This is also a good opportunity to explain the consequences if the flag remains in place, so that if the alum would like to have it removed permanently, she can so indicate in the same letter. If there is no telephone number, one should contact the institution's alumni office for help or call information at the last address and try to trace the student, although, because of name changes due to marriage, this may be difficult. If all else fails, one could write to the last address on file and mark the envelope "please forward." Of course the letter would arrive too late to help in this situation, but it could prompt the alum to take the action necessary to preclude future problems.

Alternatively, if there are problems locating the former student, the records officer could contact the potential employer. Presumably the employer is in contact with the former student. Without revealing whether or not the individual has been a student, the records officer could indicate that, in order to release any information, a written and signed release must be received from the prospective employee. The records officer could then forward a release form to the employer to give to the former student, and then wait to be contacted by the former student.

Finally, it would be sensible for the records officer to write an article for the alumni newspaper detailing FERPA-related problems and inviting alums to initiate the action required to lift the "do not release" flag. And because this is such an ongoing problem and FERPA is most likely the last thing on a graduate's mind, it would be prudent to put a FERPA notice in each commencement program and even ask the bookstore or other rental agencies to place such a notice with each graduation cap and gown rental.

Sexual Harassment

Case: One of your senior male colleagues engages in sexual humor and, when talking to you (a female colleague), frequently touches your hand, arm, or shoulder. You reject this behavior, and he subjects you to derisive comments in meetings and belittles you to your staff. You are unwilling to pursue the *harassment* issue through formal avenues for fear of retaliation. Is it unethical for you to warn other female colleagues of his behavior?

Discussion: Unfortunately, such cases are not unusual in academe. The principles of fairness, doing no harm, and benefiting others come into play here. The male colleague's actions are certainly unfair to you, and to do nothing could cause continued harm to you and your female colleagues. Unless the perpetuator is officially confronted, it would be unethical to surreptitiously warn your colleagues about his behavior. As an employee, you may not feel comfortable reporting these types of harassment to your supervisor, so you could turn to the affirmative action or Title IX officer for consultation, advice, and action.

In any case, it is imperative that corrective action be taken and that the perpetrator be told what specific behavior offends others and what corrective action is required. Moreover, if, after being confronted, the offender continues his harassing behavior, more serious action must be taken. To put it more succinctly, to spread the word to colleagues without first filing an official complaint means that you are simply damaging someone's reputation "behind his back." Your comments are bound to get back to the offender, and even though you are the victim, you leave yourself open to criticism and legal action for defamation and other claims. In effect, the offender can claim that he has been convicted and his reputation damaged without "due process," i.e., an opportunity to respond.

It should be noted that, if an official complaint is filed with management and no action is taken, management gives the appearance of condoning sexual harassment, and management thereby becomes subject to legal action. Most employers are highly aware of the legal consequences.

Reports of sexual harassment should always lead to investigative action by management, and if the findings warrant further action, immediate disciplinary action must be forthcoming. Such disciplinary action could include counseling, mandatory attendance at and participation in workshops on "sensitivity training" and related topics, or dismissal, based on published institutional policy.

Convicted Murderer Applies for Admission

Case: A convict, incarcerated for twenty years for his involvement in the gang-style murder of eight people, is paroled under unusual circumstances. When interviewed by the media, he states that in the fall he intends to enroll at your institution. The news spreads like wildfire, and parents of current students are outraged, demanding that, for the safety of their daughters and sons, you not admit the parolee. Also, many prospective students call to say that if the parolee is admitted, they will not attend your institution and will demand that their advance payments be refunded. As the dean of enrollment management, you query other admissions professionals, only to be told that, under university policy, if the paroled murderer meets all academic requirements, he must be admitted. What can you do?

Discussion: A case such as this challenges our approach to ethical decision-making. Can we respect the autonomy and be just to the applicant without being unfair or unfaithful to our current and prospective students? Ethically, we sometimes have to weigh the rights and safety of an individual vis-a-vis the rights of the group. And we need to state publicly that we are always concerned about the safety and welfare of *all* of our students. Moreover, we must be concerned about perceptions as well as facts. If parents perceive that the enrollment of this convicted murderer places their daughters or sons at risk (and you can be sure that many parents will think that), then we must be sensitive to that perception.

Perhaps the first step the dean should take is to confer with the university attorney and then contact the appropriate law enforcement officials to determine the precise information about the case and the conditions (if any) that apply to the parolee.

Then, if the parolee actually applies for admission, ensure that the applicant's academic records are carefully evaluated to determine if he is academically eligible for admission. He has been in jail for twenty years or more, so it is quite likely that he would not meet current academic requirements for admission. If he does not, the case is closed.

If the applicant is academically eligible, then it would have to be determined whether, if admitted, he would represent a clear and present danger to others on campus. To make this determination, the dean should work with the various law enforcement authorities, including prison authorities. For example, the experience of prison authorities with the applicant over the previous twenty years would be relevant. Were there additional problems in prison, or was he a model prisoner, who has demonstrated rehabilitation in a number of ways? Details about the original crime may also play a role in the decision. Was the applicant convicted because he was a member of a gang, present at the scene? Did he kill anyone himself? Was he one of the gang leaders. How old was he at the time of the crime? If, as a result of this investigation, it appeared there would be a clear and present danger, the applicant should not be admitted.

If it appears that admission is appropriate, you may want to consider as a separate decision whether student housing should be offered. The level of risk posed by an individual coming to classes may be quite different from the risk of one housed full-time with younger, less experienced students.

In summary, the final decision becomes a judgment call, and it would behoove any dean or director to involve others in the decision, including the attorney and the faculty-student admissions committee. In the final analysis, it may be necessary to rule in favor of the rights of the many (student body) over the individual rights of the applicant. In so doing, we are being *faithful* to the promises made to the other students, we would *benefit others* rather than the individual, and we would be being *just* to the current and prospective students, their parents, and the university.

Also, if possible it would be humane and just to the denied applicant if the dean were to announce the decision in a counseling-type interview while providing helpful advice to the applicant. For example, it might be pointed out that his enrollment on any residential campus would spark opposition and mistrust and the candidate's academic success would be in jeopardy. Conversely, if the candidate were to enroll at a downtown campus in a metropolitan setting and live off campus, the probability of his academic success would be increased.

This case should also remind all enrollment professionals to be sure that there is a written institutional policy on citizenship, so that such an applicant could be denied admission without the institution ending up in court. The wording in most admissions policies, "must be in good standing," applies to more than grades and credits, but it would be prudent if we were all more specific in our literature, so that all prospective students would understand that "in good standing" applies to citizenship as well as academics.

Final Examination Accommodation

Case: The final examination schedule is published well before the end of the semester. Shortly after it was published, a student petitioned her instructor for more than the scheduled two hours to complete the final, citing a documented learning disability. The instructor denied this and several subsequent requests, stating that special exceptions for one student would not be fair to the others and could jeopardize the integrity of the examination. The department head agreed with the instructor and the student turned to you, asking for help. Do you intervene?

Discussion: Positive intervention action will prevent harm to the disabled student and ultimately benefit other students with similar problems. And if such a case can be later used as an example (without identifying the student or faculty member) in training sessions for faculty, benefits can be maximized. However, unless you are the properly designated official to handle such cases, your role should be one of referral to the proper individual or agency. Perhaps the instructor and department head are not aware that the federal Americans with Disabilities Act (ADA) of 1990 establishes a national nondiscrimination law that provides comprehensive protection to individuals with disabilities. This includes students with visible disabilities such as mobility, hearing, and vision impairments, as well as those with learning disabilities and psychological disorders.

Chances are the campus president or chancellor has already designated an appropriate administrator to handle these problems, and the case can and should be referred to that person. In fact, the ADA mandates that campuses adopt policies and procedures that will facilitate the fullest participation possible for people with disabilities, including making proper accommodations for examinations. The director of disabled student services should be working with the registrar and faculty to smooth the path for the disabled. And as an enrollment professional, consideration should be given to preparing and submitting a comprehensive recommendation to revise the institution's final exam policies to address such cases. As an example, the final exam policy might be revised or amended as follows:

> Students with verifiable disabilities that require examination modifications will be accommodated in compliance with state and federal laws. This includes students with mobility, hearing, and vision impairments, as well as those with learning disabilities, psychological disorders, and other functional impairments. Student Services personnel will determine whether modifications are necessary and, in consultation with the instructor, arrange for the needed modifications. Students may choose to make such arrangements directly with the instructor or seek help through the Office of Disabled Student Services.

On some campuses, faculty representatives may insist that they be involved in any conflict between a faculty member and administrators over the academic accommodation of a student. The ground for such insistence is that what goes on in the classroom is the special prerogative of the faculty. While this is so, the law imposes accommodation obligations and legal liabilities on the institution, not individual faculty members.

One possible solution when conflicts cannot be resolved directly with the faculty member involved is to have an "appeals panel" of faculty members and administrators with expertise in disability issues. The faculty as a whole could agree in advance that the decisions of such a panel would be binding.

Posthumous Degree

Case: A graduate student has completed all but two courses, passed the preliminary examination, and submitted her dissertation in draft form to her committee. She subsequently is killed in a tragic accident. Her grieving spouse asks the dean to award her the Ph.D. posthumously, even though all degree requirements have not been completed. You are the registrar and the dean asks for your advice. What do you advise?

Discussion: As unfortunate as it is, it is unusual if an institution doesn't lose a student in this way from time to time. Honoring this request would be just, would benefit others, and would do no harm. Moreover, it would mark the college or university as a caring institution and be a very positive public relations move. But how does one go about it? If an institutional policy on posthumous degrees is in place, one simply follows the policy. If not, then the enrollment services professional ought to take the lead in the development of such a policy, so that the specific request can be granted and guidelines established so that future requests can be handled in a fair and consistent manner.

If time allows, you might poll some of your colleagues to ascertain if and how other institutions handle posthumous awards. In any case, the enrollment services professional might draft a recommended policy and submit it through regular channels for consideration and approval. Institutions are normally reluctant to grant degrees unless all academic requirements have been met, so separate policies on various types of awards might be recommended, such as:

1. Candidates for posthumous awards must have applied for graduation and be in the senior year (undergraduates) or final year (graduates) of their degree work.

2. If the deceased meet the criteria in 1. above and the appropriate faculty have approved the degrees, their names will be listed in the commencement program as usual, with a parenthetical note (Posthumous Award) listed with the names. In all cases, the official academic record (transcript) will be marked "deceased," with the date of death recorded. The degree award(s) will be one of two kinds:

    (a) Actual Degree awarded in the case when all or most requirements have been met, provided the cognizant faculty vote for approval.

    (b) Memorial Certificate awarded when the student has too many credits and requirements unmet. The certificate will carry the seal of the institution and the signatures of the president, registrar, department chair, and respective dean. The certificate will have a common format with personalized information inserted between the lines, "Present This Memorial Certificate" and "Given at (city and state)." The cognizant academic department will be asked to provide the personalized information and the certificate will be prepared by (person preparing). The certificate will carry the same date as the diplomas.

3. In all cases it is recommended that representatives of the institution, the department, the Office of Student Affairs, and/or student colleagues of the deceased present the degree or memorial certificate to the family in person, rather than during any commencement ceremony.

Diversifying the Admissions Staff

Case: As director of admissions, you are making a full-court press to diversify your admissions outreach staff. You want to hire a Native American. Two applicants make the final cut. One is a non-Native American with five years of outreach experience and excellent credentials and recommendations. The other is a recently graduated Native American with no experience at all but great potential. What can you do?

Discussion: Our ethical principles of fairness, being just and faithful, and keeping contracts come into play here. As we all know, we cannot make race a requirement in hiring. We can, however, indicate in our recruitment announcement something like, "Native American candidates are urged to apply." In this case, when the applications were in, the candidate list narrowed down to those to be invited for interview, and the interviews completed, there were only two candidates remaining. To be considered, both need to meet the advertised requirements for the job. Assuming that they do both meet the requirements, it would be difficult for the employer to hire the inexperienced Native American candidate, given that the credentials of the other candidate appear to be so far superior in every respect. The only reason for hiring the Native American would be race, and this is not appropriate as the sole reason for hiring someone.

The Native American candidate with no experience but great potential faces a serious problem that is familiar to all in admissions and records: "You can't get the job without experience, and you can't get experience without the job." A solution that would solve this dilemma and set a course that would help future candidates would be to create an admissions or student services trainee position, at the entry-level salary. The trainee position might include training/learning duties in a series of settings that would help the candidate tool up for a future professional position. The trainee position should be for a limited time, perhaps one or two years. An example of a training program would be to assign the trainee to work in admissions outreach from September through December, in the admissions evaluation section from January through April, and in the new student orientation section from May through August. With this pattern, the trainee could get valuable experience in a full cycle of admissions-related activities. If such a position were created in this instance, the qualified candidate with five years' experience could be hired in the professional position, and the recent Native American graduate could be placed in the trainee position. There should be no guarantee of employment after the training period is over. However, if successful, the trainee should soon become qualified to apply for a professional position at this or any other institution seeking admissions recruiters.

It may not be financially feasible for a single office to fund a trainee position. In spite of that, the admissions office is only one sector of the larger student affairs or academic affairs division. Consequently, it should be possible for the head of the division to identify enough funds to finance a trainee program. Such a program would provide opportunities for candidates from underrepresented groups to gain the experience necessary to qualify for professional positions in admissions, records, and student services.

Ethical Considerations and Decisions — a Macro-Approach

As any professional knows, there is a never-ending supply of issues to resolve and problems to solve, often affecting large groups or audiences. Some are aggravating problems that seem to resist solution. Others are major issues that come to the surface because of new legislation at the state or federal levels, changes in practice within the college or university, or new trends that tend to sweep higher education on a regular basis. In such cases, admissions and records professionals should provide leadership and ensure that they, and their colleagues, make appropriate ethical recommendations and decisions. Suggested actions in the case studies that follow address ethical issues on a macro-basis and illustrate leadership activities on the part of seasoned enrollment professionals.

Imposing Limits on the Number of Majors

Case: An academic department offers several of the most popular majors on campus, and enrollment has grown exponentially over the past ten years. Departmental budgets are based largely on student credit hours taught and full-time equivalent students (FTE's) enrolled, so the department is well off financially. At the start of the semester, with little warning, the department announces a plan to reduce enrollments and majors. Dozens of students are being turned away, and there is no procedure for appeal. What can be done?

Discussion: During the glory days of higher education, funds were readily available to public institutions, and departments could continue to grow and accommodate more students. However, since the early to mid-1980s, funding has become more scarce, and the limitations mentioned above have become commonplace. All of the ethical guideposts are called into question when decisions like this are made, and faculty and administrators ought to be concerned about the student as a consumer. Is such action just? Are the departmental decision-makers being faithful to their students? Have existing obligations been met? The answer to each of the three questions is a resounding "No!"

This case provides an excellent opportunity to focus on the leadership of enrollment services professionals. An immediate solution would be to seek support from the top, enlist the help of the campus ombudsman and others, and try to reason with the department chair, dean, and provost — in that order. It might be possible to get the departmental decision rescinded or at least delayed until a reasonable plan can be developed. Yet, a long-term, proactive solution is called for, and the enrollment services professional should exert maximum effort to prevent such unilateral actions in the future. One might point out that literature and promises made by the admissions office and material printed in the course catalog, if relied upon by students, create obligations that may be legally enforceable. The institution and the department must, if at all possible, honor these obligations.

The affected undergraduates fall into two categories: (1) first-year students and possibly sophomores who have not been certified into the major, and (2) certified or declared majors who are well into their respective programs. While it is quite possible to redirect the as-yet-uncertified students, the institution has an ethical obligation to those who have already completed the basic requirements for certification. Such students should have every right to expect to graduate in the major. Even those individuals who have not been certified into the major may have chosen to attend the institution based on representations in the catalog and elsewhere about the availability of the major. Thus, there may be obligations to these students as well.

The enrollment services professional, serving in her or his capacity on the key academic policy-making committee or committees, can take the lead in developing, through the normal governance structure, policies that will protect students as well as the reputation of the unit in question and the institution. Important ethical goals would be to advocate for the students and to provide the leadership necessary to convince the governance structure that this is an institutional issue. Departments should not be allowed to act unilaterally in such cases, given the consequences for the whole campus. A unit that, for justifiable reasons, wishes to reduce enrollment should petition through appropriate channels for approval to impose limits and should be required to present solid evidence supporting the petition. Steps in the process might include:

1. Unit submits a careful analysis of its ability to accommodate students, including limitations (if any) of staff, operating funds, equipment, and space, including laboratories.

2. Unit provides data on the probable effects of the proposed limitation. Such data might include estimates of the numbers of prospective majors who would be turned away, the numbers of non-majors whose academic programs require courses to be taken in the unit, and identification of other academic departments that might be expected to certify or enroll the students turned away.

3. Governance structure develops criteria for selecting majors in any program wishing to impose enrollment limits. Then, if the proposed limit or some other negotiated limit is approved, the unit will be expected to develop a limitation plan that meets at least the following criteria:

    (a) More than one criterion is required for selection (e.g., cumulative GPA, grades in specific courses, interviews, portfolios, etc.).

    (b) Procedures must include provisions to ensure certification of candidates from underrepresented groups.

    (c) Criteria and procedures approved during a given academic year may not be implemented until at least the fall term of the following academic year (allowing the admissions office to stand by its published information and ensuring access to those already in the pipeline). Even better would be to "grandfather" all currently enrolled students and to have the new criteria and procedures apply only to new students.

    (d) Appeal procedures must be provided for applicants who are not accepted into the major.

(e) Information about certification limits must be included in the catalog and all recruitment literature well before such limits are imposed.

Registrars and directors of admissions serve as academic officers of the college or university, and their role in the development and implementation of policy is crucial. The leadership provided by these professionals can ensure that policy issues are well-grounded and thoroughly researched and that ethical decisions in the micro- or macro-sense are based on the best and most recent research available from colleagues and through AACRAO and other resource agencies. Moreover, serving as the conscience of the institution, the enrollment services professional can ensure that all concerned parties are apprised of the issues and informed of new and changed policies, and that student consumers are always treated in fair and equitable ways.

Institutional Responsibility

Case: The economy in the state has gone from bad to worse, and several agencies have been given financial priority over higher education. Consequently, the university budget has been cut 20 percent. Following careful and exhaustive study, the institution has decided to drop what has been determined to be a small and unproductive degree program. Several senior majors are cut off at the "academic pockets" and appeal to you for help. What can you do?

Discussion: This ethical dilemma is not unlike the one involving limits on majors, but in this case, the institution has evidently declared a state of financial exigency and, according to the administration, such radical action is required. The ethical issues include doing harm (to the majors, as well as to, perhaps, the faculty), being just and faithful, keeping promises, and meeting commitments. The enrollment services professional can and should advocate for the students and initiate the appropriate appeals. However, because of the financial exigency, the appeals will probably be unsuccessful, and solutions must be found to assist the students on an individual basis. To provide some "consumer protection" and help minimize such occurrences in the future, the enrollment services professional might use all of her or his leadership skills to convince the academic leaders of the institution to approve a statement of institutional responsibility to students. Once approved, such a policy statement should be featured prominently in the catalog and other academic publications. An example might read as follows:

> *Institutional Responsibility Statement:* Undergraduate students who are certified majors can assume that a degree will be granted if they maintain continuous enroll-

ment and meet all requirements as listed in the catalog. However, because of serious reductions in financial support, loss of faculty, or for other significant reasons, the institution may from time to time find it necessary to discontinue a degree program. When this occurs, further admission into the degree program will be frozen effective with the official action discontinuing the degree, and every effort will be made to allow currently enrolled majors to complete their degrees within a reasonable period of time. To facilitate this process, department and program chairs have the obligation to provide for the individual academic needs of these students:

(1) Students may be encouraged to complete their requirements in similar or related degree tracks;

(2) Although general education requirements and the minimum total hours for the degree may never be waived, the student's major department may waive or substitute departmental degree requirements;

(3) Undergraduate students may be allowed to complete remaining requirements at another institution. In all cases, all financial obligations will continue to be the responsibility of the individual students involved.

Automated Prerequisite Checking

Case: Your faculty have approved and the administration has funded a new on-line enrollment system utilizing voice response technology and the touchtone telephone. Once it is implemented, students will be able to enroll in classes by telephone. The faculty senate voted to have part of the new enrollment package include automated prerequisite checking and insists that students must satisfy all prerequisites or be denied enrollment. If the prerequisites are rigidly enforced, you know that many otherwise eligible students will be frozen out of classes. What do you do?

Discussion: The concept and reality of academic course prerequisites have been a part of higher education for a century or more. Prior to the advent of on-line enrollment, prerequisites were generally viewed as advisory in nature and were often the subject of negotiation between professor and student. With interactive student information systems and on-line enrollment, it is now possible to enforce prerequisite completion programmatically. But is it fair and just to students, especially juniors and seniors, to do so without some sort of warning or phase-in period?

A serious oversight in the thinking of some who want to rigidly enforce all prerequisites is that there are ways other than taking specific courses to satisfy prerequisites. Thus, a likely first step in this case would be for the enrollment services professional to take the lead in developing an institutional prerequisite policy that would recognize the various methods of satisfying prerequisites. Working through the proper academic channels, one might propose a catalog policy something like the following:

> When applicable, prerequisites are listed in this catalog within the description for each course. Prerequisites may be levels of competence, or courses that a student must have completed, or the status that a student must have achieved prior to enrolling for a specific course. For example, Math 171 (calculus) requires a prerequisite of Math 107 (precalculus), meaning that the student may not enroll for Math 171 until successfully completing Math 107.
>
> Prerequisites may also be general, such as "one semester of chemistry or concurrent enrollment in chemistry." Prerequisites may include a level of expertise or a specified major, e.g., students may not enroll in Spanish 324 without first being fluent in Spanish, or students may not enroll in an advanced seminar before achieving senior standing in the major.
>
> Questions concerning prerequisites should be referred to the instructor of the course. Students who have not met all prerequisites may be excluded from the course, or the instructor may waive the prerequisite based on demonstrated competence or equivalent academic experience. In summary, prerequisites may be:
>
> 1. Courses that must be completed in advance
> 2. Levels of competence
> 3. Class standing (e.g., junior status)
> 4. A placement examination successfully passed
> 5. A specified academic major
> 6. Levels of expertise
> 7. Concurrent enrollment in a co-requisite course
> 8. Demonstrated competence

9. Equivalent academic experience
10. Consent of the instructor

Once the prerequisite policy has been adopted, the enrollment services professional will have the tools necessary to demonstrate to faculty and unit heads that there are alternate methods of satisfying a given prerequisite, many of which are not programmable. With this knowledge at hand, one might then initiate a drive to convince faculty that many of the prerequisites listed in the current catalog are simply advisory in nature, and that programmatic enforcement of all prerequisites will simply place many unnecessary hurdles in the paths of students. Working with faculty, it will then be possible to eliminate "cosmetic" prerequisites and retain only those that are absolutely necessary (such as in the sciences). This approach will help reduce the numbers of students turned away from desperately needed classes. Moreover, prerequisites such as "class standing" and "specific major" will help students successfully enroll in the proper classes and graduate on time.

The enrollment services professional should warn the faculty of the negative consequences of imposing the rigid prerequisite checks that the faculty want. The upshot would surely be that hundreds of students denied enrollment would descend on the faculty seeking "consent of the instructor" access. After several semesters of confusion and added workload, faculty and departments would soon begin eliminating unnecessary prerequisites and other roadblocks to enrollment. This approach, however, would mean that many students would be academically traumatized before the system could be cleaned up.

Prayer at Commencement

Case: As one of the chief academic officers of a public institution, you are in charge of the commencement ceremony. Traditionally, the ceremony begins with an invocation and ends with a benediction. The benediction was eliminated a few years earlier in the interest of time. Now, criticism is growing over the invocation and the issue of separation of church and state, as well as the concern that non-Christian religions are seldom considered. Recently, a small group of faculty representing the American Civil Liberties Union threatened action if the invocation is not discontinued. You suspect that eliminating the invocation will please a relatively small group while offending the majority, but you also know that the courts generally rule against such prayers in public situations. Do you eliminate the invocation?

Discussion: Our ethical principles of fairness and being just and faithful apply in this case. One must also be sensitive to the fact that non-Christian religions are recognized infrequently, if ever, and therefore, there is a solid case for reconsidering current practice. Moreover, if the truth be known, there have been many instances of grumbling and dissatisfaction among the various Christian denominations when one priest or minister is selected over the others. However, tradition is always important. The parents of graduating students and the public generally expect commencement to begin with prayer, and many would be disappointed if it did not.

If the status quo is allowed to continue, are we being fair to the minority? Are we to be just and faithful to tradition and the majority, or to the wishes of those opposed?

This appears to be a lose-lose situation, but it need not be. The professional in charge of commencement does not have to make the decision alone. Surely she or he has a commencement committee, and the issue should be referred to the committee. The committee should then send its recommendation to the president or chancellor for a final decision (the president or chancellor because that officer usually presides at commencement and will be the recipient of criticism or praise regarding the ceremony). A recommendation that could turn the issue into a win-win situation would be to eliminate the invocation but replace it with a formal "moment of silent prayer." In this instance, the president, at the end of the faculty march, posting of the colors, and playing of the national anthem, would convene the ceremony and make an announcement somewhat as follows:

> It is appropriate at this time for us all to remember the parents and relatives of our new graduates and to thank them for helping to make this great day possible. Let us then pause for a moment of silent prayer. I ask each of you, in your own way, to express your gratitude and thanksgiving for this important milestone in our students' lives.
>
> (The president maintains silence for an appropriate time, then says, "Thank you" and goes on with the ceremony.)

If the recommendation is followed, the tradition of prayer is maintained, no single religion is favored over another, and we are being "just" and "fair" to all concerned.

Epilogue

One need only read the local newspaper or watch national news on television to be aware of what often appears to be a complete absence of ethical principles and sound ethical practices in business and government. Higher education is not immune to the problem either. The famous educator, Clark Kerr (1994, 11), outlined the problem succinctly, stating, "I still marvel at the large literature by academics on ethics in general and on medical and legal business ethics in particular as compared with the slight literature on academic ethics."

The literature on "Ethics and Ethos" abounds with high-sounding ethical platitudes, but there is relatively little printed on the application of ethical principles to everyday problems. Thus, the foregoing chapter outlines several sets of principles that can be used when one is faced with ethical decisions and then presents numerous case studies with proposed ethical solutions. Even though the authors offer only one or sometimes two solutions to each dilemma, readers are reminded that there is seldom only a single solution to any problem, as answers often vary depending on the institution (e.g., public or private, two- or four-year) and the form of governance. Finally, readers are challenged to apply sound ethical principles in their work and record their decisions in the form of "policy notes" or "decisions made," so that current and future staff members will have an ethical roadmap to follow, helping to ensure continuity and fairness in academic and student services decision-making.

Further Reading and Study

John Kultgen explores various "ethical premises" in *Ethics and Professionalism* (1988). Neil Miller (1990) outlines the role education should play in moral and ethical development in "Ethics 101?" In *Applied Ethics in Student Services* (1985), Canon and Brown provide a basic primer on ethical problems in daily practice and on ethical principles and ethical decisions in student affairs. Good background information on the "Principles of Wise Choice" can be found in *Ethics* by Charles A. Baylis (1958). *Fair Practices In Higher Education*, a report of the Carnegie Council on Policy Studies in Higher Education (1979), provides sound information on institutional and student rights and responsibilities. And in *The Book of Virtues*, William Bennett (1993) provides an insightful compendium of articles, stories, and poems on the "bedrock issues" of ethics and morals.

For an interesting examination of ethical matters and ethical decision-making, the enrollment services professional should read *Ethics in Higher Education*, edited by William May (1990). For those who want to study additional case studies similar to those in this chapter, a dozen or more ethical dilemmas are discussed in "Ethical Practices in Academe," a chapter in Quann and Birnbaum (1996) *Records Management for the 1990s and Beyond.*

References

American Association of Collegiate Registrars and Admissions Officers. 1995. Professional practices and ethical standards. In *AACRAO Member Guide 1995-96.* Washington DC: American Association of Collegiate Registrars and Admissions Officers.

Baylis, Charles A. 1958. *Ethics: The principles of wise choice.* New York: Henry Holt and Company.

Bennett, William J., ed. 1993. *The book of virtues: A treasury of great moral stories.* New York: Simon & Schuster.

Canon, Harry J., and Robert D. Brown, eds. 1985. *Applied ethics in student services.* San Francisco: Jossey-Bass, Inc.

Carnegie Council on Policy Studies in Higher Education. 1979. *Fair practices in higher education.* San Francisco: Jossey-Bass.

Clement, Linda M. and Scott T. Rickard. 1992. *Effective leadership in student services: Voices from the field.* San Francisco: Jossey-Bass, Inc.

Kerr, Clark. 1994. Knowledge ethics and the new academic culture. *Change, The Magazine of Higher Learning* (January/February) 26:1.

Kitchener, Karen S. 1985. Ethical principles and ethical decisions in student affairs. In *Applied Ethics in Student Services,* edited by Harry J. Canon and Robert D. Brown. San Francisco: Jossey-Bass, Inc.

Kimbrough, Ralph B. 1985. *Ethics: A Course of study for educational leaders.* Arlington VA: American Association of School Administrators.

Kultgen, John. 1988. *Ethics and professionalism.* Philadelphia: University of Pennsylvania Press.

May, William W., editor. 1990. *Ethics and higher education.* New York: Macmillan Publishing Company.

Mayhew, Lewis B. 1979. *Surviving the eighties.* San Francisco: Jossey-Bass, Inc.

Miller, Neil. 1990. Ethics 101? *UCLA Magazine.* Los Angeles: University of California-Los Angeles (Summer).

Quann, C. James, and David Birnbaum. 1996. Ethical practices in academe. *Records Management for the 1990s and Beyond.* Westport CT: Greenwood Publishing Group, Inc.

Robinson, George M., Janice and Moulton. 1985. *Ethical problems in higher education.* Englewood Cliffs NJ: Prentice-Hall, Inc.

Chapter 10

Career Mobility

by William R. Haid

Introduction

Enrollment services is a field that offers many opportunities for career advancement. A look into these professions will reveal many long-time employees and many managers who have moved up through the ranks. Entry into an enrollment services office, such as admissions, registrar, or financial aid, usually occurs at the clerical or counselor level. Some will enter an enrollment services office at a supervisory or management position, but this is unusual.

Supervisors and managers in enrollment services tend to be people who have moved up in the organization, either at the same institution or at another. Few directors of admissions or financial aid and even fewer registrars had their present positions as a career goal when they finished college or began their work experience. This is also true for assistant and associate directors and registrars. Most started in some entry-level position, or even as a student employee while in college, and were promoted and advanced into permanent, supervisory, and management positions.

Enrollment services has not tended to be a field that many can enter at higher levels without direct related experience. However, as enrollment management becomes a broader campus activity attracting the interest

---

William R. Haid is Registrar at the University of Colorado at Boulder. Before assuming that position in 1990, he served as Registrar at the University of New Mexico for eight years and as Assistant and Associate Registrar at Arizona State University for seven years. In 1994, he was elected to the AACRAO Board of Directors as Vice President for Professional Development, Research and Publications, after serving as Vice President and President of ACRAO regional groups. He has also worked as a consultant in the areas of customer service and staff development.

of faculty and academic administrators, the pool of potential candidates for positions in enrollment services has increased. This is encouraging news to some and discouraging to others. Clearly, opportunities for advancement occur within the field of enrollment services, but there are also problems along the way for both those who are promoted and those who aren't. This chapter will discuss specific ways that individuals can improve their prospects of moving up and being successful when they do.

In today's marketplace and economy, new jobs are scarce and people are holding onto their present ones longer. Finding a new job and changing fields are not as easy as they once were. Learning and perfecting transferable skills alone does not ensure job transferability, whether in higher education or, more specifically, in enrollment services. Informal and unscientific surveys conducted by the author revealed that the average length of employment in enrollment services among 200 conference attendees was 12.2 years, and that the average between promotions was four and a half years. Those who have recently landed such jobs may wish to consider the possibilities of staying in this line of work for ten to twenty years. It can be very satisfying work in a stimulating environment, even if upward mobility is not a goal. However, advancement and promotion can greatly enrich the job satisfaction and career experience.

This chapter will discuss opportunities in enrollment services, the skills and behaviors needed for advancement, the factors associated with moving out as well as moving up, how to know when you are ready for a new move, getting that next job, and contributing to the profession.

Opportunities in Enrollment Services

Enrollment services is an atypical field. Except in the very broadest sense, advanced education is not available as a credential for entry into enrollment services or promotions to the management ranks. Advanced education, however, is expected as a credential of higher education for upper-level positions. Most promotions come from within the field and often from within the current organization. The skills and abilities most desired in enrollment services are not of a technical nature, as in accounting or engineering. Experience and exposure to the problems and solutions involved in enrollment services, such as recruitment and retention strategies within the environment of higher education, are essential.

The functions of enrollment services — admissions, financial aid, registration and records, and the others noted in Chapter 1 — are essential functions of any institution of higher education. A new emphasis on enrollment management, the strategic planning for optimum campus enrollment, has brought increased attention to the integration of these functions on campus and, especially, the role of its leaders. As institutions and professional associations give even more attention to the domains of enrollment services — including enrollment management, instructional management, information technology, and student services — the need for professionals in these areas will grow, and with it the opportunities for advancement. The only pitfall ahead is that internal competition for the advancement opportunities will come from your colleagues and friends.

Skills and Behaviors

The challenge to all who strive to move up in enrollment services is to distinguish yourself in a positive way from your peers and position yourself for the tasks and responsibilities of advancement. Following are the author's thoughts on the skills and behaviors that can help a person advance and perform at increasing management responsibilities. These skills may apply universally, but they are written with enrollment services offices in mind.

The categories selected to convey these skills are intentionally simple and straightforward. There are six important steps to consider and remember when working to move up in the organization or to put into practice when you do move up: Work hard, take care of people, keep your priorities straight, don't be afraid of change, do the right thing, and take care of yourself.

Work Hard

The old saying, "Work smarter, not harder," should be, "Work smarter AND harder" in the context of moving up in enrollment services. While most managers and supervisors are promoted from within the ranks of enrollment services staff, only a few actually move up this way. There are obviously fewer management positions available, and many enrollment services staff are not promoted at all. The best some can do is move laterally within an organization to get different experiences or working environments. To be one of the few who moves up, working harder is a way to distinguish yourself from your peers. There are several ways to do this.

First, set an example, especially if you are a supervisor. Others will be encouraged to follow suit, and many problems can be avoided in the workplace. A supervisor cannot expect on-time arrival at work if he or she doesn't get to work on time! Others can be motivated more easily if they can see what good performance looks like. Next, be productive at work. Getting work done is not to be competitive, but to strive for higher levels of output, set an example and become a leader among your peers. Whether processing applications, recruiting students, or doing enrollment verifications, develop a reputation for getting work done and don't accept the minimum expected. Exceed it!

Be willing to accept new responsibilities eagerly. If you are asked to join a project, chair a committee, or offer a new service, say yes and don't hesitate. This may strike you as taking on more work, but it broadens your experience and sets you apart from your peers. Also, never stop learning while you work. Whether a new procedure like sending transcripts through electronic data exchange, new computer software such as a degree audit system, or a new office management concept like business process transformation, keep an open mind about learning something new. There is no one in our organizations who can't learn something new, and no one who will advance without learning something new. (See Chapter 7 on professional development for more discussion of both formal and informal learning.)

Learn to write and write often. Writing is such a useful and underutilized skill that a good writer can easily be distinguished from others. Write exceptional memos, procedures, reports, and articles. Your value to the organization will increase noticeably. Writing, though, will require discipline and good time management. Both of these are necessary to working smarter and harder.

Volunteer for new tasks and assignments, and get involved in professional activities. Many opportunities are available for younger (and older) staff members to offer their services and time to professional activities. State or regional associations present such opportunities, but do not overlook campus opportunities, such as coordinating the building blood drive or giving tours to visitors on campus. Participation in activities beyond your job will broaden your experience and make you valuable to your organization. You *can* work smart and hard.

Along the career way, find an area that becomes your specialty. Become the campus expert on something. Expertise on student privacy laws such as FERPA, enrollment management, student information systems, recruiting strategies, office management, records management, and staff development further distinguish you and make you valuable to and recognized by your institution and the profession.

Take Care of People

Second, one of the most important aspects to moving up is how well you take care of people. Customer relations is important and, as a supervisor or manager, you will be evaluated on how well your unit takes care of customers. Develop a love for good customer service and you will stand out in a world that too easily accepts mediocre (or worse!) treatment. Though customer service is important, employee relations are even more important. If you take care of employee relations, your employees will take care of customer relations. As your responsibility for people in the organization increases, so must your attention to how well your staff is treated. Taking care of people is a sign of good leadership.

Clearly communicating expectations to employees is the single most important leadership function of a supervisor or manager. Verbally and in writing, people should know what is expected of them and what good performance looks like. Communicate in three ways that help employees know where they stand:

1. Routinely monitor performance and provide feedback to staff, not just on the annual performance evaluation.

2. Praise and reward them when they have done something well.

3. Reprimand and redirect them when they have failed to meet clear expectations.

To be effective, both praise and criticism must be timely, specific to what caused it, and given fairly and consistently. Communicating expectations is the proper role of any leader, and one who does this well will be in demand.

Keep Your Priorities Straight

The third area is keeping your priorities straight. Often, people work hard, and even smart, but lose track of their priorities from not having set clear goals and objectives to focus on. Set long-term and short-term goals and write them down. Write down career and personal goals. Keep your goals before you in some fashion. A sign on your wall, a note on your desk, and a card in your pocket are ways to do that. Without a goal, there is no direction. Make this a priority!

Once you have your goals, work toward them. Short-term goals need objectives, which are the specific steps that will lead to the goal. They are the basis for your work plans. Make a work plan each week to keep you on track with your goals and objectives and then monitor your progress. Plan your work and work your plan, or you will simply work and work and work, without a plan or worthwhile results!

Keeping your priorities straight and maintaining consistency in office relationships can be difficult. For example, you have worked hard and taken care of people. You have shown good skills in your duties and responsible behavior. You are promoted, and now you are a supervisor. You have responsibility for people who were previously your peers and your friends. Imagine trying to supervise and evaluate recruiters who previously were your traveling companions. Many people in this position have found it hard to shift roles and keep work relationships separate from friendships. As a supervisor, you must realize that you cannot please everyone. To do so almost always involves inconsistency and leads to further feelings of unfairness. You will please more of your staff by being consistent than by pleasing everyone. Respect, understanding, caring, and fairness are more important values to employ in your treatment of people than trying to please everyone.

Don't Be Afraid of Change

The fourth area has to do with change. Don't be afraid of change. Change is the one thing in today's workplace that you must make your friend. Times are changing, people are changing, technology is changing, and needs are changing. If you want to move up, you must be able to embrace change. As an employee or a supervisor, be ready for changes that come your way. Or, better yet, be a change agent yourself. Be creative and experiment. Allow your staff to do the same. Reward creative failure — don't punish. The best ideas are not developed on the first try. Use change for continuous improvement. Measure the results and adopt and reward what works. Don't change for change's sake, but don't accept status quo for status quo's sake. People who move up are people who can change!

Do the Right Thing

The fifth area is called "doing the right thing." In work, as in life, you will decide how ethically and honestly you conduct yourself. Practicing intellectual honesty in your work as well as your personal life means more than not telling lies. It means being honest about everything. It means full disclosure. It means being vulnerable at times. It means being real! Don't shirk responsibilities. Be willing to do the hard thing. If you are a supervisor or manager, accept and execute the responsibilities that have been given to you. If a tough decision needs to be made, make it. If a negative performance evaluation needs to be given, give it. If a person needs to be terminated, terminate him or her. It won't be pleasant, but you will be respected for doing the right thing. Consult Chapter 9 for excellent insights into this goal.

Take Care of Yourself

The last area is about you. You must know yourself and be yourself. Develop a "style" and live that style at work. If you are a compassionate person, be a compassionate leader. If you are funny, use humor at work. If you have a deep faith, live your faith at work. You got where you are by being who you are. Don't change because you are at work. Take care of yourself and take time for yourself. Working hard was the first area discussed. Taking care of yourself may mean playing hard when you play. It means keeping family priorities and developing meaningful friendships. It means making time for personal interests and vacations. You should be pleasant and even fun to be around — which you will be if you take care of yourself and keep work in perspective.

Moving Out

Not all opportunities for advancement in enrollment services occur by moving up without moving out. A single organization is limited in advancement opportunities. And while promoting from within is a common practice at the first and second stages of advancement, hiring externally is more likely at the higher levels. Both kinds of opportunities can occur.

People who move up are often people who can move. Of course, not everyone is in a position to make such a change, and there are many factors to consider. But whether a move means to another state, another institution within your state or area, or another department on your campus, sometimes you have to move out to move up. In many departments, turnover is very low and advancement opportunities are limited. In other situations, a person will have done all that can be done in that department and will need a different experience to broaden opportunities. The best opportunities often require a move of some sort.

Knowing When You're Ready

Considering a change in jobs in the course of a career in enrollment services is natural. Whether that change is a new job assignment, a push for an advancement, or a change of scenery, knowing when and how to evaluate your readiness for change is important. Informal surveys of conference participants revealed that four and a half years was the average length of employment before a major change took place. Also revealed was a trend of four to five distinct jobs assignments in careers that spanned twenty years or more. Job changes are likely to be more frequent in the future, as technology advances and higher education transforms to a information age. See Chapters 4 and 11 for more discussion on this topic.

The length of time in your present assignment is one factor to consider. If you have been doing the same job for over four years, it may be time to evaluate your readiness for movement. Consider the challenges of your assignment. Are you challenged in your work? Or has it become routine? Do you look forward to Mondays? Or dread another week? Have you recently completed a major project? Has it been too long since there has been a major project? All of these questions can help you determine if a change would be healthy for you.

Also, consider your "worth" to your present institution. Are you valued for your contribution and sought after for special assignments? Do your supervisors and colleagues listen to your opinions? What has been your salary history in your present job? If you have not been receiving adequate salary increases, is it associated with your performance or other budgetary issues at your institution? Are you receiving higher or lower salary increases than your peers? What is happening in other departments or institutions? Sometimes, a check of the marketplace via educational journals and professional associations can give you an idea of your worth.

Some of the considerations for a job change are objective, but most are not. This is often the time for a "gut check." What is your intuition telling you? Are you riding high? Or are you in a slump? What are your mentors saying? Check in with friends and family for their reading on your outlook and prospects.

Getting the Next Job

If you've come to the conclusion that you are ready for that next job, the job search and interview process will require some attention. Job openings can be found with an active or inactive search.

An inactive search is one in which you wait until something comes to your attention via your regular information channels, such as newsletters, electronic listservs, and announcements from colleagues. This sort of a search has merit in that such job openings that may interest you may seem meant for you in a providential way. The drawback is in missing opportunities that don't come to your attention but could also be "just right" for you. An inactive job search can be effective when time is not a priority.

An active job search will include the regular information channels as above, but will be an effort directed at additional information channels. This includes reading or scanning the job announcements in the newspapers, journals, and newsletters for the field and area in which you are interested. Enrollment services positions are regularly posted in *The Chronicle of Higher Education*, in AACRAO's Data Dispenser and *NetNews*, and on electronic listservs such as REGIST-L and ENROLL-L. Informing trusted friends and colleagues will broaden the search and often produce good referrals that come to their attention. Be aware, though, of negative effects on your current job status if your supervisor and colleagues know you are "looking." Informing your supervisor is a matter of very special timing. To avoid possible problems, do not inform your supervisor or colleagues of a pending job opportunity until you are a finalist for the position or unless they are likely to be called as a reference.

If nothing of interest develops for you, the process may take longer or require an even broader search. Some employment agencies claim to broker positions in higher education. Proceed with caution if utilizing "professional" agencies, as fees are usually required and can be substantial.

Your résumé should be updated periodically, but especially before a job search. Make it accurate and attractive. Use the résumé to chronicle your education and work experience and to highlight your strengths. Be complete in describing your positions, but do not go into great detail. The time for detail and explanation is during the interview. Your résumé is your first and best opportunity to demonstrate your ability to communicate. No other rules for résumé form or content apply! Do not finalize the résumé until you are ready to submit it for a specific job opening. Specifically address the position you are seeking.

A cover letter is absolutely essential when submitting your résumé for a position. The broader the search and the larger the applicant pool, the more important your letter and résumé are in the process. Your letter should accomplish several things. It should have an excellent appearance. It should communicate your interest in the position and describe your special qualifications. It should address the specific needs expressed in the job announcement and demonstrate your ability to communicate in writing. It should be absolutely unique for the position applied for and quickly set you apart from the countless others who apply. Your cover letter and résumé are the only way from the application process to the interview. They must pass the screening and reading of busy people and, often, a search committee. The importance of presenting yourself in writing requires that you give it great attention. Consult some of the many career self-help books available in bookstores and libraries on how to prepare effective cover letters and résumés.

Listing references is a tricky business. References listed can be an important indicator to a reader of your résumé, but calling the reference list is rarely how serious reference checks are accomplished. Colleagues and associates are more likely to be called than the names you provide, if reference checks are included in a search process. A list of references should be included with your résumé only if references are requested in the application process. One way to handle the references if you are not conducting an open or active search is to state that references will be provided if you become a finalist for the position. Never send unsolicited letters of reference.

Special thought should be given to your references, depending on the position you are seeking, and, of course, you should secure advance permission from each reference cited. Your list should include both internal and external names and should include your immediate supervisor or someone in your chain of command. If your job search is not known to your superiors, you may choose to include a former supervisor. Each person will make this decision based on his or her circumstances. Omitting the name of someone in your chain of command is a warning signal to many readers and will almost always require an explanation at a later point. At some point in this process, you should inform your supervisor. He or she could be called without your knowledge, which could be embarrassing and counterproductive to your present and future employment.

When you are called and invited for an interview, you can expect the full range of emotions about a job change to kick in. With excitement and anxiety, your most serious preparation in the job search process begins. Find out as much as you can about the situation for which you are interviewing. Use public information, such as college catalogs and World Wide Web pages. Read any background information that may be sent to you ahead of the interview, and consider requesting any materials you do not get and consider important. Call someone you know in that department or institution and ask him or her for information about the situation. If you don't know anyone there, call someone who may. The point is to find out what their real needs are and to be prepared to show that you are the one to meet those needs.

Once the preparation is done and the interview begins, the key is to relax and be confident in yourself. Be prepared to give a statement about your thoughts on various aspects of the job, such as how recruiting is the first step in retention or the role of technology in delivering student services. Be prepared to answer the same question several times, such as why you are interested in this job and your "management style." Be prepared to talk about yourself but also to listen to and understand the problems being presented to you. Do not attempt to solve their problems, but identify with them. If meeting with different groups, anticipate and address their different needs. Staff groups will want to know your work style. Management groups will want to know your performance history. Academic administrators will want to know that you understand their role in the institution and their interest in your position.

The interview is an exciting and exhausting event. Some positions will require a multiple-day interview with evening meetings and meals. You are certainly on display during the interview, and you must rise to the occasion. You also must evaluate the position from a firsthand view. You should be prepared with significant questions to ask along the way, from "What is your expectation of this position?" to "How accessible are you to your subordinates?" Try to determine, both in advance and during the interview, what you need to know about the position or the situation in order to make a decision if you are offered the job.

Notice that salary, benefits, and other negotiated items have not been discussed during the interview, and they should not be until an offer is made or about to be made. Negotiated items can include budget, staffing, computer support, faculty rank and tenure, teaching load, moving costs, temporary housing, spousal employment, and certain benefit packages. You may engage in some conversations as these issues come up, but don't commit or exclude yourself too early in the process over negotiated items. Starting salary can be negotiated for most positions. Once you are identified as the selected candidate, you are in the best position to state your salary needs and any other requirements, such as previous commitments and physical adjustments. The new employer will let you know if your needs are beyond the institution's ability to meet. At this point, it wants you and it will work to get you. Be honest and reasonable in stating your needs and you should reach a satisfactory agreement with your new employer.

Making the Transition

When you have reached a satisfactory agreement and accepted the position, the excitement really begins — and so does the celebration! Congratulations are in order, but time is not on your side. Not only do you need to plan for the move to your new position, but you must also notify your current employer and plan for the transitions that are ahead. Always leave with professionalism, and don't burn your bridges. You will want to finish or hand off your current projects. Determine a realistic work plan for the time remaining and don't neglect essential duties, such as performance appraisals for staff. Talk openly and frankly to staff, associates, and superiors about the state of your affairs so that good decisions about your successor can be made. Make recommendations and offer advice, but don't expect to make the decisions. You will find that "lame ducks" get to handle items of decreasing importance as their time to departure nears. Be available and gracious about farewells and sendoffs. Closure is important for your colleagues as well as for you.

Arriving on the new job offers many opportunities. The "honeymoon" is really a time for getting to know your new environment in a very forgiving period. You will have opportunities for sharing your thoughts and plans as you meet people and attend meetings for the first time. The more you have thought about and planned for your new beginning, the faster you can establish yourself. Do not be surprised if you are considered an expert or asked for advice. New people always have a fresh perspective to offer, and your new colleagues will be interested in your ideas early on. Be cautioned to not make big decisions or commitments too early that you may regret as you become better informed later. Recall the earlier comments in this chapter on the skills and behaviors for moving up and re-employ them in your new job. They apply equally now as then.

Contributing to the Profession

You know that your mentors have been helpful to you in your career path in enrollment services. What you may also notice is that you are becoming a mentor to others. This is an important role and should be taken seriously. As you advance in the profession, you have more and more to share with others. Mentoring younger professionals is one way to do that. Participating in professional associations is another. Professional associations often provide the vehicle for writing and speaking on your expertise. Adding to the body of knowledge and advancing the profession are the responsibility of all who benefit from it. Consider participation and leadership in your professional association. It is a very fulfilling activity. For a more extended discussion of professional development and these topics, read Chapter 7.

Participation in professional activities also gives you an opportunity to build your professional network. Your network is who you know, who knows you, and who will support you. It is an essential part of many job advancements. It helps you increase your value to your employer, as you will have access to other "experts" at various times. Professional association activity gives you an opportunity to network via programs, contacts, recognition in the profession, "résumé-building" with your contributions, etc.

Final Thoughts

The leadership of enrollment services offices in the next five to ten years will more than likely come from the ranks of those employed in these fields now. Younger employees should prepare themselves now for these positions by working hard and distinguishing themselves from their peers. Assistant and associate directors and registrars should employ the steps to take care of the people in their areas and build a record of success for the future. The road to moving up in enrollment services is there for those who want to take the journey. Have fun moving up!

Chapter 11

Future of the Profession

by Nancy C. Sprotte

Introduction

In October 1995, the AACRAO Task Force on the Role and Mission of Student Enrollment Services met in Chicago. These senior campus administrators had shared initial thoughts and concepts on the topic by e-mail. When they finally met for two days of discussion, they were able to clearly articulate a number of conclusions about the future of enrollment services. From this, they addressed how our professional colleagues must step up to the new challenges facing us. I came away from that discussion with a great optimism that, within AACRAO, we have visionary leaders who can guide us in our journey.

The members of that Task Force have many years of service to higher education, and they represent many types of institutions. I thank them for their contributions to my own thinking and the work of AACRAO. The Task Force members, in addition to myself, are:

> David J. Harbeck (Chair), Vice President, Information Systems and Admissions and Records, Tulsa Junior College

---

Nancy C. Sprotte has served San Diego State University for fifteen years as the Director of Admissions and Records and, most recently, as Assistant Vice President for Student Affairs. Prior to that, she was Assistant Admissions Officer at San Jose State University and Registrar at San Francisco State University.

Culminating six years on the Board of Directors for AACRAO, she served as President in 1994-1995. During her term of office, the Association expanded activities in international education and began to redefine the role of enrollment services in higher education. She continues to contribute to these areas as well as the expanding role of virtual learning environments.

John M. Finney, Associate Dean and University Registrar, University of Puget Sound

Glenn Irvin, Dean of Instruction, California Polytechnic State University, San Luis Obispo

David C. Lanier, University Registrar, University of North Carolina-Chapel Hill

Millard (Pete) Storey, Director of Admissions, University of Wisconsin-Madison

Jerry Sullivan, Director of Financial Aid, University of Colorado, Boulder; on assignment for 1995-96 as Director, Systems Development Task Force, U.S. Department of Education

James Wager, University Registrar, Pennsylvania State University-Main Campus

Causes of Change

There are several broad areas in which we are experiencing changes, and they are expected to continue into the future. These include student demographics, information technology, and politics and economics.

The "babyboomlet" of students coming through the elementary and secondary systems will soon be entering higher education. The rates of change vary from state to state, but generally, the ethnic and racial backgrounds of these students are increasingly diverse across the country. This second tidal wave is occurring just at the moment when economic stresses on the country and the states are causing reductions in funding to higher education, which will limit access.

Our colleges and universities will continue to be challenged by demographic changes. They will require that we rethink traditional learning styles as the student population becomes even more diverse. Students from diverse cultures and languages will tax our ability to remain culturally aware of and sensitive to differences in an ever-growing ethnocentric environment. Colleges and universities must find ways to help everyone understand that differences are to be appreciated — not feared.

Many students have other responsibilities that limit their ability to be traditional students, attending classes on a full-time basis for four years, in order to complete a degree. Many colleges and universities, especially public institutions, find that large numbers of their students work half-time or more; others have family responsibilities that interfere with their ability to attend school on a full-time basis. Some students are returning to school for training in new fields, as economic or corporate downsizing has eliminated their jobs. Our institutions will need to find new ways to deliver instruction to students who cannot routinely come to campus but who wish to complete a degree or update their formal education.

The revolution in information technology has caused fundamental changes in many aspects of our endeavors. America now finds itself competing in a technology-driven, global economy that has eroded the premise of high-volume, standardized, stable mass production. The rapid advances in information technology have affected the colleges and universities. Information of all types that formerly had limited distribution is now widely available across — and outside of — institutions of higher education. Increasing numbers of our students have grown up with access to computers or interactive video games. This experience has changed the tasks we perform daily, our service expectations, and the ways we relate and communicate with one another.

Changes in the politico-economic system, driven largely by the revolution in information technology, are requiring greater access to educational services. If the coming onslaught of students does not receive adequate education and they do not become full participants in the politico-economic system, the future and security of all citizens are uncertain.

Over the last several years, state and federal support for higher education has been dwindling, causing increased tuition rates in both public and private institutions. Reduced resources have begun to affect the ability of many colleges and universities to ensure that all who qualify academically will be able to enroll without regard to their socio-economic status.

Direct support to public institutions in most states has declined. At both the federal and state levels, student financial aid has not been able to keep up with the increasing costs. More emphasis is placed on loans to make up the difference between need and available grants and scholarships; therefore, students are leaving college with alarmingly high levels of debt. Increased pressure will be felt to find ways to hold costs down, in order to maintain and increase educational opportunity.

Resulting Changes

A number of specific changes have resulted from these broad causes. We have seen an increase in the *rate* of change. Communication and technology are moving through a rapid time of change. Easy access to worldwide information sometimes makes it difficult to sustain reflection and conversation. Advancements in science and technology (particularly in genetics, biomedicine, etc.) are so rapid that we spend little time questioning the ethics and social consequences of this technology. How will colleges and universities ensure that this critical questioning takes place against what arguably is potential economic growth?

It appears that the public is losing confidence in postsecondary education. Numerous stories in the media express doubt and concern over major college athletics, faculty productivity, and the relevance of academic offerings. Coupled with these concerns is the constant reminder that postsecondary education costs annually exceed the rate of inflation. Student-Right-to-Know legislation requires colleges and universities to report graduation rates for their students, so that parents and students can compare outcomes among institutions. It is likely that publics will expect colleges and universities to be introspective and to institute processes that will ensure that critical analysis is being done to improve quality. Failure to do this will create even more suspicion from legislatures, educational agencies, corporations, parents, and students.

The term "workplace" is taking on a whole new meaning. Emerging information and new systems are opening the way for new methods of processing data and doing work. More and more employees will find themselves working "at home" and will not need to work at a central location. How will this influence traditional management functions? Does this mean that middle management will no longer be needed? Will the concept of departments and divisions be eliminated, because those functions are now being done through advanced technology? Will higher education be at the forefront in the preparation of the workforce for this change? To survive, colleges, and universities will be required to meet this challenge.

The interest in internationalism is increasing on campuses. Students will have to be prepared to work in international environments and markets. Social, cultural, political, and economic interactions between America and other countries will become more common and fluid. Many institutions are increasing efforts to internationalize their curricula and to develop international exchange programs for faculty and students. Some colleges and universities are also seeking to increase international student enrollment for fiscal reasons.

Customer orientation is growing on our campuses. Colleges and universities, like the organizations outside them, will be more concerned with providing quality services. Stakeholders in institutions will demand greater access, responsiveness, and accountability. Accountability will increasingly take the form of demonstrating value for investment to the educational consumer.

There will be more differentiation of institutions. Major institutions can no longer be all things to all people. Institutional missions will be more sharply focused and resources aligned accordingly. Student markets will be more segmented and defined.

We will be called upon to develop and expand postsecondary/K-12 relationships. The "K-16 system" will achieve greater articulation, with students at earlier ages accessing knowledge not normally available until they reach higher education. Transfer of information and records from K through 16 will become more efficient and streamlined.

Colleges and universities will face increased competition from other providers of knowledge and training. An excellent example is the virtual university promulgated by the Western Governors Association. While the structure and functions of this are in the process of being determined, one criterion will be "independent — not controlled by those who represent established interests with regard to either the delivery of education or its certification." The governors are seeking to provide incentives for technologies to be used more fully in teaching and learning activities and to establish methods of assessing and certifying competencies and learning acquired via advanced technology. These opportunities would not be limited to our traditional colleges and universities.

Resulting Themes for Higher Education

From these changes some general themes emerge that will be central to higher education over the next decade. Institutions will be faced with continued pressure from the government, parents, and students to contain costs. Colleges and universities will seek to continue efforts to develop diversified faculty, staff, and student populations. This will occur during a time of significant changes in the demographics of our population and also when questions are being raised about affirmative action efforts that have helped campuses achieve these objectives in the past. Finally, questions are being asked about the level of preparation of large numbers of students entering our institutions.

Colleges and universities will be faced with continued pressure to contain costs, and that pressure will come from the government, parents, and students. They will expect us to operate our institutions in a much more effective and efficient, "business-like" manner. Most ongoing costs are related to faculty; therefore, we can expect increased interest in faculty workload and the use of mediated instruction as a way to reach more students with fewer faculty resources. We can then expect strong faculty and union backlash as traditional pedagogical processes are challenged. Enrollment services will be held to high standards of quality and timeliness, but new resources will rarely become available.

Financial aid resources will continue to erode, and students and parents will be expected to contribute more of their personal resources toward college expenses. Families will question high costs and probable indebtedness for higher education. It is very critical that we carry the message that a college education is a worthwhile investment. The 1995 *Economic Report of the President* (1995, 174) found thatthe income gap between male high school graduates and those with four-year college degrees increased by nearly 20 percent between 1979 and 1993, as measured in 1993 dollars.

Colleges and universities will continue efforts to develop diversified faculty, staff, and student populations in order to reflect changes in the demographics of the population we serve. This will occur at a time when legal roadblocks are being erected against affirmative action efforts that have helped campuses achieve these objectives in the past. As campus leaders in the area of enrollment services, we must continue seeking a diversified campus. We will also need to convince many others outside the institution that it is in the best interest of the students we seek to educate and for society as a whole. At the same time, we must develop admission requirements and processes that select students who can most benefit from the education we offer them and who will contribute to the campus community and society in general after they leave us. If we lose legal support for affirmative action, we will have to be aggressive and creative in our strategies to recruit, enroll, and graduate students from underrepresented groups.

Finally, there is concern about the level of preparation of large numbers of entering students. More students educationally disadvantaged during their K-12 years are arriving at our institutions without adequate preparation to begin a full load of college-level courses. This is a particular problem for state colleges and universities that lack selective admission requirements. In most cases, students may meet published minimum admission requirements, but they lack sufficient language and mathematics skills to be competitive in college courses; they may not be able to progress at the rate students and educators alike would like to see. These students may have the motivation to succeed, but they lack a strong academic preparation or the study skills needed to succeed in a competitive college environment. They may come from an impoverished high school or community; they may have language problems because they are recent immigrants or live in households where English is not the primary language; they may have diagnosed learning or physical difficulties or they may have learning disabilitiest that have gone undiagnosed. As leaders in the enrollment services area, we must increase our early outreach activities to help these students prepare for college. When they arrive on our campus, we must provide the support needed to allow them to catch up with other students and to compete successfully.

New Expectations for Enrollment Services Professionals

It is critical that we move the student enrollment services profession from a track of being too technical and specialized. We must recognize that those who have roles in the traditional areas of the registrar, admissions, financial aid, institutional research, and others are needed to provide leadership, coordination, and cooperation. Without this, these positions will not be seen as important players on the campus and we will be relegated to minor professional roles.

New organizational structures and changing theories of leadership and management help define our roles. We see more integration of the various functions that support the academic mission of the university or college. A broadly defined area of enrollment services can be envisioned by AACRAO as an expanded set of intersecting circles representing the four domains of enrollment services work:

- Enrollment Management
- Instructional Management
- Information Technology
- Student Services

(Note: two other domains — professional stature and leadership — are discussed in chapters 1, 2, 5, and 7.) Within each circle, we find traditional role, as well as new or redefined functional areas of work.

Enrollment Management

A number of activities have been identified as those that must be addressed if a college or university is to meet its enrollment objectives. Traditionally, this began with admissions and recruitment activities.

More recently, responsibility for financial aid, housing, testing and placement, and orientation have been among those included within a broader range of enrollment management activities.

From the beginning, our admissions colleagues must be part of defining the institution's image: we have the best knowledge of applicant, parent, and counselor needs, desires, and perceptions. We must improve our skills in analyzing the source of students and determining where our students will be coming from in the future. The admissions officer must be accurate in determining what types of students are needed by the campus, and then guide the campus in achieving its enrollment targets. It is critical to build teamwork with the financial aid officer, for student aid is an important factor in attracting and retaining students. We must better articulate the best recruitment strategies to the CEO or the board. We must master new skills in development of marketing strategies, be very clear, collect and interpret the data, and build a persuasive case for the recruitment and admissions plans.

Instructional Management

The functions of the registrar have expanded from those of enrolling students and recording their grades. Many have assumed responsibility for institutional research activities. Curricula planning and advising bring together student and faculty activities.

Registrar professionals must improve interpersonal skills and become proactive in providing leadership in building systems and providing the coordination of efforts in delivering student services. We cannot be comfortable being only technical in nature. Rather, we must be innovators for systematic improvements, and we must be seen as a source of information for campus-wide decision making.

Information Technology

Computers have changed almost everything we do in enrollment offices. Formerly, central functions of the campus computing center, now many activities are within our offices. Computers are now used extensively in student learning support services, language and design labs, and the library.

We must explore new technologies that will enhance efforts to provide student services and support campus functions. We must have the necessary skills to provide needed leadership to an increasingly technical staff. Legal issues will continue to develop and evolve along with the technological environment of the campus, and we must lead the campus community in addressing these.

Student Services

Many student support services are now considered critical to the total campus recruitment and retention program; in many cases, they have been integrated within enrollment management areas. Examples of these activities include career planning and employment, health services, residence life, and student activities.

Providing a safe and nurturing environment supports student learning and improves retention. Programs to prepare students for the world of work or graduate study will contribute to student satisfaction and help meet future enrollment goals. As professionals in these areas, we must lead the campus in providing high-quality support programs that are appropriate for the needs of our students, and we must encourage their full integration into the academic fabric of the campus.

Within the universe of the college or university management system, these domains may report to any area of the campus. Often, some or all of these functions will report to the chief academic officer or the chief student affairs officer. The reporting structure is not as important as the working relationships that are established.

As we think about AACRAO membership, it is also possible to envision layers within that model. Although we represent different institutional types, we operate within one of the four domains; with experience and expertise, we move into the professional stature and leadership domains. We may work at four-year institutions, professional schools, community colleges, international programs, proprietary institutions, or high schools. In some cases, we, or the functions we perform, may even move between layers, if we are involved in activities that assist students moving between sectors. An example of this might be those who work in high school and college articulation efforts or those who work in the overseas program of a U.S. College or university.

Membership in professional associations such as AACRAO can help us shape the future of higher education. Professional programs and workshops, publication resources, and the network of other professionals allow us to keep abreast of trends that affect students and our institutions. Through knowledge, we are in a better position to help formulate and influence policy at the national, state, and local levels. However, we must first fully understand past policies and practices, trends in demographics, the changing social and political environment, and emerging technologies that can affect our students and our institutions.

Active participation in associations such as AACRAO gives us an opportunity to be players in this. We may gain experience in research and development of public policy or institutional processes. The professional networks we develop become far-reaching resources to tap as we face specific issues in our work at the college or university. Many colleagues can already attest to the value of posing a question or problem on a professional electronic list. Inquiries to such lists as AACRAO-NASPA's EN-ROLL-L can result in immediate feedback that has helped colleagues design or defend a process or policy the campus was considering.

As we move within and between domains, we may also find it valuable to look at the offerings of other associations or those offered in conjunction with AACRAO's professional development programs. For example, if we function within a student affairs arena on the campus, we may want to consider membership or participation in the National Association of Student Personnel Administrators; we may want to attend local programs or subscribe to literature sponsored by NASPA. If we work in instructional management activities, participation in the Association for Institutional Research (AIR) or the National Academic Advising Association (NACADA) may complement our knowledge and skills. *The Chronicle of Higher Education* publishes information about professional programs. If you want to develop a particular area of expertise in your current job, if you seek career changes, or if you want to look at your own work from an outside perspective, it is possible to identify programs of interest.

The future of the profession will be exciting. Changes in student demographics, developments in information technology, and political and economic changes will affect how we move our institutions and higher education into the next century. Effective leaders will be knowledgeable about the domains occupied by the enrollment services professional, and they will exercise leadership within the campus and higher education communities. It will be important for us to continue a program of lifelong learning and professional development. We must seek formal and informal training from a variety of sources, and we must read and consult extensively to be aware of trends in education, students, and technology. You are to be commended for your commitment to higher education, and I encourage you to step up to the challenge of the exciting future ahead of us.

References

Western Governors' Association. 1996. *A western virtual university*. Denver CO. http://www.westgov.org/smart/vu/vu.html.

Economic report of the President transmitted to the Congress February 1995. 1995. Washington DC: United States Government Printing Office.

Appendix A

AACRAO as a Resource

The American Association of Collegiate Registrars and Admissions Officers, founded in 1910, serves enrollment officers via its products and services and provides an outstanding vehicle for members to learn, share, network, and achieve personal and professional growth.

As a nonprofit, voluntary professional association, AACRAO serves the educational community by promoting the advancement of education and the professional development of its members. More than 2,400 institutions and 8,800 individuals make AACRAO a dynamic, member-driven organization.

AACRAO's policies and priorities are established by its Board of Directors and guided by its Constitution and Bylaws. The Association's mission and strategic plan are carried out by committees and task forces coordinated by an elected board made up of nine officers. Daily administration is conducted from the National Office at the National Center for Higher Education, One Dupont Circle, in Washington, DC.

Products and Services

Professional Development

The Annual Meeting is AACRAO's premier event, bringing together some 2,500-3,000 enrollment services officers from the U.S., Canada, and many other nations. It is held in early to mid- April at various large cities whose hotels and convention centers can accommodate its members and their needs and interests. Some 200-300 half- and full-day workshops and program sessions offer the latest in theory as well as practice, ranging from leadership and management development to new trends and legislation to technology applications. Keynote and Plenary Sessions bring in top speakers on major issues confronting the profession. The Technology Center offers demonstrations of cutting-edge advancements, while the Exhibit Hall provides opportunities for the 100+ vendors of enrollment-related goods and services to interact with attendees. Tours, events, and social gatherings afford ample opportunities for attendees to share ideas, network, and refresh themselves during their time away from campus.

AACRAO also offers a variety of focused workshops, conferences, and seminars throughout the year. Some are clearly the premier event for their specialty, such as the annual Strategic Enrollment Management (SEM) conference, the Electronic Data Interchange (EDI) in Education conference, or the FERPA workshops. Others may be more broad-based and offered on an irregular or one-time basis. Watch AACRAO publications and promotional materials for topics, dates, descriptions, locations, and registration information.

AACRAO members receive discounts on registration fees for association professional development events.

Committees and Task Forces are the action units in which the real contributions of members are made. Volunteers serve on groups in their specific areas of interest, ranging from developing program sessions for the Annual Meeting to making recommendations to the Association on major issues requiring member input and expertise. Involvement ladders allow members to move quickly from beginning committee members through senior officer positions, gaining new knowledge, skills, and friends in a challenging, interesting, and often fun process.

Publications

Membership in AACRAO brings with it the following publications of timely importance on subjects of great interest to enrollment leaders:

The AACRAO Data Dispenser, the general newsletter published ten times per year, covers everything from association news to publication announcements, new federal legislation, feature articles, and advertising.

College & University, AACRAO's quarterly refereed journal, provides a variety of articles related to all enrollment-related areas, including emerging issues, new techniques, and technology in higher education.

AACRAO NetNews, a monthly electronic newsletter, features news and articles of interest to members with electronic mail.

AACRAO's Web Site (www.aacrao.com) is a dynamic, user-driven compendium of information about all of the association's events, publications, and services.

The *AACRAO Member Guide*, the annual member directory, helps take the work out of networking.

Transfer Credit Practices of Designated Educational Institutions describes transfer credit acceptance practices within each state.

And finally AACRAO members receive substantial discounts on all publications as they are released.

Services

The AACRAO Membership Services Department stands ready to assist members with any issues relating to their membership, as well as to respond to policy or procedure questions on enrollment issues.

The Consultant Referral Service, upon request, connects members to experienced education administrative consultants for advice and direction and offers a vehicle for members to serve as consultants themselves.

The Office of International Education Services guides members in foreign credential evaluation through counseling, training, conferences, and extensive publications.

The SPEEDE Project offers guidance, training, and support to member institutions using or hoping to use electronic data interchange to automate receipt of admissions applications, exchange of academic records, and other administrative data exchange processes. The AACRAO Standards Council provides monitoring, information, and oversight for national and international EDI standards.

AACRAO Corporate Members include corporations, companies, and individuals which offer enrollment-related products and services used by member campuses. Their participation in exhibits at various meetings, support through sponsorships, and advertising of offerings places people, information, and applications at the ready as members seek to purchase, lease, or outsource from these partners in enrollment success.

Professional and Private Practice Liability Insurance, essential to any administrator making decisions that affect students, is available through the Trust for Insuring Educators.

Additional insurance programs are offered, including term life, accidental death and dismemberment, major medical, disability income, and hospital helper insurance, headstart, cancer, short-term medical, excess major medical supplement, and long-term care insurance.

The Awards of Recognition Program acknowledges members for their achievements in and contributions to the profession.

Other Associations

Enrollment services leaders also have other associations available to enhance their professional development. Many of the following, which are meant to be suggestive, but not inclusive, offer a variety of valuable experiences depending on individual's interests, abilities, and career plans:

ACT
2201 North Dodge St.
P.O. Box 168
Iowa City, IA 52243
Telephone: 319/337-1028
Fax: 319/337-1059

American College Personnel Association
One Dupont Circle, NW, Suite 300
Washington, DC 20036
Telephone: 202/835-ACPA (2272)
Fax: 202/296-3286

The College Board
45 Columbus Ave.
New York, NY 10023-6992
Telephone: 212/713-8000
Fax: 212/713-8255

NAFSA: Association of International Educators
1875 Connecticut Ave, Suite 1000
Washington, DC 20009
Telephone: 202/462-4811
Fax: 202/667-3419

National Association for College Admission Counseling
1631 Prince St.
Alexandria, VA 22314
Telephone: 703/836-2222
Fax: 703/836-8015

National Association of Student Financial Aid Administrators
1920 L St., NW, Suite 200
Washington, DC 20036
Telephone: 202/785-0453
Fax: 202/785-1487

National Association of Student Personnel Administrators
1875 Connecticut Ave., NW, Suite 418
Washington, DC 20009

Telephone: 202/265-7500
Fax: 202/797-1157

Note: While the associations noted above tend to involve many enrollment professionals, a large number of education associations that are not cited here may also provide activities, resources, and publications of interest. Contact the AACRAO National Office at 202/293-9161 for more specific areas of association interests.

Appendix B

Professional Practices and Ethical Standards: Code of Ethics

The American Association of Collegiate Registrars and Admissions Officers (AACRAO) is vitally concerned with the advancement of postsecondary education and the standards and conduct of those who are involved in the professions at all levels. To provide guidance to these professionals, AACRAO has adopted the following principles which exemplify those qualities and attributes that distinguish members of the association both past and present.

AACRAO members shall:

Believe in and be loyal to the philosophy and goals of the profession and the institutions we serve.

Understand and respect the civil and human rights and responsibilities of all individuals while supporting and protecting the principles of due process and confidentiality.

Adhere to the principles of equality and nondiscrimination without regard to race, color, creed, gender, sexual orientation, age, disability or national origin.

Represent an institutional or Association perspective without vested interests or personal bias.

Initiate policies which support the goals of our profession.

Assert ourselves when policies or practices are proposed which seem to be contrary to the philosophy and goals of our professions and our institutions.

Participate in and contribute to professional activities and their development to ensure effective and efficient management of resources, data, and personnel.

Communicate an accurate interpretation of our institutions's admissions criteria, educational costs, financial aid availability, and major offerings to assist prospective students and their parents in making an informed decision.

Assist in improving educational standards and methods of evaluation at the institutional, state, and federal level so that grading is meaningful in reflecting the academic achievement of students.

Understand and appreciate the dynamics of interpersonal relationships when dealing with students, parents, faculty, administration, associates, and the public.

Develop and implement effective management systems which will ensure integrity, confidentiality and security of institutional records and provide an accurate interpretation of such information.

Dedicate ourselves to the ideals and principles that will enable students to develop their talents and interests to become responsible citizens and contributors to the improvement of society.

Practice honesty and integrity in our professions and in our lives.

Glossary

This glossary[1] defines the terms commonly used across the enrollment services profession that you may hear frequently. Please keep in mind that these are "generic" definitions — that is, general understandings of their meaning as used widely throughout the United States. Some campus-specific definitions may vary considerably from broader usage in the profession. And you will find that other institutions or organizations may define or apply them somewhat differently as well.

academic advising: assistance from faculty or professional staff to help the student choose (based on an evaluation of courses taken, including transferred courses) and register for courses leading to a chosen academic goal, degree, and career.

academic dismissal or suspension: indicates an individual's involuntary separation from the institution for failure to maintain academic standards. Academic suspension differs from academic dismissal in that suspension implies or states conditions under which readmission will be permitted. The transcript should clearly note academic dismissal or suspension at least while the suspension, and dismissal remain in effect.

academic forgiveness or bankruptcy: a policy employed at some institutions whereby certain portions of a student's prior educational history are removed from the computation of the student's cumulative credit and grade point average totals. A typical institutional policy includes the removal of all or a portion of the prior academic record from the cumulative totals after a specified period of nonattendance at that or other institutions. Most policies on academic forgiveness or bankruptcy require

---

[1]Copyright 1993, Council for the Advancement and Support of Education. Adopted with permission from *Training New Admissions Recruiters: A Guide for Survival and Success*, edited by Roger Swanson and Christine Kajikawa Wilkinson, pages 67-72.

Copyright 1996, American Association of Collegiate Registrars and Admissions Officers. Adopted with permission from *AACRAO Academic Record and Transcript Guide*, prepared by the AACRAO Task Force on the Academic Record and Transcript Guide, pages 34-37.

the student to request this process; it is not usually automatic. On the other hand, many institutions have a "repeat policy" which allows the first or all prior attempts of the same course to be excluded from the cumulative totals and cumulative grade point average. It is important that the history be removed only from the cumulative totals. No courses or grades should be deleted from the academic record or transcript.

academic probation or warning: denotes that a student's academic performance is below standard as defined by the institution. Although helpful for advising purposes, academic probation notations on the transcript are of questionable value because of the irregular duration of this status, the lack of uniformity of applications, and the frequent misinterpretation of its significance by recipients of transcripts. It is recommended that notations about this status not appear on the student transcript.

academic record: that document or electronic image maintained by the office of the registrar that reflects the unabridged academic history of the student at the institution. It contains a chronological listing of the student's total quantitative and qualitative learning experience and may include any information pertinent to the evaluation.

achievement tests: tests offered by the College Board that measure content knowledge in selected discipline areas; may be required for admission by some institutions.

ACT Code: assigned by the American College Testing Program to colleges and universities in the United States and Canada.

admission: acceptance as a student for a degree program who may enroll for classes, pay fees, earn credit, etc.

admission certificate/notice: the notification, usually mailed, confirming an applicant's approval for admission.

admission (eligibility) index: a combination of academic indicators (e.g., GPA or class rank and test score) used as an admission standard.

admission standards/requirements: **minimum criteria** that applicants must meet in order to be admitted.

advancement or admission to candidacy in graduate degrees: denotes that a graduate student has achieved advancement to degree candidacy. The notation on the transcript includes the date of the achievement.

Advanced Placement (AP): a series of tests that high school students can take to receive college credit, or the courses designated to prepare them for these tests.

Glossary

alumni rep: an alum who volunteers to represent his or her college or disseminate information in a variety of settings (e.g., college night).

ANSI or the American National Standards Institute: an organization whose purpose is to set standards of all types in the United States. One of its many committees is the Accredited Standards Committee X12, which sets national standards for the exchange of electronic data.

applicant for admission: one who has submitted an application and fee to be considered for admission; completion of the application process may require additional materials for evaluation or admission (e.g., transcripts, test scores).

application fee (and waiver): amount of money (nonrefundable) that the applicant must send with the application to be reviewed for admission; some institutions may grant waivers for economically disadvantaged students.

articulation agreement: a list of academic courses that two institutions have agreed are of equivalent academic content and credit, usually for determining fulfillment of graduation requirements; most useful for a community college student who is planning to transfer to a baccalaureate institution and is selecting courses to meet its graduation requirements.

average college costs or budget: the total estimated academic year costs of attending an institution, including registration fee/tuition, room and board, books and supplies, transportation, and personal expenses; will vary depending upon whether the student lives on or off campus; used to offer cost comparisons among institutions.

basis for admission: usually, either high school graduation or equivalent, or transfer from another college or university. Other bases of admission may include admission by examination, individual approval, and conditional admission.

calendar system: defines the type of academic session (e.g., semester, quarter, trimester, or term).

career placement: services to prepare and assist students to find jobs and fulfill career goals.

CEEB Code: assigned by the Educational Testing Service and authorized by the College Entrance Examination Board, commonly known as The College Board. The CEEB code is assigned to colleges and universities in the United States and Canada.

Glossary

CIP, or the Classification of Instructional Programs: a coding structure administered by the U.S. Department of Education National Center for Education Statistics to classify academic programs by content.

class rank: describes the position of a student in an academic grouping. Class rank should not be released unless accompanied by a statement that defines the basis of computation.

CLEP (College Level Examination Program): a series of tests by which people (often nontraditional) can earn college credit; acceptance varies by institution.

college fair: an event at which college and or alumni/ae admissions representatives from several institutions are available to provide information to prospective students and/or their families; it could occur at a high school, community college, business, civic organization, etc.

college night: an evening college fair.

college prep courses: courses having specific academic content (e.g., algebra, English) required as minimum preparation for admission.

college rankings: the relative position of institutions that are supposed to be the best in given categories (e.g., regional liberal arts), as determined annually according to criteria of a variety of publications; such recognition of your college may be an element of your marketing effort.

common application form: a single form used by more than one institution: a student can file for financial aid at nearly any school on a common form, while common admission forms are usually used by campuses within the same "system."

concentration/specialization: an area usually within a major that clusters selected courses around a common theme, focus, or orientation.

concurrent enrollment: a special registration category that allows a student to enroll for courses even though that student is not admitted to a degree program and may be enrolled at the same time at another institution.

Continuing Education Unit (CEU): represents 10 contact hours of participation in an organized continuing education experience under responsible sponsorship, capable direction, and qualified instruction. CEUs are not academic credits and are not applicable toward an academic degree.

co-op education: a program in which students are placed in career positions in which they learn skills and knowledge, gain experience, and receive a salary and, perhaps, academic credit.

course identification: typically includes the discipline or department abbreviation, course number, descriptive title, and number of credits associated with the course. An explanation of the numbering system specifying remedial or developmental, basic, intermediate, advanced, and graduate level courses, as well as lower and upper division offerings, or other variations or classifications in local use (e.g., courses open to both undergraduate and graduate students) should be included in the transcript key. The specific descriptive title by which each course was designated in that year's catalog should be given. The level and subject of any practice teaching should be clearly indicated. Abbreviations often are necessary, but care should be taken to make them intelligible.

credit conversion: from quarter hour credits to semester hour credits; done by multiplying the number of quarter credits by two-thirds. Conversely, to convert from semester hour credits to quarter hour credits, multiply the number of semester hour credits by 1.5. If an institution changes its credit hour type, then a remark should be placed on the transcript at the time the conversion is done to indicate that all entries from that point on are in the new units of credit.

credential program: a specified group of academic courses and, perhaps, other criteria (e.g., student teaching) that result in meeting the standards of an external agency related to professional qualification or recognition (e.g., teacher certification); may or may not be related to completion of degree requirements.

credit hour: the unit by which an institution measures its course work. The number of credit hours assigned to a course is usually defined by the number of hours per week in class and the number of weeks in the session. One credit hour is usually assigned to a class that meets fifty minutes a week over a period of a semester or quarter; in laboratory, fieldwork, drawing, music, physical education, or similar types of instruction, one credit hour is assigned for a session that meets two or three hours a week for a semester or quarter. Quarter credit hours and semester credit hours are the two most common systems of measuring course work. A credit hour earned over a ten-week quarter is equivalent to two-thirds of an hour earned over a sixteen-week semester.

cultural diversity/pluralism: broad representation of various cultural and ethnic groups for the enrichment of the campus climate.

database: in the broadest sense, includes all data collected and maintained by the institution in any form (paper, computer, microfilm, optical disk, etc.) It more commonly refers to those items of data that are maintained in the institutional computerized database for the student. Many of these data elements are stored as coded values in the computerized database.

dates of attendance: the starting and ending dates of the term or the course within the term. It is recommended that actual dates (month, day, and year) be designated for each course or term on the transcript whenever possible. If it is not possible, approximate dates may be designated by the academic year (i.e., Fall or First Semester and year). Summer sessions are generally by the calendar year. When designating terms on the academic year as first, second, etc., it is generally understood that they are numbered with the beginning of the academic year, i.e., the fall term. For special terms or sessions that do not fit the traditional calendars, it is even more important that the exact beginning and ending dates (day, month, year) be indicated.

deficiencies: areas in which an applicant is lacking and that must be made up prior to or following enrollment (e.g., a math course).

degree audit: an internal advising document that typically includes both degree and program requirements and also an extract of the academic history of the student. A typical degree audit program matches the requirements for the student's degree and program with the courses that the student has completed and is currently enrolled in. A degree audit frequently includes the academic status of the student, test scores, proficiencies completed, etc.

demographics: the social science of studying characteristics of people in groups (e.g., where they live and come from, who they are, statistics relating to them and their behavior).

demonstrated competencies: non-classroom experiences for which credit is awarded. Examples include military experience, life experiences, CLEP, AP, PEP, other nationally standardized examinations, and institutional examinations.

demonstrated proficiencies: typical degree or program requirements such as English or math proficiency, foreign language proficiency, public service, etc., that have been completed by the student. The institution maintains records of these proficiencies on the institutional database, but since no credit is usually awarded as a result of the completion, these demonstrated proficiencies are not included on the transcript.

denied: rejected for admission.

deposit: a fee required to confirm an admitted applicant's resolution to enroll; see intent-to-enroll; could also apply to other confirmation fees (e.g., for housing).

direct mail: targeting individually mailed letters or publications to prospective students who fit predefined qualifications, to elicit interest, application, or enrollment.

disadvantaged: those who, through lack of economic or educational opportunity, do not have full preparation for or access to college-level admission and academic success.

early action: a program in which the applicant applies to the institution of top choice and receives a decision well in advance of regular spring response dates.

early decision: a program in which a commitment is made by the applicant that, if admitted, he or she will enroll at the institution.

early outreach: efforts to educate and motivate elementary school students to higher education opportunities and advantages.

early semester system: fall semester starts around mid-August, and spring semester extends through mid-May.

educational equity: having percentages of particular classes (e.g., ethnic or gender groups) enrolled in the campus population proportionally equal to their percentages in the potential applicant cohort or in the general population.

Electronic Data Interchange, or EDI: the electronic exchange of documents directly from one computer to another using previously agreed upon, standard formats. One example of EDI is the use of the SPEEDE format to exchange student transcripts over an electronic network.

eligible to continue or re-enroll: an academic status which indicates the student may continue enrollment or may re-enroll at the institution without any special action required on the part of the student or the institution. The absence of any statement to the contrary on the transcript indicates that the student is academically eligible to continue or re-enroll for academic reasons. This status is appropriate whether or not the student is on academic probation at the institution or has been suspended or dismissed for other than academic reasons. The status of eligible to continue or return denotes academic status, only the record does not reflect ineligibility to re-enroll or continue because of disciplinary or other reasons than academic. If the student is ineligible to return for academic reasons, this should be clearly noted on the transcript.

ethnicity/ethnic identity: a person's self-identification (sometimes with required documentation) as to race/culture, usually during the admissions (optional) or registration process.

exchange student: a visiting student, often part of a formal academic program or contract with another campus, who enrolls for courses at the host institution for a limited period of time but plans to return to and graduate from his or her home institution.

faculty/student ratio: number of students per faculty member (e.g., 1:20), derived from enrollment divided by total faculty; used as an indicator of personal attention a student might expect from faculty (e.g., the lower the ratio, the more attention).

Federal Interagency Commission on Education (FICE) Code: federal agency administered and maintained by the U.S. Department of Education's National Center for Education Statistics. It is used to identify institutions of higher education in the United States.

fee payment: cash, check, money order, credit card, financial aid, etc., payment that allows the student to register for courses and entitles him or her other services and programs of the institution.

FERPA statement: a recommended statement to be included on the transcript to comply with FERPA requirements. A sample statement would be "The attached information has been forwarded to you at the request of the student with the understanding that it will not be released to other parties. The Family Educational Rights and Privacy Act of 1974, as Amended, prohibits release of this information without the student's consent. Please return this material to us if you are unable to comply with this condition of release." Other abbreviated statements that convey the same message are acceptable.

filing period: inclusive dates of a period during which applications for a given term are accepted for maximum consideration (e.g., November 1 through 30 for admission to fall quarter the following year).

financial aid: loans, grants, work-study, and/or scholarships used to pay for various costs associated with attending college, awarded by the institution; may be need-based or not.

general education/certification: areas of coursework (e.g., social sciences, science and mathematics, fine arts) required for graduation that provide academic breadth and depth; certification means these areas have been evaluated as being completed.

GPA (grade point average): an arithmetic ratio denoting the overall quality of a student's academic record; used in comparisons of the student with either a standard or with other students. The GPA is commonly calculated by (1) multiplying the credits for each course by the grade points associated with the grade earned, (2) totaling the points earned for all courses, and (3) dividing the total points by the total number of graded credits attempted as defined by the institution.

grade: a qualitative rating or evaluation of a student's achievement. Most frequently, it is expressed on a letter scale or in percentages. Grades of A, B, C, D correspond in a general way to the terms excellent, good, satisfactory, and lowest passing quality. The grade of F represents failure and is unacceptable for credit in a course. Some institutions use a plus or minus to further delineate a letter grade. Other grades sometimes used Pass/Fail, Pass/No Record, Satisfactory/Unsatisfactory, Credit/No Credit. (See narrative evaluation.)

grade points: numerical values assigned to letter grades in order to provide a basis for determination of grade point average; most common usage is the four-point system: A=4, B=3, C=2, D=1, F=0.

graduation statement: a remark on the transcript identifying degrees awarded by the issuing institution, including dates, majors, and honors, if applicable.

guaranteed admission: when a prospective student is promised admission contingent upon fulfillment of specified criteria (e.g., a minimum GPA, number of courses, etc.).

high school equivalency test: a test (e.g., the General Educational Development test, or GED) that, if passed, is accepted as demonstrating the equivalency of graduating from high school.

immediate outreach: recruitment of high school juniors and seniors and community college transfers to apply and enroll at an institution of higher education, usually within a year.

immunization: inoculation or other method to prevent contraction of an infectious disease; a requirement related to measles/rubella at many colleges.

impaction/oversubscription: a condition at an institution or within a major in which the number of applicants exceeds spaces availalble.

intent-to-enroll/register: indication by the response/reply date that an admitted applicant plans to enroll or register, often accompanied by a deposit.

intermediate outreach: efforts to educate and motivate freshman and sophomore high school students to higher education opportunities and advantages.

Glossary

International Baccalaureate: a formal academic program that offers an approved curriculum equal to college prep courses and a college-level entrance exam; it can be taken in many countries (and U.S. high schools) and is recognized worldwide; some college credit may be granted.

internship: a structured, time-specific learning assignment taken for academic credit with defined parameters and outcomes; often off campus.

key to the transcript: information provided to the recipient of the transcript to properly interpret the transcripted record. It is recommended that the key be printed on the back of the transcript, but it may be a separate document that accompanies each transcript issued.

last entry notation: the printed or stamped message or series of symbols signifying that no further entries should follow on a student's transcript.

learning disabled: one who has been certified through testing as having identified learning disabilities (e.g., dyslexia).

legacy: the child of an alum.

location and identification of the institution: includes the street address, city, state, ZIP code, and country, if applicable. It may also include other helpful identifying information, such as telephone and fax numbers, FICE, CEEB, and ACT codes.

macro-issues: refers to relationships with larger sectors, such as issues that affect all students.

major area of study: denotes the degree program within an academic discipline in which the student is enrolled. Similar terms sometimes used are minor, concentration or emphasis. One means of communicating this area is by the use of the U.S. Department of Education's National Center for Education Statistics Classification of Instructional Programs (CIP) codes.

major: a student's primary academic concentration as defined by courses (content and quantity) in the same or closely related departments.

marketing plan: the overall strategy by which an institution seeks to recruit its applicants; it is the product of demographic research, data-based decisions, and evaluated methodologies, and it is used to attract and enroll students with optimal qualifications as defined by the institution.

matriculation: after admission, enrolling in courses leading to completion of a degree.

micro-issues: refers to particular or singular cases or issues, such as individual students.

minor: an area of lesser academic concentration; different in content form but can be related to the major.

name changes: see name of student.

name of the institution: its corporate or legal name. In complex institutions, the names of separate administrative units and their locations may be different from the main campus.

name of student: information which includes family name and all other given names. Nicknames may be included in the institutional academic database, but are not used on the transcript. Institutions have no obligation to record name changes for students not currently enrolled, except as related to legal, documented sex changes. Name changes should be recorded only when requested and there is evidence of a legal basis for change.

narrative evaluation: a faculty assessment in written form of the quality and characteristics of student performance. The narrative may stand alone or supplement the conventional evaluation information; it usually includes a description of student performance and achievement.

nontraditional learning: college-level learning that takes place free of space and time limitations.

nontraditional student: one who differs from the profile of typical college-age students (e.g., older, disabled, or ethnic minority); outreach strategies to this kind of student tend to be very different, as they must respond to the needs of each unique group or even the individual being recruited; see returning re-entry student.

Nota bene: a Latin term meaning note well or take particular notice; often abbreviated as NB.

official transcript: a copy of a student's academic record that has been verified, usually by an institutional seal; an unofficial transcript is not so verified and will usually not be accepted by admissions offices.

on-line: an adjective that describes the relationship of an instrument such as a terminal or telephone to the computer that interprets and executes instructions.

open house/preview day: an on-campus recruitment event where a college hosts prospective students and their families to showcase the campus;

includes tours, academic programs, faculty presentations, food and entertainment, sports events, etc.

orientation: programs usually preceding the start of classes that help admitted students prepare for a successful academic, environmental, social, etc., adjustment to college; orientation may include social activities, advising, campus visits and tours, registration, and educational activities.

placement tests: tests to determine at what level or in what specific course a student should enroll, particularly in English, mathematics, and foreign languages.

post-bac student: a holder of one baccalaureate degree who enrolls for a second degree.

posthumous: after death, as in posthumous degree, a degree awarded after the recipient's death.

prior postsecondary education: includes names and locations of all colleges and universities previously attended, with periods of attendance and degrees.

privacy act ("Family Educational Rights and Privacy Act" or "Buckley Amendment" or "FERPA"): a 1974 federal law guaranteeing enrolled students confidentiality and access to their academic records, including all information related to a student's history and results of enrollment in courses plus any other information (e.g., residency data, counselor notes, disqualification actions) in the student's institutional record files.

private/independent/proprietary institution: an institution with no governing or fiscal ties to state or local government; may be a for-profit or not-for-profit institution.

prospect/prospective student: a person who has the potential of becoming a student at a particular institution.

provisional/conditional admission: the status whereby a student will be fully admitted if he or she fulfills one or more conditions (e.g., completes a specified course, forwards a final transcript).

public institution: one that is governed by a publicly appointed or selected board and funded in whole or in part by tax dollars.

quarter system: an academic calendar that divides the academic year into three roughly equal three-month periods; the summer quarter often equals each of the others in length.

rank in class: a student's academic standing vis-a-vis others in the class (e.g., upper 10 percent, 75th percentile, 25th out of 134.

regional rep: an admissions recruiter who lives in a geographical area distant from the institution he or she represents, and who functions primarily in that region (e.g., a "West Coast" regional rep who lives in San Francisco and recruits for a New England college).

registration: selecting and enrolling in classes and paying appropriate fees to earn academic credit for them.

rep: representative.

residency: at public institutions, the determination by review of evidence (e.g., driver's license, tax statements, voter registration, etc.) of the intent of a student to live or establish permanent residency in a given state for the privilege of paying lower tuition; often, a year or longer is required once intent has been determined before lower fees ("resident" or "in-state") are approved.

returning/re-entry student: a nontraditional student who is "older than average" (usually 25 or older) and/or has once been in college and is now enrolling or planning to enroll.

roadrunner/road warrior: an admissions recruiter who travels extensively.

rolling admissions: a method of admissions processing in which applicants are admitted or denied when their materials are complete and reviewed, right up to (or through) the beginning of classes.

secondary school graduation: the date of graduation and name and location of the secondary school from which the individual received a diploma.

selective admission: admission based on specific criteria by an institution with more applicants than spaces for them; can be institution wide or by major.

semester system: an academic calendar in which a student enrolls for an approximate four-month period in both fall (e.g., mid-September through mid-December) and spring (e.g., mid-January through early June); a summer term is usually shorter; see also early semester system.

SPEEDE/ExPRESS: AACRAO Committee on Standardization of Postsecondary Education Electronic Data Exchange (SPEEDE) and Exchange of Permanent Records Electronically for Students and Schools (ExPRESS). The combined standards are now known as the SPEEDE/ExPRESS formats.

Glossary

special admit: a student who does not meet regular admissions requirements, but whose special skills, preparation, advantages, etc., meet alternative and/or equivalent criteria.

student identification number: any unique number assigned to the student by the institution. If utilized as the student identifier, the Social Security number should be labeled as the student identification number.

student profile: a data-based description of characteristics of an institution's student body (e.g., 57 percent female, 43 percent male, who live within 100 miles of campus, rank on average at the 75th percentile of high school graduating classes, etc.).

student reps/volunteers: enrolled students who volunteer to participate in recruitment efforts (e.g., making school visits, giving campus tours, meeting prospective students).

supplemental admissions requirements: additional criteria that certain groups of applicants (e.g., international students) must meet.

telemarketing: recruitment effort in which representatives of an institution (e.g., admissions staff, alums, student volunteers, faculty) contact prospective or admitted students by telephone to interest them in applying or to confirm their enrollment.

test scores: most often, scores earned by students completing either or both of the two major college aptitude tests, the SAT (Scholastic Aptitude Test) or the ACT; could also refer to any other aptitude or placement test scores.

TOEFL: Test of English as a Foreign Language, administered to non-native speakers of English to measure their English language proficiency; many colleges have TOEFL minimum scores required for admission.

transcript: a copy of the student's academic record extrapolated from the academic record and forwarded to persons or agencies for their use in reviewing the academic performance of the student. It is a legal document which contains the signature of the certifying official, the institutional seal, and the date of issue. Uncertified copies of academic records which are generally issued to students, advisers, and deans for the purpose of academic advising should not contain the signature or seal and should be clearly identified as "internal use only" documents.

transfer day: a day when college reps visit a community college to meet with prospective transfer students.

transfer student: a student who begins at one college and intends to enter or who has been admitted and/or enrolled at another; a lower-division transfer student is one who transfers at the freshman or sophomore level, upper-division at the junior or senior level.

transferable courses: academic courses and units at one institution that are acceptable at another; may or may not count toward specific degree requirements.

trimester system: an academic calendar that divides the year into three roughly equal four-month periods; summer trimester equals each of the others in length.

type of credit: a means of awarding credit for nonclassroom experiences such as military experience, life experience, nationally standardized or institutional examinations, or television and correspondence courses. Off-campus credit should be labeled only if institutional policy so dictates.

underrepresented: a lower percentage of members of a particular class (e.g., women, ethnic minorities) compared to the enrollment than the percentage who exist in the applicant cohort or in the general population.

visiting/unclassified/transient student: an admission/enrollment category describing nonmatriculating (non-degree-seeking) students who seek a limited number of courses for career advancement, personal interest, etc.

wait list: names of applicants who may be admitted depending on the number of admitted students who confirm their intent-to-enroll by the reply date.

yield: the ratio of one group to another (e.g., applicants to admitted applicants, admitted applicants to enrollees); a critical measure of recruitment effectiveness and of projecting a given term's future enrollment.

yield activities: types of recruitment efforts designed to increase yield (e.g., a regional party hosted by alumni/ae volunteers to increase the enrollment rate of admitted students).

Index

A

AACRAO Member Guide	218
AACRAO's code of ethics	223, 224
academic advising	8
academic advisor	8
access	110
admissions	5
categories of openness of	5
admissions staff	
diversifying	182
Allen, James	37
Americans with Disabilities Act (ADA)	179
Applied Ethics in Student Services	173
Association for Institutional Research (AIR)	216
Association of College Admissions Counselors (ACAC)	2
associations, for enrollment services professionals	220, 222
Audio-Tutorial Instruction (ATI)	119
authority	101, 154
crisis of	89
formal	152

B

Baylis, Charles A.	191
bedel	1
Bennett, William	191
Book of Virtues, The	191

C

ceremony, significance of	164
Chronicle of Higher Education	140, 147, 201, 216
code of ethics	223, 224
organizational	172
College & University	147, 218
commencemnt ceremony	
prayer at	189
communication	28
environmental factors and	57
grapevine	51
informal	50
leadership and	33
nonverbal	53
perception and	41, 43
personal distance and	57
self-perception	40
teamwork and	59
written	50
competition, for institutions of higher education	211
Computer-Based Instruction (CBI)	120
computer-mediated communications	74
conferences, for enrollment services	
personnel	218
counseling skills	15
credentialing	138
cross-impact analysis (CIA)	124
curriculum delivery	119
curriculum development	117
customer service and leadership	197
Cyberspace	74

D

Data Dispenser	147, 201
decision-making, ethical	173
disabled students	179
Drucker, Peter	53

241

Index

E

educationally disadvantaged students	212
Eisenhower, Dwight D.	155
Electronic Data Interchange (EDI)	80
electronic publishing	75
See also World Wide Web	
Emerson, Ralph Waldo	33
ENROLL-L	141, 201, 216
enrollment management	152, 157
language of	166
enrollment services	3
advancing in	199
entering the profession	16, 22, 193
future of	17
history of	1
leadership in	22, 88
opportunities in	194
within academic arenas	163
within student affairs	163
enrollment services professionals	
associations	220
computers and	13, 82
education and	24
dean	136
director	136
legal issues and	14
marketing and	15
responsibilities of	4, 213
skills needed by	27, 195
enrollment, fluctuations of	17
enrollment, predictions of	17
ethical decision making	173
ethical decisions	
principles governing	173
Ethical Problems in Higher Education	173
ethics	191
micro-issues	173
macro-issues	173
Ethics in Higher Eduction	191

F

Faculty and	
politics	155
faculty develpment	10
Fair Practices In Higher Education	191
Family Educational Rights and Privacy Act (FERPA)	12, 175
financial aid	7, 212
financial aid officer	7
formal authority	152
Fulghum, Robert	51

G

Getty, J. Paul	38
goals, enrollment	124
"great man" theory	90
Groupware	76

H

High Performance Computing Act	72
How College Affects Students	119
hypertext	75

I

image, professional	56
information	
market research	162
information management	160
information superhighway	
see also Internet	72
institutional research	10
institutional responsibility	186
institutional responsibility statement	186
intelligent agents	77
Internet	35, 72
publications	142

J

James, William	37
job search	201, 202

K

K-16 systems	211
Key Performance Indicators (KPIs)	123
Kitchener, Karen	173

L

language	
or enrollment management	166
politics and	165
leaders	
qualities of	172
leadership	152
and being a role model	65
and business terminology	92
attitude and	39
authority	101

communication and	33	*See also* information superhighway	
contingency theory of	95		
creativity and	101	*NetNews*	147, 201
current definitions	94	networking	142
customer serivce and	197	networks	112
definitions	89	interpersonal	166
educational	93	learning and	110
followers and	96	Nixon, Richard	151
in enrollment services	88, 153	nontraditional students	109

O

objectives, defined	124
organizational chart	154
organizational culture	152
organizational design, evaluating	127
organizational politics	152
organizational structure	154
organizations	
as social settings	166
orientation	8

in higher education 88
management 92
modernistic 92
politics and 153, 164
purpose and 88
skills necessary 99
theory 90, 92
transactional 95
Leadership Challenge, The 93
learning assistance centers 9
learning products
marketing 121
listening
active 58
communication 58
listservs 141

M

management
in education 93
leadership vs 92
theory 94
market research
SEM and 123
marketing 15, 18
maximizing benefits, principle of 173
May, William 191
Moulton, Janice 173
multimedia 77

N

NAFSA: Association of
International Educators 220
National Association for College
Admission Counseling 2, 4
National Association of Academic
Advising (NACADA) 216
National Association of Student
Financial Aid Administrators 4
National Association of Student
Personnel Administrators
(NASPA) 216
National Research and
Educational Network (NREN) 73

P

paralanguage	54, 55
perception	46, 47
communication and	41, 43
Perelman, Lewis J.	71
perpetual learning	109
network based	113
personality types	60
Personalized System of Instruction (PSI)	120
perspective and communication	44
physically challenged students	179
politics	
information managemt and	160
language and	165
organizational life and	166
prerequisites	
checking	187
precedent, historical, and policy making	159
principle of fairness	173
of maximizing benefits	173
of universalization	173
professional development	138, 148, 217
Professional Development Guidelines for Registrars: A Self-Audit	23
Professional Practices and Ethical Standards	172
professionalism	24, 25, 29
proficiency-based education	18

Project Learning 2000	71	
publications	147, 218	

R

Race and hiring	182
Records Management for the 1990s and Beyond	192
recruitment	108
REGIST-L	201
registrar	2, 11
origins of	1
responsibilities of	214
registration	
see touchtone telephone	11
residence life	9
retention, defined	108
ritual in higher education	164
Robinson, George	173
Rockefeller, John D.	38
Roosevelt, Theodore	38
Rusk, Dean	59

S

Seldin, John	34
self-perception and communication	40
SEM	129
Seven Blind Mice	42
sexual harassment	176
Strategic Enrollment Management *see* SEM	
student services	215
Student-Right-to-Know	210
students, nontraditional	109

T

technology	209, 210, 214
compression	79
enrollment services and	82
touchtone telephone registration	11
tracking	117
Transfer Credit Practices of Designated Educational Institutions	219
transfer students	6
Twain, Mark	53

U

unity of voice	166

V

video-on-demand	79
videoconferencing	78
virtual reality (VR)	80
virtual univeristies	18, 113
vocal interferences	56

W

Winograd, Terry	76
workshops, for enrollment professionals	218
World Wide Web	18, 74, 142

Y

Young, Ed	42